Scoring Points

Scoring Points

Politicians, Activists, and the Lower Federal Court Appointment Process

NANCY SCHERER

Stanford University Press
Stanford, California
2005

Stanford University Press
Stanford, California

© 2005 by the Board of Trustees of the Leland Stanford Junior University. All
rights reserved.

Printed in the United States of America on acid-free, archival-quality paper

Library of Congress Cataloging-in-Publication Data

Scherer, Nancy.
 Scoring points : politicians, activists, and the lower Federal Court
 appointment process / Nancy Scherer.
  p. cm.
 Includes bibliographical references and index.
 ISBN 0-8047-4948-5 (cloth : alk. paper)—ISBN 0-8047-4949-3 (pbk. : alk.
 paper)
  1. Judges—Selection and appointment—United States. I. Title.
KF8776.S34 2005
347.73'2034—dc22   2005004650

Original Printing 2005

Last figure below indicates year of this printing:
14 13 12 11 10 09 08 07 06 05

Typeset by G&S Book Services in 10.5/12.5 Bembo

ISBN 978-0-8047-4948-0   ISBN 978-0-8047-4949-7

For Oscar and Susan Cohen

Contents

Tables and Figures

FIGURES

Acknowledgments

I THANK MY dissertation committee for their insightful comments while this project was in its infancy: Michael C. Dawson, Dennis J. Hutchinson, John Brehm, and a very special thanks to Gerald N. Rosenberg. I also received much valuable input and support along the way and thank the following individuals: Gregory A. Caldeira, Lawrence Baum, Elliot E. Slotnick, Sheldon Goldman, Cass Sunstein, Harold J. Spaeth, Wendy Martinek, and Amy Steigerwalt. And I thank my editor, Amanda Moran; she believed in this project since I was in graduate school and remained patient as I undertook a major rewrite of the original dissertation. Finally, I thank my parents, Paul and Janice Scherer.

Scoring Points

Why Has the Lower Federal Court Appointment Process Become So Politicized?

FOR MOST OF OUR NATION'S HISTORY, judicial scholars and politicians almost exclusively have focused their attention on understanding the interaction of politics and the nation's highest court: the Supreme Court of the United States. Thus, social scientists sought to answer such questions as: What influences a president's Supreme Court nomination decision (e.g., Caldeira and Wright, 1998; B. Perry, 1991)? When is the Senate most likely to reject a Supreme Court nominee (e.g., Cameron, Cover, and Segal, 1990)? When will the Supreme Court emerge as an issue in a presidential election (e.g., Stephenson, 1999)? And, perhaps most significant, do Supreme Court justices decide cases in accordance with the Constitution, statutory interpretation, and controlling precedent—certainly the prevailing view taught in our nation's law schools—or in accordance with their own personal political philosophies (Segal and Spaeth, 1993)?

The emphasis on the Supreme Court is not surprising, given the visibility of its decisions and appointments. However, both Supreme Court appointments and decisions are relatively rare events. Each president makes, on average, only two Supreme Court appointments per four-year term (Fleming and Wood, 1997); during the tenure of Chief Justice William H. Rehnquist, the Court has, on average, decided fewer than one hundred cases per term. Much less attention has been devoted to understanding the political significance of the lower federal courts. This is true notwithstanding the fact that each president makes hundreds of lower court appointments each term and that the lower federal courts decide thousands of cases daily.

I would argue that, today, the lower federal court appointment process has become even more politically relevant than that of a Supreme Court jus-

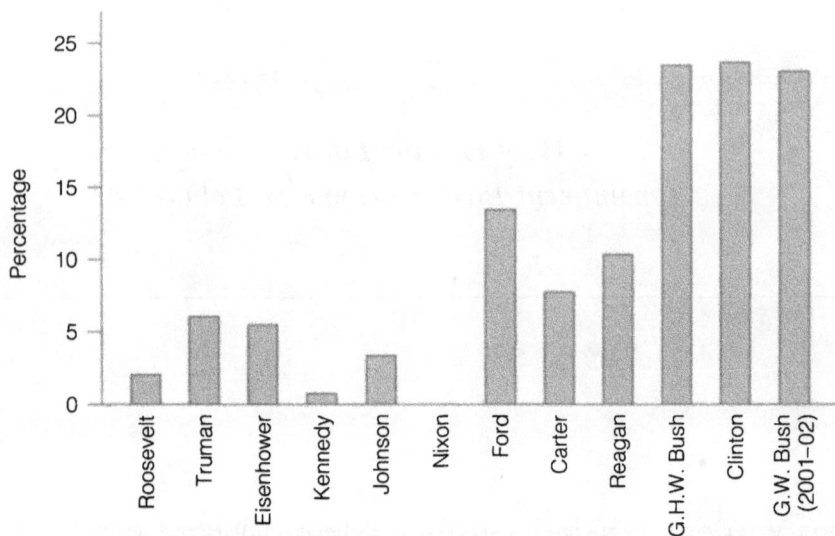

FIGURE I-I. Percentage of Lower Court Nominations Not Confirmed (Rejected by Vote or Procedure) by Senate, 1933–2002
Source: *New York Times*, November 15, 2003, p. A10.

tice, given the infrequency of Supreme Court appointments and decisions. One need only look to the intense partisan fighting over lower court nominations during the past decade to see how important the composition of the lower federal courts has become to key political elites on both the right and left of the ideological spectrum. Perhaps no one event epitomizes the intensity that this issue has taken on than the unprecedented thirty-eight-hour debate held on the floor of the Senate on November 12–13, 2003. Venting their frustrations with a judicial confirmation process that they say is terribly broken, Republican senators decried the Democratic minority's filibusters of four George W. Bush nominees to the U.S. Courts of Appeals. Ignoring the Republicans' demands to give all lower court nominations up or down confirmation votes, Democrats launched two more filibusters only one day after the marathon session ended, bringing the total of G. W. Bush nominations subjected to filibusters to six. By the end of 2004, the number of filibusters had risen to ten.

A host of other indicators point to an increase in the politicization of the lower court appointment process over the past few decades. For example, as shown in Figure I-I, the percentage of lower court nominations *not* confirmed by the Senate has increased dramatically in the past two decades, beginning in the George H. W. Bush administration.[1]

Similarly, the number of days for a lower court nomination to get con-

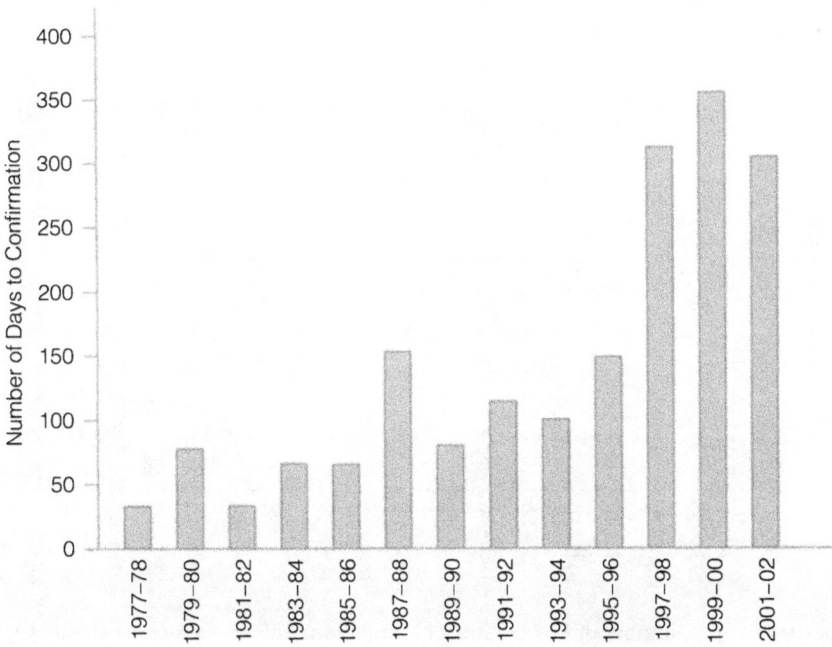

FIGURE 1-2. Number of Days From Nomination to Confirmation, U.S. Courts of Appeals Judges, 1977–2002

Source: Goldman, 36 *University of California Davis Law Review* 695, 709, 711 (2003).

firmed has increased significantly since the Jimmy Carter administration (data were not available before this time). As shown in Figure I-2, for non-presidential election years,[2] the average number of days for a court of appeals nominee to be confirmed increased from 33.3 days during the Carter administration to 313 days during William J. Clinton's second term in office and 305.4 days during G. W. Bush's first two years in office.

The number of lower court nominations challenged by interest groups has also increased steadily in recent decades. As shown in Figure I-3, before the modern political era, interest groups did not launch public campaigns against lower court nominations, although interest groups were active in the Supreme Court appointment process for most of the 20th century (Maltese, 1995). Then, during the Richard M. Nixon and Gerald R. Ford administrations (1973–76), we see that one appeals court nomination was the subject of interest group opposition; two appellate nominees faced interest group opposition during the Carter administration, and two more during Ronald Reagan's first term. But beginning in Reagan's second term in office, we see a notable increase in the number of interest group fights over lower court nominations that remained fairly steady through the end of the Clinton ad-

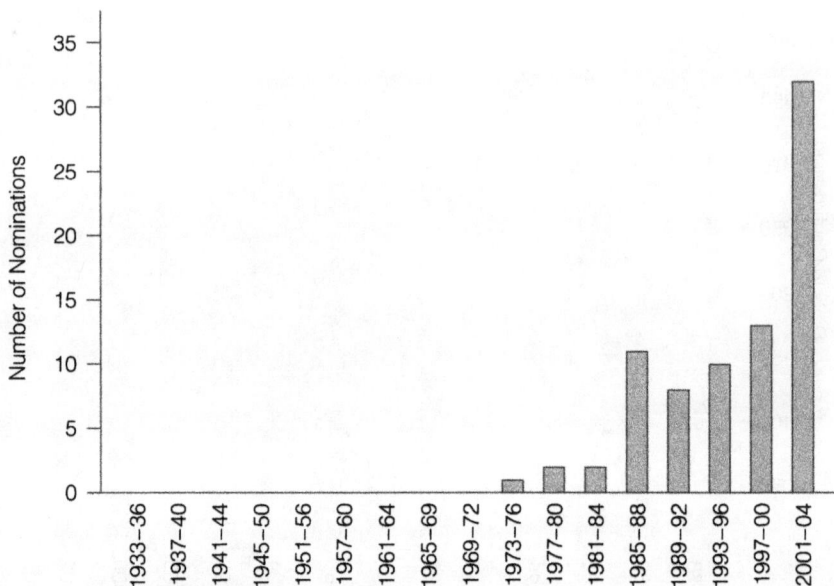

FIGURE I-3. Number of Lower Court Nominations Subject to Interest Group Opposition, 1933–2004

ministration. Finally, we see a dramatic increase in lower court confirmation fights during the administration of G. W. Bush.

Another indicator of increased politicization of the lower court appointment process may be gleaned from Figure I-4, which shows the number of editorials and op-ed pieces that appeared in the *New York Times* and *Wall Street Journal* on lower federal court appointments between 1933 and 2004. Before Reagan's second term in office, there were fewer than ten such articles per four-year presidential term. Then, beginning in 1985, we see a significant increase in the attention given to this issue on the editorial pages of these two nationally distributed newspapers. And following the same pattern previously noted, during the first four years of the G. W. Bush presidency, the number of editorials nearly triples compared with the number written during the eight years of the Clinton presidency.

Clearly, given the level of attention that politicians, interest groups, and the media give to lower court appointments, the time has come for judicial scholars to turn their attention to studying the political implications of today's complex lower court appointment process. And so, in this book, I tackle this critical question: Why has the lower federal court appointment process become so politicized in the modern political era?[3]

My basic theoretical and historical arguments are presented in Part One.

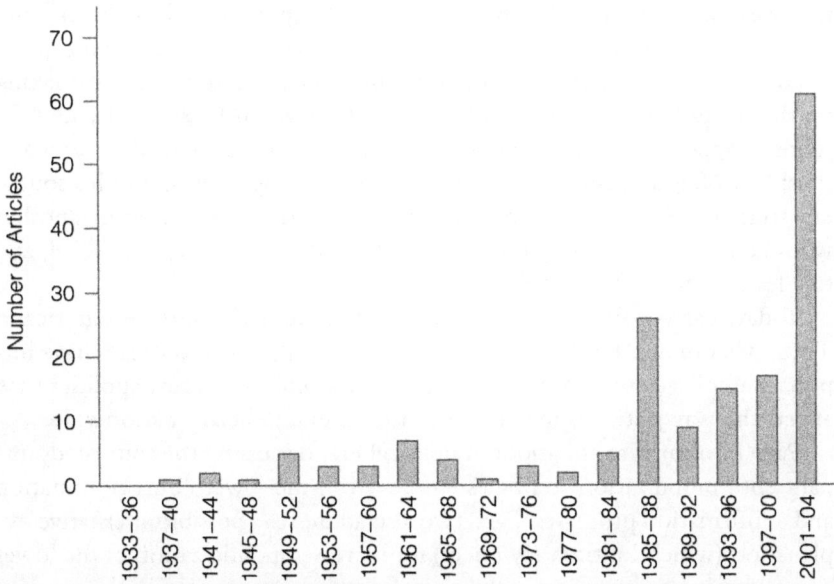

FIGURE 1-4. Number of Editorials and Op-Ed Pieces on Lower Court Appointments, Combined Total, *New York Times* and *Wall Street Journal*, 1933–2004
Source: ProQuest Historical Newspapers.

Chapter 1 sets out the theory of *elite mobilization*, which explains why the lower court confirmation process has become more politicized in the past few decades. This theory states that politicians (primarily senators and the president) have always used lower court appointments for electoral purposes—that is, to garner support from their respective parties' activists. However, because of two historic changes to American institutions beginning in the 1950s—the old party system began to break down and the federal judiciary became particularly receptive to expanding individuals' constitutional rights—politicians switched from an appointment system dominated by patronage to one dominated by new policy-oriented strategies. Collectively, I refer to these new policy-oriented strategies as *elite mobilization strategies*. Once policy was injected into the appointment process, the once sacrosanct "gentleman's agreement" among senators and the president—which allowed lower court judges to be selected and confirmed swiftly under the patronage system—began to break down. In its place is an appointment system rife with partisan politics, as politicians exploit lower court judgeships to "score points" with their elite constituents.

Chapter 2 expands on the temporal argument set out in Chapter 1. Specifically, using data of judicial decision-making from the New Deal era, the Great Society era, and through the present—periods before, during, and after the two critical changes occurred in the American political landscape— I demonstrate that there was no significant party-polarized decision-making on the lower federal courts until the late 1960s when President Lyndon B. Johnson appointed judges who would uphold the 1964 Civil Rights Act and President Nixon appointed judges hostile to civil rights as part of his southern strategy.[4] After Nixon, policy-based strategies of one kind or another would come to dominate judicial selection at the court of appeals level, and to a lesser extent, the district court level.

Today, party-polarized voting in the lower federal courts is significant. Thus, what these data also reveal is that elite mobilization strategies have important implications beyond the politics of Washington, as party politics now affects the way justice is meted out in the federal judiciary nationwide.

Part Two turns to the modern political era, discussing the four predominant elite mobilization strategies employed in the lower court nomination and confirmation processes. Part Two also addresses a possible alternative explanation (which I ultimately reject) for increased politicization of the lower court appointment process—the rise of divided government in the modern political era.

Chapter 3 addresses modern-day presidents' reliance on ideological litmus tests in the selection of lower court nominees. Although this practice may have been used intermittently before the 1960s (particularly during the administration of Franklin Delano Roosevelt [FDR]), its first systematic, widespread, and public use would not come until the election of Nixon in 1968, when he made an express campaign promise to appoint "law and order" judges at all levels of the federal judiciary. Later, Reagan and G. H. W. Bush would take up this tactic in promising to appoint lower court judges who would overturn the decision of *Roe v. Wade* (1973), while G. W. Bush has again shifted the emphasis of the Republicans' litmus test from one focusing on abortion to one focusing on the appointment of "restrained" judges. Although Democratic presidents Carter and Clinton seem to have paid close attention to their judicial nominees' support of a woman's right to choose an abortion, the exploitation of ideological litmus tests remains predominantly a Republican elite mobilization strategy.

Chapter 4 turns to another elite mobilization strategy: the president's use of affirmative action in the selection of lower court judges. This strategy is predominantly a Democratic strategy, as it seeks to appease demands of minority and female activists—critical constituencies in the Democratic Party—for greater diversity on the federal bench. Carter first used this strategy in the 1970s, and Clinton picked it up again in the 1990s. Although at first glance it appears that both Democratic presidents operated under a single diversification strategy, on closer inspection, it seems that Clinton was much more strategic in his appointment of minorities to the bench. In attempting to portray himself as a moderate, Clinton alienated black leaders with many of his policies; by appointing liberal blacks to the federal courts, Clinton was able to satisfy important policy demands of this critical constituency.

Chapters 5 and 6 address the rise of obstructionist confirmation tactics in the U.S. Senate as a way to appease important interest groups and party activists. This strategy differs from those the president uses because it is aimed at defeating rather than choosing judicial candidates and also because it targets specific nominees rather than setting out general criteria for guiding judicial appointments. Interview testimony from key political activists involved in confirmation politics reveals that they uniformly express the need to know which senators from their affiliated parties stand by them and which are willing to compromise ideological values—information that they will later use to mobilize voters behind the politician in the next election, to mobilize voters against the politician, or perhaps not to mobilize voters at all.

Chapter 7 looks at the use of lower federal appointments by political challengers for public office. Here we see how candidates challenging incumbents—in both presidential and senatorial campaigns—also attempt to "score points" with elites about the lower court judicial appointment process even though they currently have no involvement with that process. In short, this elite mobilization strategy requires that political challengers go on the record, at the behest of policy activists, as to whether they will employ the correct judicial selection or confirmation tactics on behalf of their activists if elected. For presidential challengers, this means announcing the use of an ideological litmus test or affirmative action policy; for senatorial challengers, this means announcing support for or opposition to an embattled judicial candidate. Once satisfied that the candidate will adopt the correct elite mobilization strategy when in office, activists kick into gear and mobilize voters for the candidate.

Chapter 8 considers an alternative hypothesis: that the predominance of divided government in the modern political era (rather than the rise of issue activism among party elites coupled with the expansion of individual rights) has caused heightened politicization of the lower court judicial selection/confirmation processes. What we find is that the use of elite mobilization strategies continues with equal force whether government is divided or unified but that the specific tactics politicians use may vary according to the type of ruling regime in place. Thus, moving from divided to unified government, or vice versa, has no impact on the litmus tests presidents use to choose nominees or on the likelihood of confirmation by the Senate. One change we do see in moving from divided to unified government, however, are the types of tactics senators use to obstruct confirmation of judicial nominees.

Chapter 9 summarizes the book's main findings and assesses the state of the lower federal court appointment process in the current political environment.

Several books have sought to explain why the judicial appointment process has become more politicized in recent decades, and the bulk of them are strictly focused on the confirmation phase of the appointment process. Accordingly, these books attribute increased politicization to changes in the Senate, rather than, as I do, to changes in the party system. For example, in *Judicious Choices: The New Politics of Supreme Court Confirmations* (1994), Silverstein argues that democratization of the Senate—opening up the process to interest groups and the breakdown of a hierarchical model of power—has allowed the Supreme Court confirmation process to become much more contentious. Similarly, in *Warring Factions: Interest Groups, Money, and the New Politics of Senate Confirmation* (2002b), Bell argues that the influx of money and interest groups into the Senate's confirmation proceedings—once a largely secret process—has caused problems with the appointment process.

This book takes a much different theoretical approach. Rather than atomizing the problem as solely a function of problems in the Senate's confirmation proceedings, the theory of elite mobilization starts with the premise that the entire appointment process is infected: how presidents choose nominees, how the Senate confirms nominees, and critically, how political candidates exploit controversial nominations during elections—all to please issue activists associated with the two major parties. Moreover, the theory of elite mobilization is tied to changes in the party system, rather than to institutional changes in the structure of the Senate. Although I concede that such institutional changes have occurred in the Senate, I see them as part of the breakdown of the old party system.

This theory that the breakdown of the judicial appointment process is a function of changes in the party system is a unique contribution to the literature. In short, since lower court nominations were traditionally controlled by local party elites and used strictly as political patronage, we need to ask why the political parties would be willing to cede control over these judgeships to national political leaders unless there was a change in the party system itself. Finally, this book, unlike others looking at the appointment process, presents extensive empirical data of the decision-making behavior of lower court appointees of Presidents Warren G. Harding through Clinton. By examining this data, we can see how lower court appointees, over time, have become significantly more party polarized in their voting behavior, just as the two parties have become more polarized.

PART ONE

Judicial Selection in
Historical Perspective

CHAPTER 1

The Theory of Elite Mobilization

AT THE HEART OF the question explored in this book—why has the lower court appointment process become so politicized in the modern political era?—lie two important developments in American politics that began to take shape during the 1950s and 1960s. First, there was an historic transformation of the mass party system that had existed since the Jacksonian era. Second, political activists (affiliated with interest groups and public interest law firms, e.g., the NAACP Defense Fund and the American Civil Liberties Union [ACLU]) increasingly began to turn to the federal courts, rather than federal and state legislatures, to achieve policy goals. Working in tandem, these changes would forever raise the stakes of lower federal court appointments.

Transformation of the Old Mass Party System

The two national parties under the old mass party system were actually two loosely connected systems of local party organizations, established to solve the collective action problem that politicians faced in terms of mobilizing voters (Aldrich, 1995; Mayhew, 1986). Two critical aspects of the old party system affected judicial appointment politics. First, because the activists who ran the local party organizations were predominantly interested in obtaining material incentives from politicians—that is, jobs and contracts in return for helping the candidate get elected—the activists working within the party system were seen as largely nonideological in nature (Conway and Feigert, 1968). Party activists "engaged in a conflict without principles, a struggle between the ins and outs which never becomes fanatical and creates no deep cleavage in the country" (Duverger, 1964, at 418). Characterized by a pragmatism that made them willing to compromise and strike deals in order to deliver the jobs and contracts they desired for their supporters, these old-line party activists came to be known as "professionals" (Wilson, 1962). Second, as parties were little more than a caucus of local organizations, regional conflicts abounded among party leaders; it was the job of the national organization to find ways to hold these factions together. Thus, for example, with conservative southern Democrats in Congress opposed to integration and liberal northern Democrats in Congress wanting to end Jim Crow laws, the national Democratic Party for many years avoided taking a stand on civil rights so as to preserve its national coalition (Aldrich, 1995). Simply stated, the two major parties under the mass party system were ideologically heterogeneous.

During the 1960s, the old mass party system crumbled (Aldrich, 1995). In place of the professionals came ideologically driven political activists, known as "amateurs" (Wilson, 1962) or "purists" (Wildavsky, 1965), who were characterized by their unwillingness to compromise on ideological causes (Wildavsky, 1965). "Purists consider the stock-in-trade of the politician—compromise and bargaining, conciliating the opposition, bending a little to capture support—to be hypocritical; they prefer a style that relies on the announcement of principles and on moral crusades" (Polsby and Wildavsky, 1976, at 30–31). During the 1960s, purists came to fill the ranks of both the Democratic and Republican parties (Polsby and Wildavsky, 1971).[1] While conservative activists flocked to the Republican Party—supporting Barry Goldwater and his anti–federal civil rights agenda—liberals flocked to the Democratic Party—supporting Johnson and his pro–civil rights agenda. This transformation of the key party activists—from professionals to amateurs—changed the party system in two critical respects. First, it made Democratic and Republican party activists much more ideologically polarized than they were under the old party system (Costain, 1980; Kirkpatrick, 1976; Lunch, 1987; Stone, Rapoport, and Abramowitz, 1994). This is particularly true of the party activists involved in political campaigns (Aldrich, 1995). Second, it transformed the activists of each party from a group divided by local allegiances to a group united by a uniform set of national policy goals.

Although activists in the parties had become more unified, mass voters were becoming less enchanted with the two major parties. In short, fewer Americans began identifying themselves as a Democrat or a Republican (Rosenstone and Hansen, 1993). This meant that the two major political parties were less capable of mobilizing voters on behalf of political candidates—the very reason they were originally conceived in the early 19th century (Aldrich, 1995). Interest groups picked up much of the slack in mobilizing voters for national elections (Frymer and Yoon, 2002; Gibson, Frendreis, and Vertz, 1989), particularly after the Supreme Court's ruling in *Buckley v. Valeo* (1976) (Kornylak, 2001). In *Buckley*, the Court held that under the First Amendment, a campaign finance reform statute could not preclude interest groups from engaging in "issue advocacy." Accordingly, determined to exercise influence over the outcomes of important federal elections, interest groups began spending millions of dollars on campaign advertising aimed at mobilizing voters to support their favored candidates (Frymer and Yoon, 2002). Interest groups also began to contribute volunteers and money to their preferred candidates (Gibson, Frendreis, and Vertz, 1989).

With the policy interests of organizations like the National Organization for Women (NOW), the ACLU, the National Association for the Advancement of Colored People (NAACP), and Planned Parenthood inextricably intertwined with the policy interests of the new liberal political activists in the Democratic Party, liberal issue activists (those affiliated with interest groups) became aligned with the Democratic Party (Oldfield, 1995; Rozell and Wilcox, 1999; Schlozman and Tierney, 1986; Walker, 1991). Similarly, conservative issue activists who, in the 1970s, began seeking to undo legal victories for liberal causes (most notably in the areas of abortion, affirmative action, and criminal defendants' rights) aligned themselves with the Republican Party (Oldfield, 1995; Rozell and Wilcox, 1996, 1999). Some scholars thus characterize these modern-day issue activists as the "newest wave" of purists in the Republican and Democratic parties (e.g., Green and Guth, 1988). They also shared with the new party activists a desire to push a uniform set of national policy goals. By the 1970s, the old mass party system had transformed into the modern party system.

What does party politics have to do with federal court appointments? Under both the old and modern party systems, party activists closely monitored the selection of lower court judges. But while local party activists under the old party system viewed lower court judgeships as jobs to be distributed to friends and campaign contributors, in the modern political era, party and issue activists view judicial appointments as crucial policy matters. Why did lower federal court judgeships begin to figure into the policy goals of the new breed of political activists? The reasons turn on the second historic event in American politics to occur during the 1950s and 1960s: the transformation of the federal judiciary.

Transformation of the Federal Judiciary

In the 1930s, less than 10 percent of the Supreme Court's decisions involved cases other than property rights. In short, the Court's docket was dedicated to claims brought by businesses and wealthy individuals. In stark contrast, by the 1960s, individual, constitutional rights cases made up almost 70 percent of the Court's docket (Epp, 1998). As Epp explains, interest groups did not begin bringing rights-oriented litigation in the 1950s and 1960s; that strategy began earlier in the 20th century. There is little doubt, however, that interest groups *intensified* their litigation strategy in the 1950s. This is because earlier in the century, liberal jurists on the Court disfavored judicial policy-making (Silverstein, 1994). But under the leadership of Chief Justice Earl Warren, liberal interest groups such as the NAACP and the ACLU sensed that the Court was now sympathetic to the claims of liberal activists for broader constitutional protections for individuals, particularly those denied minorities by southern state legislatures. Indeed, justices during the Warren Court era saw an active role for the judiciary in public policy-making (Silverstein, 1994). Thus, the Warren Court significantly expanded civil rights and civil liberties in accordance with the personal policy preferences of the justices sitting on that court (Segal and Spaeth, 1993).

What were the new constitutional rights achieved through federal court litigation? First, in *Brown v. Board of Education* (1954), the Supreme Court reversed an 1896 precedent, *Plessy v. Ferguson*, and held that "separate but equal" public schools were unconstitutional. Breathing new life into the Fourteenth Amendment's equal protection clause, the *Brown* decision was only the first in a line of Supreme Court rulings designed to dismantle the Jim Crow laws in the South.[2]

Second, during the 1960s, the Court turned its attention to civil liberties protections for criminal defendants under the Fourth, Fifth, and Sixth Amendments. In that decade the Court would again repeatedly reverse its own precedent and impose upon state criminal proceedings, among other things, the rule that excludes from trial illegally obtained evidence, mandatory appointed counsel for indigents in all criminal cases, and mandatory warnings for suspects being interrogated designed to apprise them of their constitutional rights.[3]

Third, during the 1970s, the Supreme Court would begin to recognize new rights for women. Pursuant to the equal protection clause, women were deemed a semi-suspect class, thus mandating heightened scrutiny of state and federal statutes that treated men and women disparately.[4] The decision that ultimately became its most controversial on women's rights was *Roe v. Wade* (1973), where the Court held that a woman's constitutional right to privacy under the Fourteenth Amendment's due process clause included the unfettered right to choose abortion during the first trimester of pregnancy.

Fourth, the Warren Court made it much easier for aggrieved parties to bring lawsuits in federal court (Silverstein, 1994). For example, in 1966, the Court amended the Federal Rules of Civil Procedure, making it easier to bring class action suits. Notions of standing to sue were also relaxed so as to afford the liberal court the opportunity to hear the substantive claims of aggrieved groups.

At the urging of liberal issue activists, then, the Supreme Court transformed the federal judiciary into the principal political institution where the disadvantaged could seek redress that they could not obtain otherwise from the elected branches, particularly in the South. But not only the Supreme Court was affected by this new wave of rights litigation. So, too, were the lower federal courts, as they would be charged with fashioning remedies to guarantee these new individual rights and with overseeing implementation of these remedies. The federal courts thus became the safe haven for the "discreet and insular minorities" to which the Supreme Court first referred in its now famous footnote four in *United States v. Carolene Products* (1937).

This transformation prompted noted scholar Alexander Bickel to observe that "all too many federal judges have been induced to view themselves as holding roving commissions as problem solvers, and as charged with a duty to act when majoritarian institutions do not" (Bickel, 1970, at 134). To this day, conservative activists see this litigation strategy as a means to bypass state legislatures:

> The clearest example [of liberals' use of the courts] is the abortion case . . . That is a question to be decided under the general police power that belongs to the states. There is no general federal police power. States in the early 1970s were already moving to change their abortion laws . . . But apparently they were not moving fast enough, and so feminist organizations went to the Supreme Court to try to obtain what they had been unable to obtain through state legislatures. And the Court gave them what they were looking for by finding a right that was dubiously among our unenumerated rights. (Pilon interview, 2002)

Whether a favorable court order standing alone—without some extrajudicial assistance in implementation—can ever deliver the policy results sought has been the subject of much scholarly debate (see, for example, Horowitz, 1977; Rosenberg, 1991; Scheingold, 1974). However, what is important is that during this period, liberal activists came to share a deep-rooted belief in the efficacy of the federal courts to achieve social change. And they continue to cling to this belief today. As Nan Aron, president of the Alliance for Justice, a liberal interest group that monitors the federal judiciary, explains:

> The way our democracy works is that poor people, people of color, disenfranchised people, [and] women have very little recourse to the Executive Branch. They don't make contributions to Democratic or Republican presidential campaigns. They tend not to know people in power. And therefore, [they] have very little access to the executives . . . of the world. They have almost no access to

members of Congress because they clearly don't contribute to congressional or senate races. The only recourse they have is to the judiciary. It's the only branch of government that will hear . . . cases brought by people without power . . . This is the only branch whereby a disenfranchised person or group has any ability to have redress for grievances. (Aron interview, 2002)

By the mid-1970s, perceiving that liberal activists had successfully achieved the policy goals they sought through federal court litigation, conservative activists began co-opting the liberals' litigation strategy (Epstein, 1985). Specifically, conservative activists began to use the federal courts to *undo* the substantial gains the liberal activists had made in the previous twenty years. Thus, conservative-sponsored litigation centered on the same issues as liberal-sponsored litigation; they asked federal courts to reconsider civil liberties protections for criminal defendants, abortion rights for women, and civil rights for minorities and women.

Some liberal activists allege that the litigation strategy of conservative activists in the 1970s and 1980s was actually driven by the same frustration with the legislative process that originally drove liberal activists to the federal courts in the 1950s and 1960s. In other words, unable to win conservative victories in Congress during the early years of the Reagan administration, conservatives started seeing the federal courts as the key to accomplishing the policy goals they could not achieve through the legislative process, notwithstanding Reagan's efforts to "pack" the lower court with conservative judges. As the director of People for the American Way, Ralph G. Neas, explains:

Going into 1981, the Republican right thought that, "wow, we have the presidency, we have the Senate, and we're really going to change things." And I think they were astonished, for example, during the [fight over] extension of the Voting Rights Act. Here was the heart and soul of the civil rights laws, and I'm convinced they thought it was a slam dunk to get either the so-called simple extension, or no Voting Rights Act extension at all. And by simple extension I mean just enacting the current language at that time without addressing a 1980 Supreme Court case that had dramatically weakened the Voting Rights Act. And what happened is that the Leadership Conference on Civil Rights led a national legislative campaign with strong bipartisan support that rejected the Reagan–Ed Meese–William Bradford Reynolds–William French Smith position, [the vote going] 85–8 in the Senate, and 389–24 in the House. And all of a sudden that commenced a string of victories [for the left] that lasted twelve years. (Neas interview, 2002)

Furthermore, the president of NOW, Kim Gandy, contends that the conservatives' desire to bypass the legislative process continues today: "they want us essentially to get down to one branch of government where basically the Judicial Branch does everything and it doesn't matter what Congress does because these right-wing judges, if they don't like them [congressional statutes], they throw them out and that's the end of that" (Gandy interview, 2002).

In sum, the rights revolution of the 1950s–1970s encompassed three broad areas of constitutional rights: race, crime, and women's rights. Critically, these were the very same issues with which the Democratic and Republican parties' new issue-oriented activists were most concerned. And so, with so much riding on federal court litigation, issue and party activists would join forces and begin monitoring the judicial selection and confirmation processes.

Activists Begin to Want the "Right" Kind of Judges Appointed

While once party activists demanded only that the president and senators seat campaign contributors and friends on the lower federal courts (i.e., patronage), policy-oriented activists have different priorities. Although they understand why a politician may want to reward a big contributor to his or her previous election campaign, the new breed of activists do not believe patronage concerns should detract from the main goal of appointing judges who can be depended on to further the activists' policy agenda. What this means is that only patrons who are known to share the activists' commitment to certain policy outcomes are now acceptable to serve on the federal courts. Aron says she understands why a politician might want to appoint someone on the basis of patronage:

> If you're a fund-raiser or you're a top campaign manager . . . [and] you're someone who is well-qualified, of course it makes sense. Why not reward your loyal supporters who also happen to be very qualified. Like a Willie Fletcher [who was Clinton's roommate at Oxford and the head of his California campaign for president, later nominated by Clinton to the Ninth Circuit Court of Appeals]. That's a good example . . . I think in theory I can understand it so long as the person is the right person for the court. (Aron interview, 2002)

For modern presidents, this means that activists affiliated with their own party may challenge judicial nominees if the activists believe the nominees to be opposed to their policy goals. In fact, this is exactly what happened to Clinton when he tried to nominate a pro-life candidate to the district court; liberal activists let him know there were to be no free rides when it comes to a lifetime appointment to the bench: "We have to be true to our beliefs and principles. If the administration nominates candidates who lack a sensitivity and commitment to constitutional principles, we will work hard to make our voice heard" (Aron, quoted in Klaidman, 1993).

Conservative activists similarly express a dislike for patronage appointments. One would go so far as to eliminate patronage completely from the judicial selection process—by barring home state senators and local Republican leaders from suggesting judicial candidates to the president, as is today the custom for district court appointments—because it detracts from what the activist believes should be the main focus of judicial selection, the judicial philosophy of the nominee:

> The Constitution says that the president nominates and appoints [federal court judges], subject to the advice and consent of the Senate . . . [Senators are] not supposed to be involved in the nomination phase. And the more that [senators get involved], the more factors enter in [to the nomination decision, and] that distracts from what I believe to be the primary criterion of judicial philosophy . . . [Patronage] distracts from what ought to be the central criterion. (Jipping interview, 2002)

As activists on the right and left make clear, what they want is for the president to nominate (or not nominate), and for the Senate to confirm (or not confirm), federal court judges who will be sympathetic to their political causes. Indeed, these activists are so convinced that their desired policy outcomes depend on litigation outcomes that today, the appointment of judges sympathetic to their causes, in effect, has become a policy goal unto itself— almost as important as achieving the underlying substantive policy goals at issue. And although their desire to secure sympathetic judges originally focused solely on Supreme Court nominations (Silverstein, 1994), for a number of reasons, activists began to shift their focus to lower federal court appointments as well.

One way that presidents in the modern political era have responded to activists' demands to eliminate patronage from the judicial appointment process is to wrest control of courts of appeals nominations from home state senators and other local party leaders. While Carter did this through merit selection committees, presidents since then have delegated the responsibility of identifying candidates for the courts of appeals to the White House Counsel's Office in conjunction with the Justice Department, moving the selection process into the White House. This is not to suggest that activists today condone patronage appointments at the district court level. They uniformly believe that the "right" kind of judges must be appointed at all levels of the federal judiciary (Aron interview, 2002; Gandy interview, 2002; Cavendish interview, 2002; Jipping interview, 2002). Accordingly, activists monitor all of a president's judicial nominations.

But as a practical matter, because home state senators or other prominent local party leaders still play a role in the selection of district court judges—they propose a list of names to the president, who may then reject or accept names on the list—pure patronage appointments are much more apt to occur at the district court level than at the court of appeals level. This is also due to the sheer volume of district court appointments made every year and the limited resources activists have to monitor these nominations. However, conservative and liberal activists have launched numerous opposition campaigns against district court nominees since the Reagan administration (see Chapter 5). In fact, liberal interest groups fought hard to keep Clinton from nominating two white male Democrats being considered for district court posts—both friends of local Democrats—because they opposed abortion (see Chapter 3).[5] This means that, while a pure patronage appointment is more likely to occur at the district court level than at the court of appeals level, senators and presidents still face the risk of a backlash from activists if these district court nominees do not also ascribe to the policy positions of the party's activists. And as more resources become available to activists to challenge more nominations, this risk increases.

Activists Shift Their Attention to the Lower Federal Courts

Why do activists focus so much attention on lower federal court appointments today? First, activists realize that there are few opportunities to affect Supreme Court appointments in the modern political era. Consider that for more than ten years after Justice Blackmun's retirement in 1994, there was no Supreme Court vacancy. In contrast, a president names hundreds of judges to the lower federal courts during each four-year term.

Second, with the Rehnquist Court hearing about half the number of cases that the Warren E. Burger Court heard, activists began to recognize that as a practical matter, the lower federal courts today serve as the final arbiter of more than 99 percent of all federal court litigation; in other words, important policy is being made every day in the lower federal courts (Songer, 1991). According to Elizabeth Cavendish, former legal director of NARAL Pro-Choice America (NARAL), this is where all important legal issues in the pro-choice/pro-life debate are being decided:

> There's a real recognition that lower court judges hold vast power over women's reproductive lives, and right now the composition of the Supreme Court is stable, and so there isn't an immediate threat to overturn *Roe*, but what is an underappreciated phenomenon is how much chipping away there has been at *Roe v. Wade* and protections for a woman's right to choose even given *Roe* and *[Planned*

Parenthood v.] Casey. Casey, in 1992 . . . empowered lower court judges because it established an undue burden standard. So it took the courts' focus away from strict scrutiny—which has been called fatal in fact to abortion restrictions—to an undue burden standard, which is obviously a mushier standard, and more fact dependent and subject to the interpretations of district and court of appeals judges. (Cavendish interview, 2002)

Neas, the director of People for the American Way, believes that certain circuits—specifically the Fourth and Fifth Circuits, generally considered the more conservative circuits—require special attention because the judges there are setting bad precedents for millions who live within those jurisdictions:

When you look at the Fourth Circuit and the Fifth Circuit and elsewhere, I think a good case can be made that they stretch precedents to the limits, and I would say defy precedents on many occasions. And thirty thousand cases are decided on appeal by those circuit courts every year, and only ninety cases or so go to the Supreme Court. So for millions of Americans, what these circuit courts decide is what the law of the land [is]. (Neas interview, 2002)

Third, in an apparent attempt to reduce uncertainty about the way Supreme Court nominees are likely to vote once becoming a justice, presidents have increasingly turned to the courts of appeals in searching for Supreme Court candidates. Indeed, seven of the nine justices on the court for the October 2004 term were elevated from the federal appellate courts. As NOW president Gandy aptly notes, the courts of appeals are now the "farm team" for the Supreme Court (Gandy interview, 2002). And so, for these litigation-oriented liberal interest groups—and those conservative groups that oppose them—having the "right" kind of judges seated on the appellate courts ensures the "right" kind of judges on the Supreme Court.

Fourth, Ronald Reagan began a trend of appointing lower federal court judges for lifetime appointments at much younger ages. While less than 3 percent of appellate judges appointed by Presidents Dwight D. Eisenhower, John F. Kennedy, Johnson, and Carter were younger than forty, 10 percent of Reagan's court of appeals appointments were in their thirties (Schwartz, 1988, at 60). As Gandy explained of the pre-Reagan era: "the idea was not that you appointed somebody [to the appellate bench] at thirty-five . . . Ford and Carter were appointing people who were in their late fifties. A [judicial appointment] was to cap your career" (Gandy interview, 2002). In short, because Reagan started a trend to appoint federal court judges earlier in their careers, judges now serve longer terms, and consequently, there is less turnover when the party changes in the White House.

The Emergence of Elite Mobilization Strategies

In the face of these new policy demands from key political activists, politicians adapted their nomination/confirmation strategies—from patronage to policy—so as to conform to the changing demands of political activists. Herein lies the core problem with today's lower court appointment process: the system turns on satisfying competing policy demands that center on the most divisive issues of the day—race, crime, and abortion. To satisfy the demands of one party's activists, by definition, means that the other party's activists cannot be satisfied. Indeed, they become extremely dissatisfied with appointment outcomes, which only leads to more contentiousness in the process. Still unanswered, however, is why politicians accede to these demands, given that the federal judiciary, particularly the lower federal courts, is not a salient issue with their constituents. Why not simply ignore these demands and continue with the old patronage system? The answer: reelection concerns.

Judicial scholars have previously suggested that there is an electoral component to the Supreme Court selection process. For example, B. Perry (1991) argues that Supreme Court nominations are often made to generate support among the mass electorate—for example, Reagan's appointment of Sandra Day O'Connor to shore up support among female voters. However, this conventional, explanation is problematic even for the Supreme Court, and certainly when we talk about lower court nominations. Consider public opinion polls, which demonstrate that the mass electorate knows virtually nothing about the Supreme Court, let alone the lower federal courts. For example, an oft-cited poll conducted by the *Washington Post* found that more people could identify Judge Wapner, former host of the television program *The People's Court*, than could identify the Chief Justice of the United States, Rehnquist (Caldeira, 1991). Why, then, would elected officials invest so much political capital in the lower court appointment process if their constituents are not paying attention?

I, too, see an important electoral strategy at play in the lower federal court appointment process, but one much different from that suggested by B. Perry. Rather than the Democratic and Republican parties using lower federal court judgeships to curry favor with the mass electorate, I would instead argue that the parties use these nominations to curry favor with only an elite constituency within each party, that is, to "score points" with elites. Specifically, I speak of the conservative activists affiliated with the Republican Party and the liberal activists affiliated with the Democratic Party. This includes both party activists and interest group activists (sometimes called *issue activists*). As stated above, these elite constituents actually care about who sits on the federal bench. More important, they are key to politicians' reelection prospects.

Why are activists the key to reelection efforts? Because they are responsible for mobilizing the party's base to get out and vote on Election Day (Katz and Eldersveld, 1961; Sorauf, 1967; Sorauf and Beck, 1988). As Steven J. Rosenstone and J. Mark Hansen explain in their classic work *Mobilization, Participation and Democracy in America*:

> Locked into struggles for political advantage, political leaders mobilize public involvement strategically. They target and time their efforts for maximum effect. They target their efforts on people they know, people who are well positioned in social networks, people who are influential in politics, and people who are likely to participate. They organize their efforts around salient issues, time them to avoid other distractions, calibrate them to impending decisions, and escalate them when outcomes hang in the balance. (Rosenstone and Hansen, 1993, at 6–7)

Edward Carmines and James A. Stimson, too, see political activists as key players in the political process: "Political activists . . . are abnormal. Their interest is atypical. Their conspicuously political behavior, in a culture of mass noninvolvement, is deviant. But we entertain the reasonable suspicion that their weight in the political process is considerably greater than their number; that in a society where few care about politics, those few are unusually important actors" (Carmines and Stimson, 1989, at 89).

Under the old party system, political activists would be willing to mobilize voters provided the candidate delivered the promised jobs and contracts—that is, a patronage-based system:

> One of the tensions facing partisan candidates is the need to solve another collective action problem, that of generating the many activists needed to secure the labor and financial (and other) resources needed to achieve mobilization. This may yield tension, because the best appeal to activists may differ from what would best mobilize voters. Resolution of such competing pressures depends in part on the activists' incentives. For example, political machines generated selective incentives for securing activists' support that were largely independent of policy appeals to the public. (Aldrich, 1995, at 50)

For winning candidates to the Senate or presidency, lower federal court judgeships were among the many plum jobs that they could bestow upon the activists—either party activists or candidate-centered activists—who helped them get elected (e.g., Baum, 1990; Carp and Stidham, 1998; Chase, 1972; Evans, 1948; Goldman, 1997, 1967).[6] Dating back as far as the Andrew Jackson presidency (Bell, 2002b), lower court judgeships were nothing more than "rewards for political service" (Howard, 1981).[7] Sheldon Goldman

(1997) also asserts that some, but certainly not all, of FDR's courts of appeals appointees were made for policy purposes. He bases his conclusion on archival evidence documenting instances where home state senators touted their constituents for lower court vacancies on the basis of their support of the New Deal agenda. However, as we are concerned in this book with the *predominant* way in which a president chooses his lower court judges—the rule, not the exceptions—Goldman's claims are not contrary to those made herein. In fact, Goldman acknowledges that lower court judges in the early 20th century, including those appointed by FDR, were predominantly chosen for patronage reasons. Under the modern party system, however, patronage appointments alone no longer satisfy political activists; rather, they want these appointments used to further policy goals. It has thus become incumbent upon politicians to develop new nomination and confirmation strategies to satisfy the activists' policy-oriented demands—leading to an appointment process based much more on ideological considerations and much less on patronage considerations.

Moreover, as previously discussed, politicians must satisfy not only the demands of party activists, but of issue activists (those affiliated with interest groups) as well. This is because the new party system marked a period of decline of the political parties and the rise of interest groups in terms of mobilizing voters. Like the policy-oriented party activists in the post-1950s era, the modern-day issue activists demand that candidates deliver policy outcomes in exchange for their electoral support. And what is one of the most important policy outcomes that these two interrelated sets of activists want? The "right" kind of judges sitting on the federal bench.

So although their efforts to shape the federal judiciary go largely unnoticed by the American public, politicians are nevertheless still engaging in electoral politics through a variety of judicial nomination/confirmation strategies—all designed to satisfy policy demands of activists. I collectively refer to these new nomination/confirmation strategies as *elite mobilization strategies* because they are specifically intended to satisfy key elites affiliated with the two major political parties. Briefly, the new policy-oriented appointment strategies to which I refer are as follows: (1) presidents choosing judges pursuant to ideological litmus tests, (2) presidents choosing judges pursuant to affirmative action criteria, (3) senators engaging in "obstructionist" confirmation tactics against nominees found ideologically objectionable, and (4) political challengers on the campaign trail exploiting an incumbent's prior selection or confirmation decision.[8] As previously stated, all of these strategies are ultimately designed to satisfy the policy demands of party elites and activists so that they will mobilize the mass electorate on Election Day.

What do these strategies have in common? They all involve strategic actions of politicians in either choosing (in the case of the president), confirming (in the cases of sitting senators), or merely taking a stand on (in the cases of political candidates) federal court judgeships. By definition, elite mobilization requires politicians to take a *public* stand regarding lower federal court appointments. Politicians signal their targeted constituents—again, the conservative activists aligned with the Republican Party and the liberal activists aligned with the Democratic Party—to let them know exactly where they stand on a particular judicial nominee or on the direction of the federal courts as a whole. In this sense, elite mobilization efforts resemble "position taking"—one of the three classic forms of congressional activity identified by David R. Mayhew in his seminal book *Congress: The Electoral Connection* (1974)—though the audience to whom the position statements are directed is somewhat different than that which Mayhew envisioned. In the case of judgeships, politicians speak to an elite audience, rather than to a mass audience.[9] As Mayhew describes it, position taking is

> the public enunciation of a judgmental statement on anything likely to be of interest to political actors. The statement may take the form of a roll call vote. The most important classes of judgmental statements are those prescribing American governmental ends . . . The congressman as position taker is a speaker rather than a doer. The electoral requirement is not that he make pleasing things happen but that he make pleasing judgmental statements. The position itself is the political commodity. (pp. 61–62)

To the extent such elite mobilization cues are successful, the political activists at whom the tactics are aimed can then be counted on to mobilize the mass electorate on the candidate's behalf come the next election (in the case of grass-roots activists) or to donate money to a candidate (in the case of grass-top elites). To the extent such elite mobilization cues are not forthcoming—or convey the wrong message—activists and elites may then choose to mobilize the mass electorate *against* a particular candidate, or alternatively, but an equally effective tactic, not to mobilize potential voters at all. As the president of NOW explained:

> There are only so many pressure points you have with members of Congress and it mostly boils down to the people who can vote for them or who can give them money . . . [Our base] is very politically active. . . . *Not only do they [NOW members] vote, but they turn out votes. And they can turn off votes, which is every bit as powerful as turning out the votes. If they [NOW members] give you a bad name in your local community, so that the women don't want to come out and vote for you, you're in trouble.* (Gandy interview, 2002, emphasis added)

Conservative activist Thomas Jipping echoed the same sentiment:

I disabused myself of the notion that because Republican senators articulate the right principles [about keeping judicial activists off the bench] that there would be spontaneous combustion. That they'd do what they said they would do [and work to fight their confirmation]. It just doesn't work. It's too much of an insider game to just work [at defeating a nominee from] . . . inside the Beltway. You have to get your constituents involved . . . The structure we were building [at the conservative Judicial Selection Monitoring Project, JSMP] was a grass-roots [structure]. That's the approach JSMP took from the beginning. (Jipping interview, 2002)

As an indication of how much politicians fear alienating key political elites, consider the Senate confirmation battle over D. Brooks Smith to the Third Circuit Court of Appeals in May 2002. Smith was strongly opposed by NOW because of his membership in a private all-male hunting club in Pennsylvania as well as his stated opposition to the Violence Against Women Act.

Notwithstanding this vocal and strong opposition from NOW, three Democrats on the Senate Judiciary Committee voted to recommend confirmation of Smith, including two who were then viewed as possible candidates for the Democratic presidential nomination in 2004: Joseph R. Biden Jr. and John Edwards (Herbert Kohl of Wisconsin was the third Democrat to vote for Smith).[10] Immediately after the committee vote was held, Olga Vives, NOW's vice president of grass-roots activism, issued a press release. The message to Biden and Edwards was unequivocal: "the field of Democratic presidential candidates narrowed significantly today" (McFeatters, 2002).

To indicate just how seriously senators fear the political repercussions of dissatisfied activists, consider Edwards's efforts to engage in damage control after the Smith vote. According to NOW president Gandy, almost immediately following his vote in favor of Smith, a member of Edwards's staff called Gandy to explain what happened:

> I [Gandy] said, "Oh, I guess you've seen our press release." And he [the staff member] said, "Oh god. It was faxed to us from all over the country." That's a direct quote . . . He said, "Look. This nomination was gone [meaning the nominee would be voted with approval by the Judiciary Committee]. Biden had already made up his mind [to support Smith]." His story was that Edwards wanted to be able to ride to the rescue, I'm paraphrasing, on bad nominations, but being from North Carolina, as he is, there are only so many [nominees] he can vote against. And that he [Edwards] was perfectly willing to vote "no" on this nominee, but that once Biden had voted "yes," and it was clear that it [the confirmation fight] was sailing away, then there was no point in using up a "no" vote. (Gandy interview, 2002)

Gandy was particularly shocked, though, that Biden, previously thought to be a champion of women's rights, voted for Smith:

We had tried [to meet] with Biden in particular because we felt that he was the key [to defeating Smith]. The [Smith] letter promising to resign [from the all-male Spruce Creek Rod and Gun Club] had been written to Biden because Biden was chair of the committee back in 1988 when Smith got the district court nomination. I thought, "[Biden's] been dissed." He took this man's word. Plus, [Smith came out against] the Violence Against Women Act, just to add insult to injury, which was Biden's baby . . . And he was a sitting judge at the time that he was opining on the constitutionality of the Violence Against Women Act, which actually could have come to him [for a decision]. It was at a time when it [the issue] was percolating. Plus, [Smith had] all of these ethical problems.

When asked what NOW would have done had they been forewarned that Biden would vote for Smith, Gandy immediately threatened electoral consequences:

We would've had every Delaware donor of Joe Biden on an airplane, and they would've been standing in his office if we had known in advance that Joe Biden was going to vote "yes" [on Smith]. . . We could've gone that far, and we would have . . . It's not rocket science to figure out who [Biden's] donors are. You call the state Democratic Party . . . and get on the phone with them. And we'd [also] be on the phone with our allies saying, "Who do you have on your major donor list—the National Women's Law Center, the Women's Political Caucus, Emily's List, whatever—who lives in Delaware who probably gives to Joe Biden, and will you call them and ask, "Do you give to Joe Biden?" . . . We'd get on the phone with our allies saying, "We just heard Joe Biden is about to vote 'yes' on this nomination. He's going to carry Edwards and Kohl with him because they don't want to use up their limited ['no' votes]." They feel they have a finite number of "no" votes that they can cast, and they don't want to use them up, and so we've got to get Biden to vote "no." But we didn't know that [he was planning on voting "yes" to Smith]. He didn't tell us. He didn't give us a clue. (Gandy interview, 2002)

Interest groups put pressure on presidential candidates as well: "By influencing the [presidential] nomination process, interest group activists can pressure candidates to adopt particular positions. As anti-abortion activists moved in the Republican Party and pro-choice groups formed alliances with the Democrats, the abortion issue became a litmus test for presidential candidates" (Rozell and Wilcox, 1999, at 33–34). Once a president is elected, interest groups then insist that he employ a litmus test for the selection of federal court judges based on the nominee's position on *Roe*.

Conclusion

Because presidents and senators are so dependent on political activists to mobilize the electorate to turn out at the polls—and key political activists are so dependent on the federal courts to achieve their desired policy outcomes— politicians are now forced to pursue nomination/confirmation strategies that satisfy first and foremost the policy demands of these highly mobilized factions (again, activists concerned with abortion, civil rights, and civil liberties). Simply stated, in the selection and confirmation of lower federal court judges, it is the politicians' pursuit of these policy-oriented strategies— which touch on the most divisive partisan issues of the modern political era—that has led to the heightened politicization of the lower federal court appointment process. The theory of elite mobilization also explains why politicians expend such an inordinate amount of political capital on the lower federal courts when the issue has no salience with the American electorate. They need to "score points" with key elite constituents.

CHAPTER 2

From Patronage to Policy

THE OVERARCHING THEORY of this book, explored in the previous chapter, is that two dramatic events unfolded during the 1950s and 1960s—both at the behest of a new breed of policy-driven political activists—that would eventually lead to a lower court appointment process rife with partisan politics. First, the political party system changed, from a loosely connected system of local, patronage-driven organizations into a national, policy-driven organization. Second, the federal judiciary changed, from a closed institution that adjudicated the property and business-oriented claims of corporations into an open institution that adjudicated individual rights claims of the disadvantaged. As a result of these two historic changes, politicians—presidents, senators, and even candidates for these offices—would cease using lower federal court judgeships predominantly for *patronage* purposes and instead, in accordance with the demands of political activists for judges who will be sympathetic to their respective causes, would begin to exploit federal judgeships as a means to satisfy the activists' *policy* demands. The various strategies are what I collectively term elite mobilization strategies. Because the parties' activists are extremely polarized, each side seeks judges who will be on the far right or left of the ideological spectrum, transforming judicial appointment politics in Washington from a collegial "old-boys" club into a partisan battlefield.

Before we turn to in-depth analyses of the various elite mobilization strategies, we should first consider how the change in the judicial appointment process from a patronage-dominated appointment system to a policy-dominated appointment system has affected the way justice is meted out in the federal judiciary. As we will see, the historic changes that occurred to the party system and the judiciary in the 1960s had an impact far beyond politics in Washington. Because the old party system left judicial selection in the hands of local party leaders and home state senators who placed their patrons on the bench, the appointees of a given president—Democrat or Republican—were ideologically heterogeneous, just as the local party leaders and home state senators were ideologically heterogeneous. For example, when a Republican president under the old party system chose his lower court judges, and most were chosen for patronage reasons, the political ideology of these individuals would vary greatly, reflecting the values of local party bosses and politicians rather than the national political agenda advocated by the appointing president. The same would be true of judges chosen by a Democratic president under the old party system versus those chosen by a Democratic president under the modern party system. Thus, given the heterogeneity of the president's judicial cohort, it is not surprising that we see no party-polarized voting when comparing judicial behavior of Republican versus Democratic patrons appointed to the lower federal courts.

Once the party system changed, and activists began demanding ideologically compatible judges according to a uniform standard—and each party's standard was quite polarized from the other's—the appointees of both Republican and Democratic presidents became ideologically homogeneous. When a Republican president under the modern party system chooses most (if not all) of his lower court judges specifically because they disavow the holding in *Roe v. Wade*, his judicial appointees will, by definition, be ideologically homogeneous. Similarly, when a Democratic president chooses most (if not all) of his lower court judges because they support *Roe*, his judicial appointees will also, by definition, be ideologically homogeneous. As these competing litmus tests are incompatible, there will also be significant interparty differences in ideology among lower court judges. Thus, under the modern party system, we see extremely party-polarized voting on the federal bench. What this means is that, in certain types of cases—for example, abortion, civil rights, and states' rights cases—a litigant will likely know how a judge will vote simply by identifying the judge as a Democratic or Republican appointee. Such was not the case when judges of each party varied greatly among themselves, just as local party leaders varied greatly.

In this chapter, we will examine judicial decision-making behavior during three distinct periods: first, the period before transformation of the parties and judiciary (the *old party system*). Here we look at voting behavior of courts of appeals judges appointed by Presidents Harding, Calvin Coolidge, Herbert C. Hoover, and FDR in labor cases. The second period is that during which the parties and judiciary were in transition (the *party system in transition*); we examine voting behavior of courts of appeals judges appointed by Presidents Eisenhower, Kennedy, Johnson, and Nixon in civil rights cases. For the third period, after the historic transformation of the parties and judiciary (the *modern party system*), we look at the voting behavior of federal appellate judges appointed by Presidents Carter, Reagan, G. H. W. Bush, and Clinton in civil rights and abortion cases. These particular types of cases were chosen for each period because of their high political salience during the given period; if party-polarized voting were to exist in any of these periods, we should find it in these types of cases.

This analysis of decision-making behavior also serves another important purpose. During any of our three periods, to the extent we find no statistically meaningful difference between Republican and Democratic judicial decision-making on political issues over which we know Republicans and Democrats in Washington were at odds, we may then reject the notion that presidents during that period were using a predominantly ideology-based appointment strategy when choosing their lower court judges, for if they were, we should see party-polarized voting.

Decision-Making Under the Old Party System: Workers' Rights

For the first forty years of the 20th century, there was perhaps no greater political and legal struggle than that over the proper role of government in regulating the economy. While traditional Republicans favored a laissez-faire approach, Democrats and progressive Republicans (e.g., Teddy Roosevelt) favored government intervention, including minimum wage and maximum hour protections for workers (Patterson, 1967; Schulman, 1991). Critical for our purposes, this important political issue was played out not only in the Legislative and Executive Branches, but in the Judicial Branch as well. Each time a state or federal government enacted a progressive labor regulation, its constitutionality would ultimately be determined by the Supreme Court. Not surprisingly, then, presidents during this period paid close attention to their Supreme Court nominees' ideologies on the labor issue (Pritchett, 1948). Given the Republican Party's domination of the Executive Branch at this time—only one Democrat, Wilson, served as president between 1900 and 1932—conservatives were the majority on the Supreme Court. As expected, these Republican appointees repeatedly held that government economic regulation—state or federal—violated the "substantive" due process clause of the Fourteenth Amendment in that it altered freedom of employers to contract with workers.[1] Later, during the Great Depression of the 1930s, Republicans would soften their position; although accepting the notion of state regulation of the economy, they still opposed the federal government's right to regulate economic matters, which they deemed to be strictly of a local nature (Leuchtenburg, 1995).

After watching a conservative Supreme Court strike down several hall-mark pieces of his New Deal economic plan on federalism grounds, FDR threatened to undermine the Court's authority by proposing legislation that would add additional seats to the Supreme Court—all to be filled by FDR himself. Although Congress never passed his "court-packing" plan, the mere threat of such legislation was apparently enough to persuade the Supreme Court to back down and allow FDR and New Deal Democrats in Congress to initiate their federal economic recovery program. In *West Coast Hotel Co. v. Parrish* (1937),[2] the Court abandoned the substantive due process doctrine and upheld a state minimum wage law. One of Congress's first legislative triumphs in the wake of *West Coast Hotel* was passage of the Fair Labor Standards Act of 1938 (FLSA),[3] which imposed minimum wage and maximum hour requirements on all employers involved in the production of goods used in interstate commerce. After the Supreme Court declared the FLSA constitutional,[4] its enforcement was largely left to the lower federal courts. Accordingly, in order to assess judicial voting patterns in the lower federal courts under the old party system, I will analyze the voting behavior of judicial appointees to the courts of appeals of Presidents Harding, Coolidge, Hoover, and FDR in labor cases decided under the FLSA.

Using the decision-making data from these FLSA cases, I compare whether judges appointed by Democrat FDR are more "liberal" in their voting behavior—that is, support the FLSA claims of workers over employers—than those judges collectively appointed by Republican presidents Harding, Coolidge, and Hoover. No meaningful difference between the voting behavior of the Democratic and Republican cohorts lends empirical support for the central proposition of this book: that presidents before transformation of the party system did not employ predominantly ideologically based appointment strategies.[5] In short, since we know that Democratic and Republican presidents during this era were diametrically opposed on federal labor regulation, an ideology-based judicial selection strategy should produce a statistically significant difference in the voting behavior of judges appointed by these presidents in labor cases. In fact, Segal and Spaeth (1993) found ideology to play a critical role in decision-making behavior by Supreme Court justices in FLSA cases—justices who we know were chosen specifically for policy purposes. Likewise, Brudney, Schiavoni, and Merritt (1999) have identified ideological voting patterns along party lines in federal labor cases decided by the courts of appeals in the modern political era—a period in which ideological litmus tests rule the day (Brudney, Schiavoni, and Merritt, 1999).

I also want to consider whether perhaps there is party-polarized voting between FDR's appointees during the period 1935–40 and the Republican

TABLE 2-1

Logit Coefficients for the Probability of a Vote Against Workers' Claim, Nonconsensual Fair Labor Standards Act Cases, U.S. Courts of Appeals, January 1, 1940 to December 31, 1947

HARDING, COOLIDGE, HOOVER, AND ROOSEVELT APPOINTEES

	Model 1			Model 2		
	MLE	Robust SE	Δ Probability[a]	MLE	Robust SE	Δ Probability[a]
Constant	-.51*	.20	NA	-.50	.20	NA
Background-Based Variables						
Appointing Presidential Party Cohort						
Republican Appointee	Baseline	NA	.00	Baseline	NA	.00
Democratic Appointee	-.28	.21	-.07	—	—	—
FDR 1935–40 Appointee	—	—	—	-.30	.27	-.07
FDR 1933–34, 1941–44 Appointee	—	—	—	-.10	.27	-.02
Southern Judge	.58*	.23	.14	.59**	.23	.14
Fact-Based Variables						
Claim Brought by U.S.	-.76**	.24	-.18	-.75**	.24	-.18

(Vote against labor coded 1; vote for labor coded 0)

N = 444
Likelihood Ratio Test (3 df) = 21.72***
% correctly predicted = 70.78
% in null model = 67.56
Proportional Reduction in Error = 11.02

N = 444
Likelihood Ratio Test (4 df) = 22.35***
% correctly predicted = 70.78
% in null model = 67.56
Proportional Reduction in Error = 11.02

*p ≤ .10; **p ≤ .01; ***p ≤ .001 (two-tailed test)

[a] Change in probability is measured as the change from a probability of .5 given the presence of that variable.

appointees. The reason for splitting the FDR cohort into two derives from Goldman's (1997) account of judicial selection during the FDR administration. Although conceding that FDR's lower court appointments, in the aggregate, were made "in the shadow of traditionally understood senatorial and party politics" (Goldman, 1997, at 17), in reviewing FDR's presidential papers, Goldman believes that FDR paid special attention to the ideology of courts of appeals appointees during the period 1935–40 (see Goldman, 1997, at 30–38). This is because, beginning in 1935, the lower federal courts—three-quarters of which were composed of Republican appointees at that time—began entering injunctions to prevent enforcement of New Deal legislation. This heightened attention to a judicial candidate's support for the New Deal, according to Goldman, waned in about 1941 when the administration was confident in the New Deal's proper implementation by the federal courts. In order to test whether the 1935–40 FDR appointees and Republican appointees of Harding, Coolidge, and Hoover exhibit party-polarized voting, I divide the FDR cohort into two groups: FDR appointees when patronage concerns are believed to have predominated (1933–34, 1941–44) and FDR appointees when policy concerns are believed to have predominated (1935–40). I then rerun the same model discussed above.

The results of the two FLSA models are shown in Table 2-1. Methods and data-related issues, as well as coding for the variables employed in these models, are set forth in Appendix A. Because I use Logit to estimate the coefficients, and Logit coefficients are not by themselves subject to interpretation, I calculate for each coefficient the change in probability of a "conservative" vote given the presence versus the absence of each variable.

As for the first model, Table 2-1 shows no statistically significant difference in the voting behavior of judges appointed by FDR and those appointed by Republican presidents. This is telling because if we see no party-polarized voting patterns among these presidential cohorts—particularly as FDR, unlike prior presidents, was said to have paid closer attention to a nominee's ideology on economic issues—then it is unlikely that partisan voting on the courts of appeals existed at any other time before transformation of the old party system.

As for the second model, although FDR's appointees in the 1935–40 period appear, as Goldman asserts, more liberal than those otherwise made by FDR, we still see no party-polarized voting between judges appointed by FDR during 1935–40 and judges appointed by Republicans. Accordingly, it would seem safe to conclude that under the old party system, we simply do not see significant party-polarized voting in the lower federal courts.

In sum, these results accord with my expectations: when presidents chose

judges under a patronage-dominated appointment system, we do not see statistically meaningful voting patterns between Republican and Democratic
appointees. This is true even though we analyzed cases raising the most politically divisive issue of the day. And this was true even of FDR, who was
generally believed to have paid more attention to ideology in making judicial selection decisions than any other president in the first half of the 20th
century. Thus, although FDR and his three Republican predecessors in the
White House may have carefully chosen Supreme Court justices according
to uniform policy standards, there seems to have been much variation
among a president's lower court appointees because such judgeships were
still largely used as plum patronage for senators and local party leaders.

Decision-Making Under a Party System in Transition: Civil Rights

Perhaps no other political issue defines the postwar period as does the civil
rights movement. As explained in Chapter 1, beginning with the Supreme
Court's 1954 decision in *Brown v. Board of Education*, the federal courts assumed an active role in racial politics in America. This was particularly true
of the lower federal courts, which were given the task of daily enforcing the
dictates of *Brown* and its progeny. Significantly, racial politics would also
transform party politics. In short, as the civil rights movement began to pick
up speed in the 1950s, the race issue came to redefine the two major parties
(Carmines and Stimson, 1989; Edsall and Edsall, 1992).

Although once the Republican Party—the party of Abraham Lincoln—
enjoyed a huge electoral advantage with African Americans, that advantage
would begin to erode during the New Deal, as blacks began to move over
to the Democratic Party as a result of FDR's economic programs aimed at
aiding the poor. This slide would continue during the Eisenhower administration, as Eisenhower's support for the civil rights movement was tepid at
best (e.g., Bickel, 1986; Burk, 1984). Although his administration filed amicus curiae briefs in support of the civil rights plaintiffs in *Brown*, it did so at
the behest of Eisenhower's attorney general, Herbert Brownell Jr., who allegedly had to persuade an unenthusiastic president to take this stand. In
fact, while *Brown* was still pending before the Court, Eisenhower defended
southern whites' resistance to desegregation to Chief Justice Warren: "These
[southerners] are not bad people. All they are concerned about is to see that
their sweet little girls are not required to sit alongside some big overgrown
Negroes" (quoted in Burk, 1984, at 142). And in the 1956 Republican platform, Eisenhower refused to let the party expressly embrace the *Brown* decision (Burk, 1984).

Moreover, although Eisenhower did take a strong stand against segregation when he sent federal troops into Little Rock, Arkansas, to ensure desegregation of Central High School, he is said to have taken this extraordinary step not because he supported desegregation efforts, but instead because he wanted to ensure respect for the rule of law, as Governor Orval Faubus of Arkansas had been flagrantly violating a federal court order to desegregate the school (Dudziak, 1997). Tellingly, Eisenhower made no efforts to pass major civil rights legislation in his eight years in office, though moderate civil rights measures were passed in 1957 and 1960.

The Democratic Party's shift to the left on civil rights actually began during the administration of Harry S Truman. In 1948, for the first time in its history, the Democratic Party platform included a strong civil rights plank. That same year, Truman signed an executive order prohibiting race discrimination in federal employment. While alienating the Democratic Party's conservative southern base, Truman's actions also garnered more votes from blacks in the North. These efforts at redefining the Democratic Party were taken up by the next Democratic president.

Risking alienation of the Democratic Party's southern base, Kennedy promised during the 1960 campaign to introduce major civil rights legislation. Although criticized early on by civil rights leaders and liberal northern Democrats for not acting sooner, Kennedy finally kept his campaign promise when he introduced the Civil Rights Act of 1963—the most sweeping civil rights legislation ever brought before Congress—designed permanently to dismantle the Jim Crow laws in the South. Kennedy would not live to see this legislation passed, but it was nevertheless shepherded through Congress by his successor, Johnson, and was passed as the Civil Rights Act of 1964.

During his first full term in office, Johnson proposed, and Congress enacted, an aggressive legislative program designed to end all forms of racial discrimination in the South. Such legislation included the Voting Rights Act of 1965 and the Fair Housing Act of 1968. These statutes, together with programs designed to alleviate poverty, came to be known as Johnson's Great Society.

Sensing that southern Democrats were becoming disaffected with the Democratic Party's sharp turn to the left on race issues under Presidents Kennedy and Johnson, Barry Goldwater sought to exploit this regional rift among Democrats in his 1964 bid for the presidency. He did so by characterizing civil rights protesters as criminal thugs (Beckett, 1997). Also central to Goldwater's strategy was to attack the Warren Court's liberal decisions on criminal civil liberties. Although Goldwater lost the 1964 presidential race in a landslide, his bundling together of the race and crime issues would prove an important turning point in American politics, for in 1968, Nixon would pick up and run with this strategy.

In 1968, Nixon would forever cement the party divide on the race issue. Playing on southern Democrats' disaffection with the Democratic Party leadership over civil rights legislation, Nixon attacked the Democratic Party's entire Great Society agenda as well as the Supreme Court's rights revolution. To this end, Nixon made an express promise in his 1968 campaign to appoint only conservative judges—those who believe in "strict construction" of the Constitution—to all levels of the federal judiciary. In other words, by promising to undo the policy gains liberals made through federal court litigation during the 1950s and 1960s, Nixon would lure conservative, white, southern Democrats to the Republican Party. In terms of an electoral strategy, Nixon's plan proved quite successful. Not only did he win the 1968 election, but he also began a trend in electoral politics that persists today. In short, conservative southern Democrats permanently switched party allegiance and became Republicans (Carmines and Stimson, 1989), while the vast majority of African Americans permanently became Democrats.

In sum, during the postwar period, we find a new legal issue coming to define the two major parties: equal rights for minorities. While Democratic presidents Truman, Kennedy, and Johnson staked out a liberal position for their party—fully aware that they would alienate southern Democrats— Republican president Eisenhower was not enthusiastic about aiding the civil rights movement, and Republican president Nixon strategically staked out a conservative position for the Republican Party on the race issue—fully aware that he would attract southern Democrats.

As was true of the labor issue during the New Deal period, the federal courts again proved a critical battleground for the political fight over civil rights for minorities. Accordingly, we will now examine decision-making behavior in civil rights cases decided during the period in which the old party system was transitioning into the modern party system. Once again, we want to determine whether judicial voting behavior in this set of highly charged political cases was split along party lines. If policy considerations were driving judicial selection decisions in this transitional party period, then we should see party-polarized voting, just as Republican and Democratic presidents were split along party lines during this period on civil rights issues. If party-polarized voting is not present, then we may reject this hypothesis.

Studies of presidential archives have indicated that Presidents Eisenhower and Kennedy chose their lower court judges strictly for patronage purposes (Burk, 1984; Chase, 1972; Goldman, 1997), while Presidents Johnson and Nixon were much more concerned with the ideology of their lower court judges, particularly in the South where judicial enforcement of civil rights laws and decisions would have the greatest effect (Goldman, 1997; McFeeley, 1987). This makes sense given the rise of issue activism specifically centered around race during the 1960s. Accordingly, in addition to looking at decision-making for all presidential cohorts in this period, we will also compare judicial voting behavior of judges appointed at the beginning of this transitional period with that of judges appointed in the latter part of the transitional period. I would expect to see party-polarized voting in the latter part of the period when litmus tests come into widespread practice, but not in the earlier part of the period when patronage appointments were still the rule, not the exception.

For this phase of the analysis, we look at race discrimination cases decided under the Civil Rights Act of 1964 and/or the equal protection clause of the Fourteenth Amendment. This category of decisions was chosen because, as detailed above, it taps into the most ideologically driven and salient issue of the 1950s and 1960s—race and the civil rights movement—an issue that came to define the two major parties during the same period in which the old party system was breaking down.[6] Specifically, we will focus on judicial appointees of Presidents Eisenhower, Kennedy, Johnson, and Nixon.

We will make three important comparisons between Democrat- and Republican-appointed judges: (1) decision-making of appointees of Presidents Eisenhower, Kennedy, Johnson, and Nixon (the aggregate model); (2) decision-making of appointees of Presidents Eisenhower and Kennedy (the beginning of the transitional period); and (3) decision-making of appointees of Presidents Johnson and Nixon (the end of the transitional period).

The results of the race discrimination models for the transitional party period are shown in Tables 2-2 and 2-3. Explanation and coding for the variables employed in these models is set forth in Appendix C. I again calculate for each coefficient the change in probability of a "conservative" vote—a vote against the minority plaintiff alleging some form of race discrimination—given the presence or absence of that particular variable for any given observation.

Turning first to the aggregate model for Eisenhower, Kennedy, Johnson, and Nixon appointees (Table 2-2), we see that there is no statistically significant difference in the voting behavior of Republicans versus Democrats. Given that Democratic presidents' policy positions on civil rights were much more liberal than those of Republican presidents during this period, this finding suggests that none of the presidents in the transitional period between the old and new party systems continued to use an ideology-based appointment strategy. However, when we turn to the disaggregated models (Table 2-3), a different story emerges. While no party-polarized voting is

TABLE 2-2

Logit Coefficients for the Probability of a Vote Against a Minority Plaintiff,
Nonconsensual Race Discrimination Cases, U.S. Courts of Appeals,
January 1, 1968 to December 31, 1974, Party System in Transition

| | EISENHOWER, KENNEDY, JOHNSON, AND NIXON APPOINTEES | | |
	MLE	Robust SE	Δ Probability[a]
Constant	−1.18*	.16	NA
Background-Based Variables			
Appointing Presidential Party Cohort			
Republican Appointee	Baseline	NA	.00
Democratic Appointee	−.22	.15	−.05
Southern Judge	−.04	.15	−.01
Fact-Based Variables			
Class Action	−.73*	.21	−.17
Equal Protection Claim	.63*	.15	.15

(Vote against minority plaintiff coded 1;
vote for minority plaintiff coded 0)

$N = 1,009$
Likelihood Ratio Test (4 df) = 27.50*
% correctly predicted = 71.75
% in null model = 71.75
Proportional Reduction in Error = .00

* $p \leq .001$ (two-tailed test)
[a] Change in probability is measured as the difference from a probability of .5 given the presence of that variable.

detected in the earlier period (Eisenhower and Kennedy appointees), for the first time, we do see party-polarized voting when Nixon appointees are compared with Democratic appointees of Johnson. With everything else held constant, a Johnson appointee is less likely than a Nixon appointee to vote against a minority plaintiff (the conservative position) by 17 percentage points.

In sum, it is not until the late 1960s that party-polarized voting becomes pronounced in the lower federal courts. Consistent with the theory of elite mobilization, this is the very same time that the old party system—one in which patrons were critical in mobilizing voters—begins to break down and the new party system—one in which issue activists dominate party politics—begins to take shape. Needing to cater to the demands of key political elites—demands centering on policy, not patronage—presidents adapt their appointment strategies, and we immediately begin to see party-polarized voting among courts of appeals judges. And as we will see below, as this new breed of issue activists gains more influence in electoral politics

TABLE 2-3

Logit Coefficients for the Probability of a Vote Against a Minority Plaintiff, Nonconsensual Race Discrimination Cases, U.S. Courts of Appeals, January 1, 1968 to December 31, 1974, Party System in Transition

	EISENHOWER AND KENNEDY APPOINTEES			JOHNSON AND NIXON APPOINTEES		
	MLE	Robust SE	Δ Probability[a]	MLE	Robust SE	Δ Probability[a]
Constant	-.71***	.22	NA	-1.70***	.18	NA
Background-Based Variables						
Appointing Presidential Party Cohort						
Republican Appointee	Baseline	NA	.00	Baseline	NA	.00
Democratic Appointee	.21	.22	.05	-.72***	.19	-.17
Southern Judge	-.50*	.22	-.12	.48*	.17	.12
Fact-Based Variables						
Class Action	-.52*	.30	-.13	-.88***	.30	-.21
Equal Protection Claim	.65**	.22	.16	.66***	.20	-.16

(Vote against minority plaintiff coded 1; vote for minority plaintiff coded 0)

N = 428
Likelihood Ratio Test (4 *df*) = 19.19***
% correctly predicted = 73.29
% in null model = 73.29
Proportional Reduction in Error = .00

N = 581
Likelihood Ratio Test (4 *df*) = 35.36***
% correctly predicted = 72.28
% in null model = 72.63
Proportional Reduction in Error = 1.27

*$p \leq .10$; **$p \leq .01$; ***$p \leq .001$ (two-tailed test)

[a]Change in probability is measured as the difference from a probability of .5 given the presence of that variable.

over the next three decades, party-polarized voting in the federal courts will become even more pronounced.

Decision-Making Under the Modern Party System: Civil Rights and Abortion Rights

As political activists became more convinced over time that the federal courts held the key to achieving their social policy goals, they stepped up their demands on presidents to appoint the "right" kind of judges. Accordingly, every president in the modern political era has articulated some form of litmus test in choosing lower court judges—litmus tests that are designed to satisfy the policy demands of leading political activists. What issues do these litmus tests turn on? Abortion, civil rights, civil liberties, and states' rights. Here, we will focus on two of these issues. First, we will analyze judicial voting behavior in civil rights cases because it allows us to compare party-polarized voting between the transitional period and the modern party period. As the Democrats have staked out a more liberal position on civil rights in the modern era, I would expect Democratic appointees to be more liberal than Republican appointees in the modern party era.

Second, because abortion is the most critical litmus test presidents use in the modern political era, we also look to decision-making in abortion cases. Simply stated, every Democratic president since Carter has expressly promised to appoint judges who would uphold the *Roe* decision, and every Republican president has expressly promised to appoint judges who would either "protect the sanctity of life"—an explicit threat to overturn *Roe*— or "strictly construe the Constitution"—a more veiled threat to overturn *Roe*.[7] Thus, I would again expect Democratic appointees to vote more liberally than Republican appointees. If such ideological litmus tests were, in fact, employed during the modern political era, then we should see party-polarized voting by court of appeals judges in abortion cases and race discrimination cases.

For this part of the analysis, we look at (1) race cases decided under Title VII, the Reconstruction Civil Rights Statutes, and the equal protection clause of the Fourteenth Amendment, and (2) abortion cases decided under the due process clause of the Fourteenth Amendment, as interpreted by the Supreme Court in *Roe* and *Casey*. I examine the votes of judges appointed by Presidents Carter, Reagan, G. H. W. Bush, and Clinton. The results of the modern party era models are shown in Tables 2-4 and 2-5, and explanation and coding for these models are set forth in Appendix C (race discrimination cases) and Appendix E (abortion cases). I again calculate for

TABLE 2-4

Logit Coefficients for the Probability of a Vote Against a Minority Plaintiff,
Nonconsensual Race Discrimination Cases, U.S. Courts of Appeals,
January 1, 1994 to December 31, 2001, Modern Party System

	CARTER, REAGAN, G. H. W. BUSH, AND CLINTON APPOINTEES		
	MLE	Robust SE	Δ Probability[a]
Constant	−.42**	.11	NA
Background-Based Variables			
Appointing Presidential Party Cohort			
Republican Appointee	Baseline	NA	.00
Democratic Appointee	−1.19**	.13	−.27
Southern Judge	.49**	.14	.12
Fact-Based Variables			
White Plaintiff	.81**	.17	.19
Pro Se Plaintiff	−1.38**	.34	−.30
Race Plus Other Claim	.58*	.19	.14
Class Action	1.04**	.32	.24
Equal Protection Claim	.83**	.20	.19

(Vote against plaintiff coded 1;
vote for plaintiff coded 0)

$N = 1,353$
Likelihood Ratio Test (8 *df*) = 185.79**
% correctly predicted = 70.85
% in null model = 62.32
Proportional Reduction in Error = 22.64

*p ≤ .01; **p ≤ .001 (two-tailed test)
[a]Change in probability is measured as the difference from a probability of .5 given the presence of that variable.

each coefficient the change in probability of a "conservative" vote—a vote against the minority plaintiff alleging some form of race discrimination or a vote to uphold an abortion restriction—given the presence or absence of that particular variable.

Turning first to the race model (Table 2-4), as expected, we find a statistically significant difference between Republican and Democrat appointees in race discrimination cases. With everything else held constant, Democrat appointees are less likely to vote against a minority plaintiff by 27 percentage points when compared with Republican appointees to the federal bench. As for the abortion model (Table 2-5), what is immediately striking is the magnitude of the coefficient. With everything else held constant, a Democrat-appointed judge is less likely to vote to uphold an abortion restriction by 44 percentage points compared with a Republican-appointed judge.

TABLE 2-5

*Logit Coefficients for the Probability of a Vote to Restrict Abortion,
Nonconsensual Abortion Rights Cases, U.S. Courts of Appeals,
January 1, 1978 to December 31, 2002, Presidential Cohorts*

| | CARTER, REAGAN, G. H. W. BUSH, AND CLINTON APPOINTEES | | |
	MLE	Robust SE	Δ Probability[a]
Constant	.68*	.38	NA
Background-Based Variables			
Appointing Presidential Party Cohort			
Republican Appointee	Baseline	NA	.00
Democratic Appointee	−2.79**	.44	−.44
Southern Judge	1.27*	.50	.28
Fact-Based Variables			
Statute Restricting Abortions for Minors	.93*	.45	.22
Post-*Casey* Decision	−.15	.44	.04

(Vote against abortion rights coded 1;
vote for abortion rights coded 0)

$N = 154$
Likelihood Ratio Test (4 df) = 45.19**
% correctly predicted = 81.81
% in null model = 50.65
Proportional Reduction in Error = 63.10

*$p \leq .10$; **$p \leq .001$ (two-tailed test)

[a]Change in probability is measured as the difference from a probability of .5 given the presence of that variable.

Party Realignment

We need to address the possibility of an alternative explanation to the above results: Could the onset of party-polarized voting in the late 1960s be the result not of party transformation and the rise of issue activism but of party realignment among the electorate? The theory of party realignment states that because of a shock to the party system, party support among the mass electorate shifts suddenly from one party to the other (Campbell et al., 1960). V. O. Key (1955) referred to these sudden shocks as *critical elections*. What causes these shocks is the emergence of a political issue that arouses extreme intensity among voters; because of the positions asserted on this critical issue by the two major parties, we see a major shift in party allegiances, making one party the predominant party. A stable period with these new party allegiances then follows. Examples include the slavery issue in the 1860 election and economic welfare programs in the 1932 election. Relevant to our study is whether the civil rights debate of the 1960s spurred party realignment.

In recent years, the theory of party realignment has been questioned. Aldrich (1995) argues that Key's theory is applicable only to the old mass party system, and not to the 1960s period. According to Aldrich, although the party system was transformed in the 1960s—making the 1960s in some sense a critical period—no realignment ensued, as neither the Republican Party nor the Democratic Party emerged as the predominant party in the United States. Instead, Aldrich asserts that after the 1964 election, a critical transformation in the party institutions themselves occurred. This transformation largely turns on the changes in the party activists discussed in Chapter 1, rather than in mass voter allegiances. It is this party transformation from which the theory of elite mobilization derives (see Chapter 1). But Aldrich and other scholars (e.g., Carmines and Stimson, 1989) do acknowledge that there were some shifts in partisan loyalties beginning in the 1960s. Although not significant enough of a shift to rise to the level of a critical realignment, beginning with the 1964 election, conservative Democrats in the South shifted their loyalty to the Republican Party because of the race issue. And as Republican Party elites continued to exploit the race issue over time in a nuanced manner, the Republican Party became more conservative and the Democratic Party more liberal (Carmines and Stimson, 1989).

Given that party loyalties among many conservative activists shifted beginning in the 1960s, we must address whether this change is driving party-polarized voting in the modern political era, rather than the rise of issue activism among party elites coupled with the onset of the rights revolution in the federal courts. According to this alternative theory, under the old party system, Democratic judges in the aggregate will appear more conservative, and Republican judges more liberal, than they do in the modern party era because conservative southern Democrats would today be considered Republicans. Because of this alternative hypothesis, I specifically included a variable to control for a judge's southern background in all models previously discussed in this chapter. What this allows me to do is hold a judge's regional background constant and then parse out just the effect of party on voting behavior. Had I not included this control variable, then the alternative hypothesis would carry more weight.

However, in order to reject this alternative explanation definitively, I will now additionally examine voting patterns of non-southern and southern judges separately across our three time periods. If the same voting patterns replicate themselves for non-southern judges—that is, if we see no party-

TABLE 2-6

Comparison of Judicial Voting by Party and Across Time Periods, Greater Likelihood of Republican-Appointed Judge Casting Conservative Vote, U.S. Courts of Appeals

	OLD PARTY SYSTEM (LABOR CASES)	PARTY SYSTEM IN TRANSITION (RACE CASES)			MODERN PARTY SYSTEM (RACE CASES)	(ABORTION CASES)
	Appointees, 1920–1944	Appointees, 1953–1974	Appointees, 1953–1963	Appointees, 1964–1974	Appointees, 1977–2000	Appointees, 1977–2000
All Circuits	.07	.05	−.05	.17**	.27**	.44**
Non-Southern Circuits	.05	.06	−.04	.16*	.26**	.45**
Southern Circuits	.12	.05	−.06	.18*	.27**	.42**

$*p \leq .10$; $**p \leq .001$ (two-tailed test)

polarized voting in the earlier periods and then party-polarized voting emerging in the late 1960s—then I can reject the theory of party realignment as driving the decision-making patterns, as the non-southern constituencies of the Democratic and Republican parties did not experience major shifts in party loyalty around the race issue. Moreover, if this alternative theory is correct, we should also see major differences in decision-making behavior between the models for southern judges only and all judges. Specifically, Republican judges should be significantly more liberal than Democratic judges under the old party system when more conservatives in the South were Democrats. If this voting pattern does not emerge, we may also reject the alternative hypothesis.

For this part of the analysis, I reran the same models shown in Tables 2-1 through 2-5 two separate times. The first time, I eliminated the votes of judges from the Fourth, Fifth, and Eleventh Circuits (the southern circuits). The second time, I included only the votes of judges from the Fourth, Fifth, and Eleventh Circuits. Table 2-6 and Figure 2-1 show the differences be-

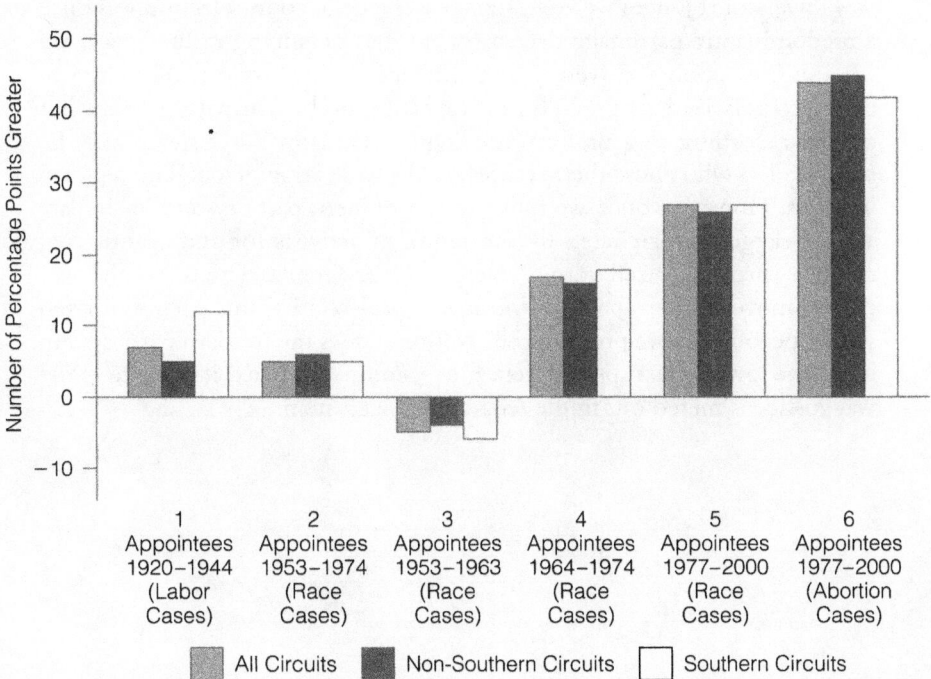

FIGURE 2-1. Greater Likelihood of Republican Judge Casting a Conservative Vote, U.S. Courts of Appeals

tween Republican- and Democrat-appointed judges' decision-making behavior across the three time periods (1) for all circuits, (2) for non-southern
circuits only, and (3) for southern circuits only. I include only the difference
in probability of a conservative vote.

As expected, the voting patterns indeed replicate themselves when the
models for non-southern circuits and all circuits are compared. Also as expected, Republican judicial appointees in the South do not vote more liberally than Democratic judicial appointees to any statistical significance before
1964. Accordingly, we can reject the alternative hypothesis that shifts in
party loyalties beginning in the 1960s—when southern Democrats moved
toward the Republican Party—are somehow driving party-polarized voting
in the modern party period.

Conclusion

Two historic transformations of American political institutions—the party
system and the federal judiciary—working in tandem led to a change in the
way lower court judges were chosen. Lower federal court selection was once
a predominantly patronage-driven system, but beginning in the 1950s, we
see a shift to a policy-driven system. Under the old party system, there was
no party-polarized voting. This makes sense, given that patrons were not
chosen according to a uniform ideological standard, but instead, like the
party leaders who chose them, represented a wide array of local and regional
interests. However, once we move to the modern party system in the late
1960s—largely precipitated by the influx of activists for and against civil
rights—party-polarized voting emerges. Over time, as activists in the two
parties move farther apart on the ideological continuum, party-polarized
voting becomes more pronounced. Not only does the modern party system
make the lower court appointment process more complex, it also affects the
way justice is meted out in the federal judicial system.

PART TWO

Elite Mobilization Strategies for the Modern Political Era

CHAPTER 3

The Role of Political Ideology in the
Lower Court Nomination Process

IN THE MODERN POLITICAL ERA, the first elite mobilization strategy to
emerge was the ideological litmus test. Starting with the Nixon administration, every president is believed to have used some form of litmus test to
choose lower court judges. But as we will see in this chapter, Republican
presidents seem to place greater weight on this elite mobilization strategy
than do their Democratic counterparts. Instead, Democratic presidents tend
to downplay the importance of litmus tests and allege to make judicial selection on the basis of merit, even-handedness, and diversity. Notwithstanding these claims, with liberal activists closely monitoring the ideology of the
judicial selections by Democratic as well as Republican presidents, Democratic presidents cannot completely shun litmus tests or else they will risk
alienating their key political activists come election time.

In this chapter, we will explore the use of the ideological litmus test by
presidents in the modern political era. Do presidents, as I predict, predominantly choose judges pursuant to a litmus test designed to satisfy the policy
demands of key activists affiliated with their party? To test this hypothesis,
we will first examine the litmus tests believed to have been used by Presidents Nixon, Carter, Reagan, G. H. W. Bush, and Clinton regarding four
politically charged legal issues: criminal defendants' civil liberty protections,
minorities' civil rights protections, states' rights, and women's abortion
rights. These issues were specifically chosen for analysis because they are the
very same issues on which judicial appointment politics have centered in the
modern political era (see Chapter 1). Once having established the presidents'
various litmus tests with respect to these four issue areas, we will then be in
a position to form hypotheses as to where each of the judicial cohorts of

these five presidents should lie on the ideological spectrum with respect to each issue under study, assuming that litmus tests were used in the selection process.

We will then examine the decision-making behavior of judges appointed by Presidents Nixon, Carter, Reagan, G. H. W. Bush, and Clinton in cases capturing the same four issue areas previously considered: search and seizure cases decided under the Fourth Amendment; civil rights cases decided under Title VII, the Reconstruction Civil Rights Statutes (commonly referred to as Sections 1981 and 1983), and the equal protection clause; states' rights cases decided under the Tenth and Eleventh Amendments; and abortion cases decided under the due process clause. If a president chooses judges pursuant to a litmus test, then we should see his judicial appointees deciding cases in a manner consistent with his espoused litmus test; on the other hand, if we find a judicial cohort's voting behavior to be inconsistent with the appointing president's litmus test, then we may reject such a hypothesis.

This empirical analysis also enables us to answer such critical questions as the following: When a president's policy agenda marks a shift from that of past presidents within his own party, do his judicial appointees reflect that of the old regime or the new regime? Do presidents pay closer attention to satisfying activists' policy demands in certain political issue areas, such as crime, over others? And to the extent a policy position of the president is at odds with key activists within his party, does judicial ideology of his appointees reflect that of the president or that of the activists?

Republicans and Litmus Tests

CRIME AND UNDOING *MIRANDA V. ARIZONA* AND *MAPP V. OHIO*

In his 1968 bid for the presidency, Nixon stated unequivocally that his judicial appointees, at all levels of the federal judiciary, "first and foremost . . . had to be men who share my legal philosophy" (McFeeley, 1987, at 26). Sensing that the nation was growing dissatisfied with the liberal rulings of the Warren Court, Nixon made it a central campaign theme that he would appoint "law and order" judges (Chernoff, Kelly, and Kroger, 1996). The subtext of Nixon's fight against "street" crime was none too subtle: He made liberal judges the scapegoat for the nation's alleged crime problem (Hoff, 1995). Nixon's stated litmus test, then, was to find judges willing to turn back the clock on the civil liberties protections accorded criminal defendants by the liberal Warren Court, instead advocating a narrow reading of the Constitution in the area of criminal law enforcement (Beckett, 1997).

Nixon's political gamble is commonly referred to as the *southern strategy*.

By playing the race and crime cards, the strategy was specifically designed to attract southern Democratic voters to the Republican Party—a party base that had been the exclusive domain of the Democratic Party since Reconstruction. Nixon carried five southern states—North Carolina, South Carolina, Tennessee, Virginia, and Florida—in the 1968 presidential election with his tough talk on race and crime. Once he was elected, conservative activists serving in the White House urged the president to make good on his campaign promise to use a litmus test when filling vacancies on the federal courts (Maltese, 2003). One often-told story about Nixon and judicial selection involves a memorandum written by White House aide Tom Charles Huston. Huston noted that judicial nominations were "perhaps the least   considered aspect of presidential power" and urged the president to set specific guidelines for choosing lower court judges. If Nixon "establishes his criteria and establishes his machinery for insuring that the criteria are met, the appointments will be his, in fact, as in theory" (Huston, quoted in Maltese, 2003, at 2–3). There is no doubt that the president was prepared to establish and use ideological criteria, for he instructed his chief domestic affairs advisor, John Ehrlichman, in a handwritten note to follow Huston's recommendation (Maltese, 2003, at 2–3).

A look at the Nixon administration's positions regarding the constitutional interpretation of the Fourth, Fifth, and Sixth Amendments reveals that Nixon advocated relatively conservative criminal law enforcement policies—ones that were certainly more conservative than the Supreme Court's or the Democratic Party's prevailing views at that time. Regarding the Supreme Court's decision in *Miranda v. Arizona* (1966)—requiring state law enforcement officials to warn a suspect of his Fifth and Sixth Amendment rights before interrogation—Nixon took the position that Congress had effectively overruled the case with passage of the Crime Control Act of 1968 (O'Neill, 2000).[1] Nixon also sought reversal of the Warren Court's exclusionary rule under the Fourth Amendment announced in *Mapp v. Ohio* (1961); he contended that this judicially constructed rule, like *Miranda*, impaired criminal law enforcement efforts (Davies, 2002).

Many political scholars believe that the Reagan and G. H. W. Bush administrations cemented the restructuring of the two political parties begun in 1968 by Nixon. Picking up on Nixon's southern strategy, both Reagan and Bush played to conservative political activists. Indeed, the Christian Coalition was instrumental in mobilizing voters for these Republican presidential candidates in the 1980s. Both presidents, like Nixon, made the federal courts the scapegoat for the crime problem. The 1980 Republican platform stated: "vital to efforts to stem crime is the fair but firm and speedy application of criminal penalties. The existence and application of strong penalties are effective disincentives to criminal actions. Yet these disincentives will only be as strong as our court system's willingness to use them."[2] Accordingly, both Reagan and Bush promised to appoint "law and order" judges to the federal courts:

> Under Mr. Carter, many appointments to federal judgeships have been particularly disappointing. By his partisan nominations, he has violated his explicit campaign promise of 1976 [to use merit selection] and has blatantly disregarded the public interest. We pledge to reverse that deplorable trend, through the appointment of women and men who respect and reflect the values of the American people, and whose judicial philosophy is characterized by the highest regard for protecting the rights of law-abiding citizens.[3]

Reagan was also the first president to aggressively try to persuade the Supreme Court to overturn the *Miranda* decision (O'Neill, 2000). To this end, in its 1988 "Guidelines on Constitutional Litigation" the Reagan Justice Department stated: "Because there is no constitutional or statutory basis for these rules [concerning *Miranda* warnings and the suppression of evidence], and because they have a detrimental effect on the search for truth in criminal investigation and adjudication, government lawyers should seek to convince the courts to construe these rules narrowly and, where possible, to limit further their scope or abandon them entirely."[4]

Like the *Miranda* ruling, Reagan also viewed the exclusionary rule announced in *Mapp* as a procedural matter—that is, strictly a rule of evidence—and argued that it "lacks a constitutional basis."[5] Believing the rule to inhibit the search for truth in a criminal trial, the Reagan Justice Department instructed federal prosecutors to seek out cases in which they could argue for *Mapp*'s reversal, or at least to "apply broadly the principles underlying the various limitations to the exclusionary rule."[6]

With the same conservative activists to satisfy, G. H. W. Bush essentially shared the same political strategy and ideology as Reagan when it came to issues of criminal law enforcement. Like Reagan, Bush took advantage of the crime issue in his 1988 presidential campaign against Michael Dukakis, focusing on Dukakis's opposition to the death penalty and support for a prison furlough program as governor of Massachusetts (Lauter, 1988).[7] The 1988 Republican platform stated: "We commend the Reagan-Bush team for naming to the federal courts distinguished women and men committed to judicial restraint, the rights of law-abiding citizens, and traditional family values. We pledge to continue their record. Where appropriate, we support congressional use of Article III, Section 2 of the Constitution to restrict the jurisdiction of federal courts."[8] Like Reagan, Bush also wanted to see *Miranda* overturned and, in fact, instructed his Justice Department to actively seek out an appropriate test case to challenge the validity of the *Miranda* holding, claiming that a 1968 congressional statute overruled the decision (O'Neill,

2000).[9] And also like Reagan, Bush took the position that the exclusionary rule was merely a rule of evidence and not a rule of constitutional significance (O'Neill, 2000).

RACE AND UNDOING THE CIVIL RIGHTS LAW

Beginning with Goldwater's bundling together of the civil rights movement and urban unrest, crime and race have forever been linked in American politics. Thus, as the crime issue began to define the Democratic and Republican parties in the 1960s, so too did the race issue (Carmines and Stimson, 1989). As discussed in Chapter 2, the Democratic Party came to be viewed as the home of racial "liberalism" and the Republican Party the home of racial "conservatism" (Aldrich, 1995, at 184–85). But even though Nixon played the race card in his 1968 run for the presidency, if one looks closely at his record on civil rights once in office, he appears to be not quite as much a hard-liner as his Republican successors Reagan and G. H. W. Bush.

On the one hand, Nixon aggressively pushed for federal affirmative action plans containing specific minority hiring quotas and compulsory timetables in which to meet these quotas (Days, 1984). One such high-profile affirmative action effort was known as the Philadelphia Plan, which required bidders on federally assisted construction contracts in the Philadelphia area to set numerical goals for hiring blacks in construction jobs—that is, quotas.[10] After the courts upheld the Philadelphia Plan, Nixon had similar affirmative action proposals inserted in all government contracts (Rose, 1989). Nixon also signed into law the Equal Employment Opportunity Act of 1972;[11] among other things, the act amended Title VII to bring state and local governments under its coverage (Belz, 1991). On the other hand, Nixon strongly opposed busing as an appropriate remedy for past race discrimination in the public schools, and even made this issue a centerpiece of his 1972 campaign for reelection (Parnet, 1990). Nixon actually proposed legislation—the Student Transportation Moratorium Act of 1972[12]—to wrest jurisdiction from federal courts over school desegregation cases so that busing orders would cease. A Democrat-controlled Congress did not, however, pass such law.

After Nixon left office in the mid-1970s, conservative activists affiliated with the Republican Party began a concerted litigation strategy to undo advances liberal activists had made in the federal courts regarding the constitutionality of race and gender preferences designed to redress past discrimination. Although originally formed to litigate strictly issues of labor law on behalf of big business, the National Chamber Litigation Center was the first group to lead this effort (Epstein, 1985). After the Supreme Court decided in 1976 to review the constitutionality of benign race-based programs in *Regents of the University of California vs. Bakke* (1978), coupled with the election that year of Carter—a strong proponent of affirmative action—came the formation of another litigation-centered anti–affirmative action interest group, the Equal Employment Advisory Council. And with the election in 1980 of Reagan, conservative litigation-oriented interest groups would find a much more sympathetic president.

Under the leadership of Reagan, the Republican Party would move far-ther to the right in its policies on civil rights than where it stood under Nixon, just as the activists affiliated with the Republican Party had become more conservative. The 1980 Republican platform clearly set out Reagan's philosophy on racial equality: "Equal opportunity should not be jeopardized by bureaucratic regulations and decisions which rely on quotas, ratios and numerical requirements to exclude some individuals in favor of others, thereby rendering such regulations and decisions inherently discrimina-tory." [13] Reagan was opposed to the use of any numerical hiring goals or timetables to remedy past race discrimination (Days, 1984). In short, he sim-ply opposed the very concept of affirmative action, taking the position that such remedies were unlawful under Title VII (Crenshaw, 1988). In terms of legislation, Reagan vetoed the Civil Rights Restoration Act of 1987,[14] but this veto was overridden by Congress. The act was intended to overrule a recent Supreme Court case [15] that, among other things, had narrowed the application of Title IX (barring gender discrimination by educational insti-tutions receiving federal funding) and Title VI (barring race discrimination in the use of federal funds). Regarding litigation strategy, the Civil Rights Division in the Reagan Justice Department essentially declined to enforce existing civil rights laws (Amaker, 1988).

Whether G. H. W. Bush privately shared Reagan's commitment to undo federal civil rights laws is harder to glean from the public record, as he flip-flopped on this issue throughout his political career. Some attribute this to Bush's lack of ideological vision on civil rights (Devins, 1991). For example, although he opposed the 1964 Civil Rights Act when running for Congress, once elected, he supported the affirmative action efforts of the Nixon ad-ministration (Morley, 1992), Later, during his tenure as vice president, Bush was often said to disagree behind closed doors with the hard-line conserva-tive positions advocated by the Reagan Justice Department (Marcus, 1992). But consistent with the theory of elite mobilization, by the time Bush ran for president in 1988, his public pronouncements on race became decidedly con-servative as he tried to court the conservative base of the Republican Party in order to ensure his election. The 1988 platform stated: "We will resist efforts to replace equal rights with discriminatory quota systems and preferential treatment. Quotas are the most insidious form of reverse discrimination against the innocent." [16] The Justice Department under Bush consistently argued against the legitimacy and legality of affirmative action in federal programs, characterizing affirmative action as "racial stereotyping that is an anathema to basic constitutional principles." [17] Bush also vetoed the Civil Rights Act of 1990. Only when he was certain to be overridden by Congress the following year did he sign into law the Civil Rights Act of 1991. [18]

STATES' RIGHTS AND UNDOING THE FEDERAL GOVERNMENT'S POWER TO LEGISLATE SOCIAL POLICY

The Republican Party has advocated increasing state power over federal power since World War II (Schreiber, 1996), but the terms of today's federalism debate were largely framed in the 1960s when Nixon began attacking the Johnson administration's Great Society programs. The cornerstone of Nixon's efforts to decentralize the federal government was his New Federalism urban aid initiative, in which, according to Nixon, "power, funds and responsibility will flow from Washington to the states and to the people" (Conlan, 1988). There were two major features of Nixon's New Federalism plan: (1) creating a revenue-sharing scheme between the federal government on the one hand and state and local governments on the other; Nixon also wanted to grant state and local governments the power to determine their own priorities with respect to the spending of any federal funds shared; and (2) moving away from categorical federal grants, in which the federal government exercises the most control over how states spend federal funds (the type of system in place during the prior two Democratic administrations), and toward a system of block grants, in which states are given considerable more flexibility to spend federal funds (Casino, 1988).

Despite Nixon's New Federalism initiatives, some argue that, to Nixon, the issue of states' rights was more about rhetoric than about decentralizing federal power (see, for example, Conlan, 1988; Schreiber, 1978). This view is based on the fact that Nixon actually *expanded* the federal government's roles in many formerly state-controlled policy areas, including consumer protection, environmental protection, and worker safety protection (Vogel, 1980). Others question Nixon's commitment to decentralizing federal power when, in fact, Nixon greatly centralized power in the Executive Branch, increasing the number of agency oversight programs during the economic crisis of the 1970s (Cross, 1988).

Reagan was the first president to reverse a long trend of expanding federal power that began with FDR's New Deal. Upon taking office, Reagan promised "to curb the size and influence of the Federal establishment and to demand recognition of the distinction between the powers granted to the Federal government, and those reserved to the States or to the people" (Lott, 1994, at 346). Critically, Reagan also promised to appoint judges to the federal bench that shared this "belief in the decentralization of the federal government and efforts to return decision-making power to state and local elected officials."[19]

Once in office, Reagan largely enacted his vision of federalism through two executive orders: Executive Order 12,372, "Intergovernmental Review of Federal Programs,"[20] and Executive Order 12,612, "Federalism Considerations in Policy Formulation and Implementation."[21] The first of these orders reformed the procedure that the Office of Management and Budget used to resolve federal state disputes over federal grants and expenditures. It directed federal officials to "accommodate" the views of the state official's position on such matters, or explain why such could not be done. The second order had a normative tone, establishing Reagan's nine "fundamental federalism principles" on the relationship between the federal, state, and local governments. For example, it stated that limiting the scope and power of the federal government preserves political liberty of the people; it declared that the states were in a better position than the national government to solve local problems; and it created a presumption of state sovereignty. In addition to these normative values, the second executive order established several critical policy-making criteria guiding the formulation and administration of future federal regulations and proposed legislation. Most notably, before an agency could issue a regulation, it must have clear constitutional and statutory authority to do so. Otherwise, it is presumed that the federal agency must defer to state sovereignty. Moreover, the order required all federal agencies to have an express grant of authority, or otherwise have firm evidence, that Congress authorized the agencies to pass regulations preempting state law.

Reagan's strategy regarding states' rights also contemplated using constitutional arguments centered on federalism and the Tenth Amendment to try to overturn major civil rights statutes of the 1960s, including the landmark 1964 Civil Rights Act. For example, the Reagan administration called the Supreme Court's decision in *Katzenbach v. Morgan* (1966),[22] which upheld the constitutionality of the act, "inconsistent" with the administration's desire to cut back Congress's ability to engage in social policy-making under its interstate commerce power.[23]

G. H. W. Bush is largely regarded as having continued the Reagan administration's policies concerning federalism—in other words, favoring states' rights over the power of the federal government (Nix, 1989; Walker, 1995). In the 1988 Republican platform, Bush stated: "Our Constitution provides for a separation of powers among the three branches of government. In that system, judicial power must be exercised with deference toward State and local authority; it must not expand at the expense of our representative institutions. When the courts try to reorder the priorities of the

American people, they undermine the stature of the judiciary and erode respect for the rule of law."[24]

In terms of substantive policy, on February 16, 1990, G. H. W. Bush released a memorandum reaffirming Reagan's Executive Order 12,612 on federalism, stressing that these states' rights principles were central to the Bush administration.[25] In addition, Bush issued Executive Order 12,803, which directed that federally financed "infrastructure assets" be regulated "consistent with the principles of federalism enumerated in Executive Order 12,612."[26] And although he signed the Gun Free School Zones Act of 1990[27]—making it a federal offense to carry a gun within one hundred yards of a school—Bush expressed concern that the statute "inappropriately overrides legitimate state firearms laws with a new unnecessary federal law" (Maloney, 1994, at 1801). This narrow reading of Article I, Section 8—advocated by the conservative pro-gun lobby in *United States v. Lopez* (1995)[28]—would later be adopted by the Supreme Court.

ABORTION AND UNDOING *ROE V. WADE*

In the years after the Supreme Court's 1973 landmark decision in *Roe v. Wade*—grounding a woman's right to abortion in the Constitution's due process clause, which guarantees citizens a right to privacy—conservative activists began to devise a long-term litigation strategy designed to overturn the decision. This effort was led by a Chicago-based interest group known as Americans United for Life (AUF) that was originally formed in 1971 to combat the lobbying efforts in state legislatures of liberal interest groups such as the ACLU, Planned Parenthood, and NARAL that were seeking repeal of state anti-abortion laws (Epstein, 1985). In the wake of pro-choice activists' victory in *Roe*, AUF shifted gears and settled on a litigation-oriented strategy to undo the decision. To this end, the group organized a staff of scholars and lawyers to articulate pro-life legal claims and to litigate pro-life lawsuits (Chambers, 1984). The interest group's goals were as follows: (1) litigating pro-life cases in the Supreme Court and the lower federal courts, (2) helping members of Congress and state legislators draft bills favorable to the movement, (3) creating a well-organized network of grassroots operations, and (4) most significantly, seeking the appointment of justices on the Supreme Court who would vote to overturn *Roe* (Chambers, 1984). By the time Reagan was running for president in 1980, these conservative pro-life forces had grown significantly in number and stature and formed the heart of a constituency that came to be called the New Right.

Reagan was only too willing to satisfy conservative activists' demands on the abortion issue. Accordingly, in the 1980 Republican platform, Reagan called for "the appointment of judges at all levels of the judiciary who respect traditional family values and the sanctity of innocent life";[29] in other words, Reagan would use a nominee's stand on *Roe* as a litmus test for judicial appointments.[30] Later, Attorney General Edwin Meese would instruct the Justice Department that *Roe* was an illegitimate exercise of the Supreme Court's power in that it created a fundamental right not contained in the Constitution.[31] Shortly before Reagan left office, one of his domestic policy advisors, Gary L. Bauer (later the head of the Christian Coalition), declared that although Reagan might not have been able to push through much of his conservative legislative agenda, he pleased conservatives by appointing many federal court judges who would adopt the policy views of the right; specifically, Bauer cited an Eighth Circuit Court of Appeals decision upholding a parental notification law for minors seeking abortions (Roberts, 1988).

Wanting to court the same socially conservative constituency that had been so loyal to Reagan, G. H. W. Bush made the exact same anti-abortion pledge to the conservative base of the Republican Party that Reagan had made in 1980: "We reaffirm our support for the appointment of judges at all levels of the judiciary who respect traditional family values and the sanctity of innocent human life."[32] Although earlier in his political career he was a pro-choice candidate, Bush instructed his Justice Department to seek an appropriate test case to seek the reversal of *Roe* by the Supreme Court. In fact, it was the G. H. W. Bush administration that came closest to getting *Roe* overturned in *Planned Parenthood of Southeast Pennsylvania v. Casey* (1992).[33]

Democrats and Litmus Tests

In stark contrast to Republican presidents in the modern political era—who openly embraced ideological litmus tests in the selection of lower court judges—the two Democratic presidents in the modern era, Carter and Clinton, were less forthcoming about whether they were using such tests. Their preferred elite mobilization tactic was diversification of the federal bench (which we will examine in Chapter 4). However, as liberal activists in the Democratic Party, particularly during the Clinton presidency, were closely scrutinizing the ideology of lower court nominees, a president who completely disregarded a judicial candidate's ideology would be risking alienating key elites in his party.

CRIME AND PROTECTING THE
MIRANDA AND *MAPP* DECISIONS

In contrast to the 1968 (Nixon), 1980 (Reagan), and 1988 (G. H. W. Bush) elections, crime was not a major issue during the 1976 campaign, except as it related to Watergate. The only indication of where Carter stood on criminal law enforcement during the 1976 campaign comes from the

Democratic platform, which suggested that Carter, if elected, would make no effort to shift traditional Democratic ideology to the right on criminal law enforcement. Instead, the platform embraced the broad civil liberty protections accorded criminal defendants by the Warren Court and emphasized eradication of poverty as a cure for any crime problem in America:

> We must restore confidence in the criminal justice system by insuring that detection, conviction and punishment of lawbreakers is swift and sure; that the criminal justice system is just and efficient; that jobs, decent housing and educational opportunities provide a real alternative to crime to those who suffer enforced poverty and injustice . . .
>
> Toward these ends, we support a major reform of the criminal justice system, but we oppose any legislative effort to introduce repressive and anti–civil libertarian measures in the guise of reform of the criminal code.[34]

Regarding interpretation of the Fourth, Fifth, and Sixth Amendments, the Carter administration stood squarely behind the rulings of the Warren Court. For example, regarding the *Miranda* decision, the Carter administration simply ignored the 1968 congressional statute purporting to overturn the Supreme Court's ruling (O'Neill, 2000). The Carter administration even supported a *stricter* warrant requirement than Supreme Court law then allowed in searches involving newsrooms (Greenhouse, 1978).[35] Thus, Carter's views on crime reflected those of liberal Democratic Party activists. The Clinton years, however, would mark a conflict between president and party activists on the crime issue.

After almost thirty years of being labeled by the American public as "soft on crime," the Democratic Party would finally turn its image around under the stewardship of Clinton. After witnessing Dukakis's 1988 defeat to President Bush largely because of Dukakis's support for "liberal" crime policies, Clinton wanted to avoid Dukakis's mistakes in his 1992 campaign for president. Clinton, however, was also aware that liberal activists affiliated with the Democratic Party—as opposed to voters—would oppose any of his efforts to steer the party to the right on the crime issue. Thus, Clinton found himself in a difficult position; he needed to satisfy liberal Democratic activists so that they would mobilize key voting blocs in the Democratic Party who opposed a "law and order" approach to crime, and at the same time he had to persuade moderate voters that he was a "new" Democrat on the crime issue. Clinton thus took a middle ground between the conservative stands of former Republican presidents and the liberal views of Democrats Carter and Dukakis. Although he supported the death penalty and enacted tough anticrime legislation, Clinton also stood by more traditional Democratic policies on drugs (i.e., focusing on drug rehabilitation rather than pure retributive measures) (Chernoff, Kelly, and Kroger, 1996). The Clinton Justice

Department also took the position that *Miranda* warnings were constitutionally mandated—a sharp break from the positions of Reagan and G. H. W. Bush—in its brief to the Supreme Court in *Dickerson v. United States* (2000).[36] Nor did the Clinton administration support overruling *Mapp* and the exclusionary rule as did Reagan and G. H. W. Bush; rather, Clinton appeared to favor maintaining limited exceptions to the rule, for example, in instances where law enforcement officials acted in "good faith" in obtaining a warrant (Leib, 1997). But what would this rift between liberal Democratic activists and the more moderate president mean in terms of Clinton's choices for the federal bench? We will want to pay special attention to the decision-making behavior of the Clinton judicial cohort when we examine judicial decision-making below.

RACE AND THE PRESERVATION OF
RACIAL PREFERENCES FOR MINORITIES

There is little doubt that Carter is located on the left of the ideological spectrum in terms of racial egalitarian policies. Carter was a staunch supporter of the use of racial preferences and racial quotas to remedy past discrimination (Finn, 1982). Indeed, he wanted to expand and strengthen the use of these affirmative action remedies through court action and extensive regulations of the Equal Employment Opportunity Commission (Belz, 1991; Devins, 1991). Carter even accepted the use of court-ordered busing to remedy unlawful racial segregation in the public schools, although only as a "last resort."[37]

As was true of the crime issue, on the race issue, Clinton again had to balance the competing interests of liberal Democratic activists—who wanted to preserve the Supreme Court's rulings of the 1970s that had upheld the use of racial preferences for minorities as "benign" preferences—and moderate voters—who opposed "reverse" discrimination against white males (many of whom were so-called Reagan Democrats). Accordingly, Clinton tried to forge a middle position between the conservative Reagan/Bush approach to civil rights and the traditional liberal Democratic Party approach of the Carter presidency. However, Clinton's positions tended to be more in line with liberal Democratic Party activists than were his crime positions. For example, although Clinton opposed the use of racial quotas in school admissions or federal contracting, he did support use of racial preferences, claiming that we should "mend [affirmative action policy], not end" federal affirmative action programs (Editorial, *Wall Street Journal*, 1997). Moreover, Clinton's Justice Department argued to the Supreme Court that minority preferences in the hiring of public school teachers were constitutional, reversing the position in this case taken earlier by the G. H. W. Bush administration in *Board of Education of the Township of Piscataway v. Taxman*.[38] Clinton also questioned the wisdom of California's Proposition 209, ending affirmative action in statewide California programs, on the ground that it would have a "devastating impact" on minorities (Brownstein, 1997).

STATES' RIGHTS AND PRESERVING THE FEDERAL GOVERNMENT'S RIGHT TO CREATE SOCIAL POLICY

The states' rights movement has a long association with racism in the South. In the earlier part of the 20th century, southerners relied on states' rights rhetoric in opposition to a federal anti-lynching legislation (Emanuel, 1996). Later, in the 1960s, southerners would turn to states' rights arguments in support of Jim Crow laws mandating segregation in the South. Not surprisingly, then, leading liberal activists, most notably the NAACP, have long favored federal over state power in the balance between the two sovereigns under our constitutional system of federalism. Indeed, not until the federal government's passage of the 1964 Civil Rights Act did segregationist policies in the South begin to unravel (Rosenberg, 1991). In the 1990s, an NAACP leader remarked that returning power to the states under welfare reform legislation harkened back to the days of Jim Crow: "Many African-Americans remember that 'states' rights' were code words for the states' denial of basic civil rights. We are concerned that this history not return in the context of welfare reform" (Henderson, quoted in Pear, 1996).

There is general consensus that Carter was firmly committed to the principle that the federal government is best equipped to handle the nation's major social problems. The 1976 Democratic platform is replete with calls for invoking federal power in areas where states had previously been primarily responsible for legislating. For example, with respect to crime, the platform states that "recognizing that law enforcement is essentially a local responsibility, we [the Democratic Party] declare that control of crime is an urgent national priority and pledge the efforts of the Democratic Party to insure that the federal government act effectively to reverse these trends."[39] Similarly, with respect to education, the platform states that the Democratic Party "should strengthen *federal* support of existing programs that stress improvement of reading and math skills . . . We should also work to expand *federal* support in areas of education need that have not yet been addressed sufficiently by the public schools."[40]

Carter's presidency also marked a peak in federal aid programs and the consolidation of regulatory power in the federal government (Walker, 1995). Carter favored a federal solution to solving the nation's urban ills; unlike Nixon, however, he preferring categorical grants over the block grants that Nixon had implemented as part of his New Federalism initiative (Martin,

1994). Like Nixon, Carter also centralized power over federal aid programs in the Executive Branch (Cross, 1988).

Although during his first term in office Clinton granted states greater discretion to experiment with certain federally funded programs, such as welfare (Dorf and Sabel, 1998), during his second term, all of Clinton's goodwill toward state governments would seemingly disappear. Without any consultation with Congress or state governments, on May 19, 1998, Clinton signed Executive Order 13,083,[41] titled simply "Federalism," which expressly revoked the policies on federalism that the Reagan and G. H. W. Bush administrations had laid down in Executive Order 12,612. Clinton's federalism order instead permitted federal agencies to formulate and implement federal policy—and at the same time foreclosed or limited state policy-making authority—under nine conditions, including the need for uniform national standards, an increased cost of decentralization, or a reluctance of states to regulate in an area for fear of losing business in the state. The new executive order also did away with the presumption of state sovereignty in the passage or implementation of federal regulations, a proposition central to the Reagan/Bush philosophy on federalism.

Clinton's federalism order immediately sparked strong opposition from the Republican-led Congress, as well as an outcry from state and local governments (Blake, 2000). When both houses of Congress sought to block the order's implementation through passage of bills codifying principles of federalism,[42] Clinton relented and revoked the order.[43] Later that year, he essentially reinstated the old Reagan/G. H. W. Bush policy with Executive Order 13,132, including the presumption of state sovereignty.[44]

Further evidence of Clinton's waning support for states' rights can be gleaned from the positions advocated by his Justice Department in several landmark Supreme Court cases involving the proper balance of power between the federal and state governments under the Tenth and Eleventh Amendments.[45] In each of these cases, Clinton's Justice Department came down squarely on the side of expansive federal power trumping state power.

ABORTION AND PRESERVING *ROE V. WADE*

Although the 1976 Democratic platform was silent on the abortion issue, Carter stood firmly behind a woman's right to choose abortion (Tribe, 1990, at 153). When it became clear that abortion would be a major issue in the 1980 campaign, the Democratic Party Platform of 1980 declared *Roe* to be "the law of the land" and stated that the party was opposed to "any constitutional amendment to restrict or overturn that decision."[46] But because the conservative anti-abortion movement was still in its infancy during the Carter years, and because Republican presidents had not yet made abortion a litmus test for federal judicial selection, liberal activists had yet to focus on the issue of choosing pro-choice judges. Thus, Carter was never pushed by Democratic Party activists in the 1970s to declare that support for *Roe* was a litmus test for federal judicial selection. However, by the 1990s, Clinton would have to make his position quite clear.

Clinton, like Carter, was a proponent of legalized abortion. The Democratic Party Platform of 1992 stated, "Democrats stand behind the right of every woman to choose [abortion], consistent with *Roe v. Wade*, regardless of ability to pay, and support a national law to protect that right." [47] Although Clinton expressly stated his intention to use support for *Roe* as a litmus test for Supreme Court nominations during the 1992 campaign, after his election, the Clinton administration indicated that it would consider nominating abortion opponents to the lower federal courts in an effort to show its evenhandedness (Lewis, 1993a). When two white males believed to be anti-choice were recommended to the White House by Democratic leaders for district court judgeships early in Clinton's first term—Gary Gaertner Jr. in Missouri (a friend of Missouri Democratic congressman Richard A. Gephardt) and William K. Downes in Wyoming (a friend of the governor's)—liberal activists kicked into high gear. Although Clinton ended up nominating Downes in Wyoming, liberal interest groups, including the Alliance for Justice, NARAL, and the Missouri State Women's Political Caucus, vigorously lobbied the administration to reject the Gaertner recommendation and nominate another pro-choice candidate for the Missouri judgeship (Freivogel, 1993). Gaertner "has a record which indicates he is extremely anti-choice, and we would hope that would fail to qualify him for the federal bench," stated the legal director of NARAL (Marcy Wilder, quoted in Freivogel, 1993). Notwithstanding the support of Speaker of the House Gephardt, Clinton refused to nominate Gaertner. After the Gaertner episode, Clinton is believed to have nominated only one other possible pro-life judge, Brian Theodore Stewart. However, Stewart was nominated as part of a log-roll—an agreement between politicians whereby each agrees to vote for the other's legislation, or in this case judicial nominee, and vice versa—between Clinton and Republican Judiciary Committee Chairman Orrin G. Hatch so as to break a judicial gridlock in the confirmation process (see Chapter 6).

Expectations of Judicial Behavior

CRIMINAL LAW ENFORCEMENT

Clearly, siding with conservative activists affiliated with the Republican Party, all three of the Republican presidents considered in this chapter stood solidly on the right in terms of criminal law enforcement. Carter also was in line with his key activists, standing squarely on the left regarding constitutional protections for criminal defendants. Clinton, however, presents a more difficult case. Although leading liberal activists in the Democratic Party continued to support the old-line Democratic Party stand on crime, Clinton was clearly more moderate. But the theory of elite mobilization suggests that Clinton would be compelled to appoint judges more liberal than he was to appease the liberal activists affiliated with the Democratic Party. Therefore, I would expect Clinton's appointees to lie close to Carter's on the left of the ideological continuum. How close remains to be seen.

RACE

On the race issue, both Carter and Clinton supported affirmative action and strong civil rights protections for minorities. Clinton did so even in the face of adverse decisions from a conservative Supreme Court, which had outlawed many governmental programs giving preferential treatment to minorities. I would thus place these two cohorts on the left of the ideological continuum.

Reagan and G. H. W. Bush clearly stood on the right on civil rights issues, in line with conservative activists. Nixon presents a more complex case. Although in the late 1960s and 1970s Democrats viewed Nixon as extremely conservative on race issues, compared with Reagan's and Bush's stands, Nixon appears to be more moderate in that he supported affirmative action to remedy past discrimination. This would be contrary to the conservative activists Nixon was trying to court as part of his southern strategy. Accordingly, consistent with elite mobilization theory, I would predict Nixon's appointees to lie on the right of the ideological spectrum near the Reagan and G. H. W. Bush cohorts.

STATES' RIGHTS

Without question, Carter stood on the left of the ideological spectrum in his unequivocal favoring of the federal government over states' rights. Although Clinton began his presidency espousing somewhat moderate views on federalism, he clearly moved to the left of the ideological spectrum by the time the Supreme Court, in 1995, began overturning sixty years of precedent in the federalism area—no longer allowing the federal government to dictate to states policy on public safety and welfare. Since Clinton needed to appease liberal activists in his party who disfavor the states' rights movement, I would expect lower federal court judges appointed by both Carter and Clinton to lie on the left of the ideological spectrum in cases involving federalism/states' rights.

On the basis of their public records concerning the proper balance of power between federal and state governments under our constitutional system of federalism, I would argue that Nixon stands somewhat to the left of Reagan and G. H. W. Bush on the ideological spectrum. Although throughout his presidency Nixon often espoused his preference for state power over federal power, his actions while in office suggest that his commitment to these principles was less than sincere. Nevertheless, as the conservatives in the South who were critical to his southern strategy favored states' rights, I would expect Nixon's appointees to vote similarly to Reagan and Bush judges in cases involving federalism/states' rights.

ABORTION

On the issue of abortion, there is little doubt that Democratic activists are pro-choice, and Republican activists are pro-life. Similarly, at least since the *Roe* decision in 1973, presidents have largely come down on the abortion issue to conform with the views of their parties' activists. More than any other issue considered in this chapter, party and issue activists would require strict conformity with a *Roe* litmus test. Nixon, the only pre-*Roe* president analyzed here, presents a more difficult case; he was personally opposed to abortion but never took an official position on the issue and clearly supported strong population controls. Moreover, unlike the post-*Roe* presidents, Nixon never expressly stated or even implied that abortion would be used as a litmus test for the appointment of judges to the lower federal courts. Accordingly, I would expect judges appointed by Democratic presidents Carter and Clinton to fall on the left of the ideological spectrum, Nixon judges to fall in the middle, and Reagan and Bush judges to fall on the right of the ideological spectrum.

Judicial Voting Behavior

We will now assess the voting behavior of the judicial cohorts of Presidents Nixon, Carter, Reagan, G. H. W. Bush, and Clinton in four different categories of cases: (1) search and seizure decisions, (2) race discrimination decisions, (3) states' rights decisions, and (4) abortion rights decisions.

Four models were constructed (one for each data set) employing a number of control variables. Explanation and coding of the variables is contained in Appendices B (search and seizure cases), C (race discrimination cases), D (states' rights cases), and E (abortion cases). We want to assess whether, consistent with the theory of elite mobilization, presidents appointed judges who represent the views of the activists in their parties and, if not, why not. The most important independent variable to focus on in this chapter is that for appointing president. The magnitude and sign of the Logit coefficients will then be compared with the policy positions advanced by the relevant group of activists involved in judicial appointment politics during that pres-

TABLE 3-1

*Logit Coefficients for the Probability of a Vote Against a Criminal Defendant,
Nonconsensual Search and Seizure Cases, January 1, 1994 to December 31, 2001*

	MLE	Robust SE	Δ Probability[a]
Constant	−.45*	.20	NA
Background-Based Variables			
Appointing Presidential Cohort			
Clinton Appointees	Baseline	NA	.00
G. H. W. Bush Appointees	.74***	.18	.18
Reagan Appointees	.79***	.15	.19
Carter Appointees	−.64***	.18	−.13
Nixon Appointees	.73**	.28	.18
Regional Background of Judge			
Compared with South			
Southern Judge	Baseline	NA	.00
Eastern Judge	−.61**	.22	−.13
Midwestern Judge	−.47**	.15	−.10
Ninth Circuit Judge	−.88***	.18	−.18
Tenth Circuit Judge	−.12	.19	−.03
Fact-Based Variables			
Location of Search Compared			
with Home			
Search of Home	Baseline	NA	.00
Search of Luggage	.52*	.21	.13
Search of Automobile	.33*	.17	.08
Search of Person	.25	.17	.06
Presence of Warrant	1.00***	.17	.23
Limited Search	.26*	.13	.06
Border Search	.13	.22	.03

(Vote against criminal defendant coded 1;
vote for criminal defendant coded 0)

$N = 1,469$
Likelihood Ratio Test (14 *df*) = 162.59***
% correctly predicted = 63.78
% observed in null model = 50.30
Proportional Reduction in Error = 27.12

*p ≤ .10; **p ≤ .01; ***p ≤ .001 (two-tailed test)

[a]Change in probability is measured as the distance from a probability of .5 assuming the presence of that variable.

ident's tenure. Because Logit coefficients are not by themselves subject to interpretation, I calculate for each coefficient the change in probability of a "conservative" vote given the presence or absence of the particular variable.

SEARCH AND SEIZURE MODEL

The results of the search and seizure models are shown in Tables 3-1 and 3-2. The most striking finding for these models is that Clinton's lower court appointees are significantly more conservative than Carter's appointees. But

TABLE 3-2

Comparison of Voting Across Presidential Cohorts, Probability That a Judge Will Vote to Uphold a Search or Seizure, Nonconsensual Search and Seizure Cases, U.S. Courts of Appeals, January 1, 1994 to December 31, 2001

	Clinton Judge	G. H. W. Bush Judge	Reagan Judge	Carter Judge	Nixon Judge
Compare a Clinton Judge with a:	—	−.18★★	−.19★★	+.13★	−.18★
Compare a G. H. W. Bush Judge with a:	+.18★★	—	−.01	−.32★★	.00
Compare a Reagan Judge with a:	+.19	+.01	—	+.33★★	.01
Compare a Carter Judge with a:	−.13★	−.32★★	−.33★★	—	−.32★★
Compare a Nixon Judge with a:	+.18★	.00	−.01	+.32★★	—
N = 1,469					

★$p \leq .01$; ★★$p \leq .001$ (two-tailed test)

it is also true that Clinton's appointees are much more likely to rule in a criminal defendant's favor than the appointees of the three Republican presidential cohorts analyzed here. That is because, like Carter, his judicial appointees lie in the middle of the ideological spectrum regarding the crime issue. I consider later in this chapter why Clinton's appointees stray from the liberal ideology of Democratic Party activists on the crime issue. Compared with a Clinton appointee (which serves as the baseline against which all other presidential cohorts are measured), we see that, with everything held constant, the probability of a vote against the criminal defendant increases by 18 percentage points given a G. H. W. Bush appointee, increases by 19 percentage points given a Reagan appointee, decreases by 13 percentage points given a Carter appointee, and increases by 18 percentage points given a Nixon appointee (Table 3-1). Critically, all of these coefficients are statistically significant.

I also wanted to investigate whether there are statistically significant differences in voting between Republican cohorts, requiring separate regressions using each of the presidential cohorts as the baseline. The probabilities obtained from these separate regressions are shown in Table 3-2; although only the probabilities for the presidential cohorts are reported, the models were specified exactly as they were for the model in Table 3-1. As expected, there were no statistically significant differences between the three Republican cohorts.

Finally, because of the possibility that in the twelve years between the Carter and Clinton presidencies the entire country had shifted ideologically toward a more anti-defendant position—although public opinion data suggest otherwise[48]—I also compare differences in ideology between Democratic and Republican presidential cohorts most proximate to each other in time (since the appointing presidents were selecting judges from roughly the same national pool of attorneys) so as to reject this alternate hypothesis. In other words, if the difference between Clinton and G. H. W. Bush appointees is smaller than the difference between Carter and Reagan appointees, then this provides some evidence that, notwithstanding a universal shift in ideology (among Democrats and Republicans) toward a "law and order" approach to criminal law enforcement, Clinton appointees are more conservative on crime issues than Carter appointees, just as Clinton was more conservative than Carter on crime issues. This comparison again strongly validates my hypotheses. Table 3-2 shows that, while the difference in percentages between a Clinton and Bush appointee is 18 percentage points, the difference between a Reagan and Carter appointee is 33 percentage points.

RACE DISCRIMINATION MODEL

The results of the race discrimination models are shown in Tables 3-3 and 3-4. As anticipated, there is no statistically significant difference in the voting behavior of Clinton and Carter appointees in race discrimination cases brought pursuant to Title VII and/or the federal Reconstruction Civil Rights Statutes (Table 3-3). Nor, as predicted, do we see any statistically significant difference in voting between the three Republican cohorts (Table 3-4). Though Nixon himself might have delivered mixed messages about racial egalitarian policies, as he promised in his two campaigns for president, his judicial appointees were more conservative in order to score points with the conservative activists he was trying to court.

As predicted, Clinton and Carter appointees lie at the left end of the ideological spectrum; G. H. W. Bush, Reagan, and Nixon appointees lie at the right end. With everything else held constant, and with Clinton as the baseline, the probability of a vote against a civil rights plaintiff increases by 28 percentage points compared with a Bush appointee, increases 28 percentage points compared with a Reagan appointee, increases 4 percentage points compared with a Carter appointee, and increases by 21 percentage points compared with a Nixon appointee (Table 3-3).

STATES' RIGHTS MODEL

The results of the states' rights models are shown in Tables 3-5 and 3-6. Consistent with my expectations, the three Republican cohorts fall on the

TABLE 3-3

Logit Coefficients for the Probability of a Vote Against a Civil Rights Plaintiff, Nonconsensual Race Discrimination Cases, January 1, 1994 to December 31, 2001

	MLE	Robust SE	Δ Probability[a]
Constant	−1.29***	.19	NA
Background-Based Independent Variables			
Appointing Presidential Cohort			
Clinton Appointees	Baseline	NA	.00
G. H. W. Bush Appointees	1.29***	.21	.28
Reagan Appointees	1.26***	.19	.28
Carter Appointees	.16	.22	.04
Nixon Appointees	.92**	.32	.21
Regional Background of Judge			
Compared with South			
Southern Judge	Baseline	NA	.00
Eastern Judge	−.36*	.17	−.09
Midwestern Judge	−.57***	.15	−.14
Ninth Circuit Judge	−.60**	.21	−.15
Tenth Circuit Judge	−.73**	.30	−.17
Fact-Based Independent Variables			
Equal Protection Claim	.84***	.20	.20
White Plaintiff	.77***	.15	.18
Pro Se Plaintiff	−1.42***	.35	−.30
Race Plus Other Claim	.53**	.19	.13
Class Action	1.18***	.30	.26

(Vote against plaintiff coded 1; vote for plaintiff coded 0)

$N = 1,408$
Likelihood Ratio Test (13 df) = 193.46***
% correctly predicted = 67.75
% observed in null model = 65.28
Proportional Reduction in Error = 7.11

*$p \leq .10$; **$p \leq .01$; ***$p \leq .001$ (two-tailed test)

[a]Change in probability is measured as the distance from a probability of .5 assuming the presence of that variable.

right of the ideological spectrum and the two Democratic cohorts fall on the left. Moreover, as we see in Table 3-6, there is no statistically significant difference between the two Democratic cohorts, nor is there a statistically significant difference between any of the three Republican cohorts.

With everything else held constant, and with Clinton appointees as the baseline, we see the likelihood of a vote against the federal government increase by 27 percentage points compared with a G. H. W. Bush judge, increase by 21 percentage points compared with a Reagan judge, decrease 7 percentage points compared with a Carter judge, and increase 16 percentage points compared with a Nixon judge (Table 3-5).

TABLE 3-4

Comparison of Voting Across Presidential Cohorts, Probability That a Judge Will Vote for a
Minority in a Race Discrimination Case, Nonconsensual Race Discrimination Cases,
U.S. Courts of Appeals, January 1, 1994 to December 31, 2001

	Clinton Judge	G. H. W. Bush Judge	Reagan Judge	Carter Judge	Nixon Judge
Compare a Clinton Judge with a:	—	−.28***	−.28***	−.04	−.21**
Compare a G. H. W. Bush Judge with a:	+.28***	—	+.01	+.25***	+.10
Compare a Reagan Judge with a:	+.28***	−.01	—	+.25***	+.08
Compare a Carter Judge with a:	+.04	−.25***	−.25***	—	−.18*
Compare a Nixon Judge with a:	+.21**	−.10	−.08	+.18*	—
N = 1,408					

*$p \leq .10$; **$p \leq .01$; ***$p \leq .001$ (two-tailed test)

ABORTION MODEL

The results of the regression analyses for the abortion models are shown
in Tables 3-7 and 3-8. Given that this issue has been the central ideological
litmus test propounded by every president since Reagan, the findings are
not surprising. Both Democratic appointees are significantly more likely to
uphold a woman's right to abortion than are the Republican appointees.
Moreover, since this issue did not emerge as a litmus test until after Nixon's
presidency, we also find, as expected, that Nixon appointees are not as conservative on this issue as G. H. W. Bush and Reagan appointees. This is also
the only issue in which there is a statistically significant difference between
two Republican cohorts (Reagan and Nixon).

With everything else held constant, and with Clinton appointees as the
baseline, the likelihood of a vote to uphold an abortion regulation increases
45 percentage points compared with a G. H. W. Bush appointee, increases
47 percentage points compared with a Reagan appointee, increases 16 percentage points compared with a Carter nominee, and increases 37 percentage points compared with a Nixon nominee (Table 3-7). Turning to Table
3-8, we see that Nixon appointees are closer to Carter appointees (18 percentage point difference) than to Reagan appointees (32 percentage point
difference) or G. H. W. Bush appointees (24 percentage point difference).

TABLE 3-5

Logit Coefficients for the Probability of a Vote Against the Federal Government,
Nonconsensual States' Rights Cases, January 1, 1996 to December 31, 2002

	MLE	Robust SE	Δ Probability[a]
Constant	−.56*	.29	NA
Background-Based Independent Variables			
Appointing Presidential Cohort			
Clinton Appointees	Baseline	NA	.00
G. H. W. Bush Appointees	1.21***	.34	.27
Reagan Appointees	.90**	.31	.21
Carter Appointees	−.29	.37	−.07
Nixon Appointees	.67	.65	.16
Regional Background of Judge			
Compared with South			
Southern Judge	Baseline	NA	.00
Eastern Judge	−.02	.36	.00
Midwestern Judge	−.85**	.31	−.17
Ninth Circuit Judge	−1.10*	.47	−.20
Tenth Circuit Judge	−.22	.67	−.05
Fact-Based Variables			
Eleventh Amendment	.63**	.27	.15

(Vote against federal government coded 1;
vote for federal government coded 0)

$N = 337$
Likelihood Ratio Test (9 *df*) = 31.26***
% correctly predicted = 64.99
% observed in null model = 50.10
Proportional Reduction in Error = 29.77

*p ≤ .10; **p ≤ .01; ***p ≤ .001 (two-tailed test)
[a]Change in probability is measured as the distance from a probability of .5 assuming the presence of that variable.

Conclusion

The first elite mobilization strategy to emerge in the modern political era was the president's exploitation of ideological litmus tests when Nixon declared that he would appoint "law and order" judges and "strict constructionists" to the lower federal courts as well as the Supreme Court. This strategy allowed Nixon to send important cues to conservative, southern political activists whom he hoped to attract permanently to the Republican Party. Reagan and G. H. W. Bush would later take up Nixon's elite mobilization strategy by going public with litmus tests based on a nominee's commitment to overturning *Roe*.

Although neither Democratic president Carter nor Clinton ever expressly stated that they would choose lower court judges according to an

TABLE 3-6

Comparison of Voting Across Presidential Cohorts, Probability That a Judge Will Vote to Uphold State Over Federal Power, Nonconsensual States' Rights Cases, U.S. Courts of Appeals, January 1, 1996 to December 31, 2002

	Clinton Judge	G. H. W. Bush Judge	Reagan Judge	Carter Judge	Nixon Judge
Compare a Clinton Judge with a:	—	−.27★★	−.21★	+.07	−.16
Compare a G. H. W. Bush Judge with a:	+.27★★	—	+.06	+.32★★	+.13
Compare a Reagan Judge with a:	+.21★	−.06	—	+.26★★	+.06
Compare a Carter Judge with a:	−.07	−.32★★	−.26★★	—	−.22
Compare a Nixon Judge with a:	+.16	−.13	−.06	+.22	—
N = 337					

★ $p \le .01$; ★★ $p \le .001$ (two-tailed test)

TABLE 3-7

Logit Coefficients for the Probability of a Vote to Restrict Abortions, Nonconsensual Abortion Rights Cases, January 1, 1978 to December 31, 2002

	MLE	Robust SE	Δ Probability[a]
Constant	−2.74★★	.89	NA
Background-Based Variables			
Appointing Presidential Cohort			
Clinton Appointees	Baseline	NA	.00
G. H. W. Bush Appointees	2.94★★★	.90	.45
Reagan Appointees	3.40★★★	.84	.47
Carter Appointees	.65	.87	.16
Nixon Appointees	1.87★	.95	.37
Southern Judge	1.13★	.50	.25
Fact-Based Variables			
Statute Restricting			
Abortions for Minors	1.21★★	.44	.27
Post-*Casey* Decision	.03	.43	.01

(Vote to restrict abortion coded 1; vote not to restrict abortion coded 0)

N = 179
Likelihood Ratio Test (7 *df*) = 50.29★★★
% correctly predicted = 74.30
% observed in null model = 51.40
Proportional Reduction in Error = 47.12

★ $p \le .10$; ★★ $p \le .01$; ★★★ $p \le .001$ (two-tailed test)

[a] Change in probability is measured as the distance from a probability of .5 assuming the presence of that variable.

TABLE 3-8

Comparison of Voting Across Presidential Cohorts, Probability That a Judge Will Vote
to Allow Restrictions on Abortions, Nonconsensual Abortion Cases, U.S. Courts of Appeals,
January 1, 1978 to December 31, 2002

	Clinton Judge	G. H. W. Bush Judge	Reagan Judge	Carter Judge	Nixon Judge
Compare a Clinton Judge with a:	—	−.45★★★	−.47★★★	−.16	−.37★
Compare a G. H. W. Bush Judge with a:	+.45★★★	—	−.11	+.41★★	+.24
Compare a Reagan Judge with a:	+.47★★★	+.11	—	+.44★★★	+.32★★
Compare a Carter Judge with a:	+.16	−.41★★★	−.44★★★	—	−.18★
Compare a Nixon Judge with a:	+.37★	−.24	−.32★★	+.18★	—
$N = 179$					

★$p \leq$ .10; ★★$p \leq$ .01; ★★★$p \leq$ .001 (two-tailed test)

ideological litmus test, liberal activists interviewed for this book expressed confidence that these presidents were, in fact, paying close attention to whether their judicial nominees supported a woman's right to choose abortion (see Chapter 5). Thus, the decision-making behavior of their judicial appointees almost perfectly dovetails with the policy agendas of the activists affiliated with the Democratic Party, with one important exception: Clinton's appointees were more conservative on the crime issue than liberal Democratic activists. Although this matches Clinton's "new" Democrat approach to crime, it is contrary to the demands of many liberal elites affiliated with the Democratic Party.

How do we reconcile the decision-making behavior of the Clinton appointees with the theory of elite mobilization? What these findings suggest is that Clinton skirted activist demands for anti–death penalty judges and judges concerned about protecting criminal defendants' civil liberties. In other respects, Clinton's appointees are just as liberal as Carter's. The reason why Clinton was able to ignore activists' policy demands for anti–death penalty judges—and yet not experience serious electoral repercussions from liberal criminal law activists—is largely due to his very effective use of the second elite mobilization strategy: that of using affirmative action to obtain race and gender diversity in the federal courts. As we will see in the next chapter, because Clinton appointed a record number of minority judges to the lower federal courts, and because these judges were more liberal on crime issues than Clinton's white appointees, liberal criminal law activists were largely satisfied with Clinton's overall appointment strategy.

CHAPTER 4

Affirmative Action and Judicial Selection

TWO NORMATIVE VALUES are commonly cited as support for diversifying the federal bench. First, as Hanna Pitkin has explained (1967), minority and female judges—sometimes referred to as "nontraditional" appointments—provide *symbolic* or *descriptive* representation. In other words, the placement of minorities and women on the federal bench is vital to minority and female litigants because it sends a message that these groups, like white males, also have access to positions of influence (Slotnick, 1983; Tobias, 1998). This, in turn, is believed to have a legitimizing effect on the federal courts as an institution because it provides confidence in the system (Goldman, 1979). As distinguished African American jurist A. Leon Higginbotham Jr. once explained:

> When all the judges come from the ranks of the ruling race, they often are viewed more as representatives or advocates for the ruling race than as judges committed to an impartial rule of law. When the public perceives the judiciary as having a vested interest in the preservation of the status quo, victims of racism . . . often wonder whether the jurist is putting a thumb on the scales of justice to make sure the system denies them full dignity. (Higginbotham, 1993, at 1035)

A second normative justification for diversifying the federal bench draws upon the work of Samuel Krislov (1974). Under this theory, it is critical to have more minority and female judges because they provide *substantive* representation to minority and female litigants. For example, advocates of this theory would argue that only black judges can effectively understand, advocate, and articulate the unique views of black litigants, having shared common life experiences. This unique perspective is then reflected in the judge's own decision-making, as well as the decision-making of others sitting on the same collegial court. As Justice Sandra Day O'Connor, the first woman on the Supreme Court, has written about Justice Thurgood Marshall, the first black person on the Supreme Court: "At oral arguments and conference meetings, in opinions and dissents, Justice Marshall imparted not only his legal acumen, but also his life experiences, pushing and prodding us to respond not only to the persuasiveness of legal argument but also to the power of moral truth" (quoted in Higginbotham, 1993, at note 34). Similarly, Higginbotham has noted that "lacking such outsiders, a court will be left with only its own self-perpetuating views, preferences and prejudices to inform its decisions" (Higginbotham, 1993, at 1450). Another black judge, interviewed by Michael Smith (1983) in the 1970s, also believed that diversity fosters better substantive representation for the legal positions commonly articulated by black litigants:

> The mere presence of the black judge is going to influence his white associates in their thinking. Secondly, because he is in, shall we say, the councils of the mighty . . . [he is] going to control the police department, the prosecutor's office, and so forth, [and] he can make the input that blacks would like to have with respect to the formulation of that policy. And if he's on his toes, he will do that. (Quoted in M. Smith, 1983, at 79–80)

More recently, Supreme Court Justice Clarence Thomas, the second African American justice in history, demonstrated how diversity on the federal bench brings diverse viewpoints. In December 2002, Thomas shared a unique perspective on the issue of whether a burning cross constitutes symbolic speech protected by the First Amendment or whether a state's statute banning such conduct is constitutional. During oral argument in *Virginia v. Black* (2003),[1] Thomas interrupted the state of Virginia's lawyer and, quite uncharacteristically for Thomas—known for not questioning attorneys at oral arguments—expressed his opinion that a burning cross is a symbol of a "reign of terror" signifying "100 years of lynching" of African Americans in the South; Thomas also told the state's attorney that he had "underestimated the power of the symbol" (quoted in Lithwick, 2002, at A35). Thomas's belief was based on personal experience growing up in segregated Georgia. According to one observer in the courtroom, his "outburst" changed the entire demeanor of the oral argument, and might well have persuaded a Court known for its guarded protection of free speech instead to uphold the statute's constitutionality (Lithwick, 2002).

Without question, a candidate's support for affirmative action in the modern political era has had a significant impact on mobilizing elites in the Democratic Party (Prysby, 1989). Conversely, opposition to affirmative action benefits Republican candidates (Pinderhughes, 1992). In this chapter, we will examine the use of affirmative action as an elite mobilization strategy. We will see how Democratic presidents Carter and Clinton used this diversification strategy as an effective means to mobilize minority and female activists—who are so critical to the electoral success of the Democratic

Party because they are responsible for mobilizing women and minority voters, two core constituencies for Democratic presidential hopefuls. By publicizing during their presidential campaigns their intention to diversify the federal courts, by continuing throughout their presidencies to publicly support the normative goals associated with diversity, by appointing significant numbers of female and minority lower court judges, and by coming to the defense of embattled black and female nominees, Carter and Clinton were able to build a reservoir of goodwill with liberal minority and female activists.

Conversely, Republican presidents have largely shunned an affirmative action strategy on the federal bench because minority and female activists engaged in judicial appointment politics are overwhelmingly liberal and demand from minority and female judicial appointees not only descriptive representation but substantive representation as well. Accordingly, unless Republican presidents appoint liberal minorities and women, these liberal activists are not satisfied; clearly, Republican presidents have been unwilling to appoint liberals to the bench, for it means violating the conservative ideological litmus tests that their conservative activists insist on.

The History of Minorities and Women on the Federal Bench

For most of our nation's history, the federal judiciary was a bastion of white male lawyers. It was not until FDR appointed William H. Hastie to serve a four-year term on the District Court of the U.S. Virgin Islands, an Article I court, that the federal bench had its first African American judge (Davis, 1989). President Truman would later appoint Judge Hastie to the U.S. Court of Appeals for the Third Circuit—making him the first black to serve on an Article III court. Women did not fare much better. The first woman to serve in the federal judiciary was Genevieve Rose Cline, appointed by President Coolidge to serve on the U.S. Customs Court (today, the U.S. Court of International Trade). FDR was the first president to appoint a woman to an appellate court, Florence Ellinwood Allen, who served on the Sixth Circuit. But progress in diversifying the federal bench was slow. Over the next thirty years, only nineteen more blacks and six women were appointed to the lower federal courts, although during this period President Johnson named the first black, Marshall, to the Supreme Court. All that would change with the election of Carter.

CARTER'S DIVERSIFICATION EFFORTS

As we will see in Chapter 5, once a president nominates a lower court judge, activists' objections center on specific nominations and are communicated directly to senators. However, regarding larger normative goals, such as increased diversity on the federal bench, activists' demands surface before a single nomination is announced, and even before the candidate is actually elected. During presidential campaigns, interest groups still have access to the future president, and this is also the time when activists wield the most influence, as candidates are extremely dependent on these activists to mobilize key voting blocs. For Democratic presidential candidates, two of the most influential special interests are civil rights and women's rights groups and thus, these issue activists exploit their influence with the future president and, among other things, demand diversification on the bench (Rozell and Wilcox, 1999).

Carter was the first Democratic presidential candidate in the modern political era to be "pressured" by women's interest groups and civil rights organizations to diversify the gender and racial makeup of the federal bench (Ness, 1978). A leading black activist, Joe L. Reed, who headed the Committee for the Appointment of Blacks to the Federal Judiciary in the U.S. Fifth Circuit, stated that Carter had assured his group before his election in 1976, and again at a meeting with his group at the White House in June 1977, that he would appoint blacks to judgeships (Special to the *New York Times*, 1977). His group also advocated that the new president allocate a certain number of judgeships in each state for blacks so as to avoid the patronage trap—where white males (with political ties to white male senators) are favored over minorities and women as part of the "old boys" network (Special to the *New York Times*, 1977).

Wanting to please these key activists, during his 1976 presidential campaign, Carter promised to overhaul the selection process of lower federal court judges (Goldman, 1997). Carter's stated goals were twofold. First, he wanted to put an end to a judicial selection process controlled by political patronage (Goldman, 1997; see also Chapter 2). Second, Carter wanted to pursue an affirmative action strategy in the selection of federal court judges (Goldman, 1979). Both goals were intended to increase the number of minority and female judges at all levels of the federal judiciary.

The Carter administration justified its diversity strategy on both normative grounds discussed above—to achieve descriptive *and* substantive representation of the nation's diverse demographic groups on the federal bench. In terms of descriptive representation, Carter's attorney general, Griffin B. Bell, said:

> The governing institutions of a democracy should reflect the spectrum of interests of the governed and this is done by dispersing the power to govern among representatives of diverse groups. In short, it is assumed that a national judiciary should resemble its national demographic constituency. Therefore, large groups which have been denied extensive representation in government should

now be given a greater degree of representation. These values cannot be tested and confirmed or refuted. One can only accept or reject them. (quoted in Slotnick, 1983)

Carter himself also stressed the need for substantive representation—wanting the judiciary to include diverse viewpoints:

> I see a Federal Court system that's filled not only with a desire for justice but a desire for understanding of the special deprivation of justice that still prevails in this country against those who are poor or inarticulate or not well organized or not well educated. We've got a long way to go in the Federal Courts where, still, money available to have competent lawyers is an obstacle to true justice. But whenever I appoint a black judge or Hispanic judge or even a woman judge, I know that they not only have committed in their own hearts a vision of what this nation ought to be but a special knowledge of the effects of past discrimination that are still there as a means to prevent equality of opportunity.[2]

Carter wasted no time in implementing his affirmative action strategy. Only four weeks after taking office in 1977, he created, by executive order, the U.S. Circuit Judge Nominating Commission.[3] The commission consisted of thirteen panels, one for each federal circuit court of appeals, that would henceforth be solely responsible for making recommendations for appeals court nominations to the president. In an effort to recruit more minorities and women, the order expressly directed that "each panel shall include members of both sexes, members of minority groups and approximately equal numbers of lawyers and non-lawyers." Accordingly, senators under this system would no longer be able to use courts of appeals appointments as patronage. Although future presidents would do away with Carter's nominating commission, they continued the tradition of exercising much more control over appellate nominations, rather than letting home state senators award these positions to favored constituents.

Carter hoped that with a diversely comprised nominating commission responsible for identifying candidates for the federal appeals courts—rather than relying on a Senate overwhelmingly composed of white males, interested in returning political favors through judicial appointments—more women and minorities would be submitted for nomination to the federal bench. Moreover, as nonpatronage appointments, all future judicial nominees, white males included, should be better qualified candidates. However, when this executive order failed to produce a single female appellate court judge in Carter's first two years in office, he issued a revised executive order intended to make his affirmative action policy for the appointment of federal court judges even more explicit. Executive Order 12,059 stated that "each [judicial nominating] panel is encouraged to make special efforts to seek out and identify well qualified women and members of minority groups as potential nominees."

Although Carter strongly urged senators to establish district court nominating commissions in their home states, his executive order did not apply to district court appointments. Having already lost control over appellate nominations, senators were naturally loath to cede their remaining power over the selection of district court judges as well; district court judgeships at this time remained largely under the control of home state senators, and continued to be used for patronage purposes.[4] However, unhappy with the Senate's unwillingness to choose district court judges with diverse backgrounds, Carter became more involved with diversification at the district court level of the federal judiciary as well. With the passage of the Omnibus Judgeship Act in 1978, which created scores of new judicial positions in the lower federal courts, Carter took affirmative steps to ensure that serious efforts would be made to fill these new judgeships with "nontraditional appointments" (i.e., minorities or women). In Executive Order 12,097, Carter authorized the attorney general to recommend candidates for these new district court positions (as opposed to vacancies on existing seats) only after considering whether "an affirmative effort has been made, in the case of each vacancy, to identify candidates, including women and members of minority groups."

Carter also continued to consult with liberal interest groups about ways in which to increase minority and female representation on the federal bench. Indeed, the Carter administration included interest groups in developing a strategy on how to achieve greater diversity in the judiciary shortly before passage of the Omnibus Judgeship Act of 1978 —which, as stated above, created 152 new lower court judgeships for Carter to fill (Lipshutz and Huron, 1979).

Although Carter's affirmative action plan as stated in his executive orders may have appeared to be no more than an outreach program, in fact, the Carter administration's implementation of this strategy looked a lot more like traditionally used affirmative action efforts of the time (see Chapter 3). For example, the administration conceded that a minority or female candidate would be chosen for the bench over a white male candidate, even though it may appear on paper that the white male was "more" qualified. Testifying before the Senate Judiciary Committee, Attorney General Bell stated that "'qualified' was the bottom line requirement for the appointment of women and minorities to the bench—even if there were more highly qualified white male candidates under consideration as well" (Slotnick, 1983, at 277). In short, Bell said that "choices of that sort had to be made to

TABLE 4-I
Number of Nontraditional Appointments

President	U.S. COURTS OF APPEALS[a]		
	Blacks	Hispanics	Women
Johnson	2 (5.0%)	0 (0.0%)	1 (2.5%)
Nixon	0 (0.0%)	0 (0.0%)	0 (0.0%)
Carter	9 (16.1%)	2 (3.6%)	11 (19.6%)
Reagan	1 (1.3%)	1 (1.3%)	4 (5.1%)
G. H. W. Bush	2 (5.4%)	1 (5.4%)	7 (18.9%)
Clinton	8 (11.6%)	7 (11.5%)	20 (32.8%)
G. W. Bush (2001–04)	4 (11.8%)	3 (8.8%)	8 (23.5%)

President	U.S. DISTRICT COURTS		
	Blacks	Hispanics	Women
Johnson	5 (4.1%)	3 (2.5%)	2 (1.6%)
Nixon	6 (3.4%)	2 (1.1%)	1 (0.6%)
Carter	28 (13.9%)	14 (6.9%)	29 (14.4%)
Reagan	6 (2.1%)	14 (4.8%)	24 (8.3%)
G. H. W. Bush	10 (6.8%)	6 (4.0%)	29 (19.6%)
Clinton	53 (17.4%)	19 (6.2%)	87 (28.5%)
G. W. Bush (2001–04)	11 (6.5%)	18 (10.7%)	35 (20.8%)

Values are *N* (percentage of each president's total appointments for that type of court).
[a]Recess appointments not included.
SOURCE: http://www.fjc.gov

alter the composition of the bench in meaningful quantities" (Bell, quoted in Slotnick, 1983, at 277). Carter also admitted to a reporter that he favored the use of quotas in achieving his affirmative action goals: "If I didn't have to get Senate confirmation of appointees, I could just tell you flatly that 12 percent of all my judicial appointments would be black and three percent would be Spanish speaking and 40 percent would be women" (quoted in Slotnick, 1983, at 277).

The results of Carter's full-force effort to diversity the federal bench were impressive. Table 4-1 shows the African American, Hispanic, and female federal appellate and district court judges appointed by Presidents Johnson through G. W. Bush. Where fellow Democrat Johnson appointed only two blacks (5 percent of all Johnson appellate court appointments) and one woman (2.5 percent) to the courts of appeals and five blacks (4.1 percent of all Johnson district court appointments) and two women (1.6 percent) to the district courts, Carter appointed nine blacks (16.1 percent of all Carter appellate court appointments) and eleven women (19.6 percent) to the courts of appeals and twenty-eight blacks (13.9 percent of all Carter district court appointments) and twenty-nine women (14.4 percent) to the district courts.

At the appellate level, Carter appointed the first black judge to sit on the Second Circuit (Amalya L. Kearse), the Third Circuit (Higginbotham), the Fifth Circuit (Joseph W. Hatchett),[5] the Eighth Circuit (Theodore McMillian), and the Ninth Circuit (J. Jerome Farris, later followed by a second black appointee, Cecil F. Poole) (Davis, 1989). At the district court level, Carter also has the distinction of appointing the first black federal court judge to sit in the South (Robert F. Collins) (United Press International, 1978). Furthermore, he appointed the first female judge to sit on the Second Circuit (Kearse), the Third Circuit (Dolores K. Sloviter), the Fifth Circuit (Phyllis A. Kravitch),[6] the Eighth Circuit (Diana E. Murphy), and the Tenth Circuit (Stephanie K. Seymour).

REPUBLICAN PRESIDENTS AND AFFIRMATIVE ACTION

Although Reagan pledged in his 1980 campaign for president to appoint the first woman to the Supreme Court—and, with the appointment of O'Connor, satisfied this campaign promise—all serious efforts to diversify the federal bench came to an abrupt halt with Reagan's election as he immediately disbanded the circuit court nominating commission set up during the Carter administration (Goldman, 1997). During his eight years in office, Reagan appointed only one black (1.3 percent of all Reagan appellate court appointments) and four women (5.1 percent) to the courts of appeals and six blacks (2.1 percent of all Reagan district court appointments) and twenty-four women (8.3 percent) to the district courts (see Table 4-1).

Reagan's Republican successor in the White House, G. H. W. Bush, essentially continued Reagan's strategy. He neither promised to diversify the courts, nor did he appoint many minorities, although women fared somewhat better than did minorities. Bush appointed two blacks (5.4 percent of all Bush appellate appointments) and seven women (18.9 percent) to the courts of appeals and ten blacks (6.8 percent of all Bush district court appointments) and twenty-nine women (19.6 percent) to the district courts (see Table 4-1). Bush was also the first president to appoint a woman to the Fourth Circuit (Karen J. Williams) and the Seventh Circuit (Ilana D. Rovner). Although many federal jurisdictions still remained with no minority representation, by the end of the G. H. W. Bush presidency, women were represented on ten of the twelve circuit courts (83.3 percent) and forty-eight of ninety-one Article III district courts (52.7 percent).

That Reagan and G. H. W. Bush made little effort to appoint minorities to the federal courts is entirely consistent with the theory of elite mobilization. In short, black political elites—those at whom a diversification strategy in the federal courts would be aimed—are overwhelmingly supporters of the Democratic Party. Were a Republican to appoint a conservative black attorney to a lower court judgeship, would this be sufficient to satisfy liberal black activists? Is descriptive representation without substantive representation sufficient to satisfy liberal activists?

As President G. H. W. Bush learned after he nominated Thomas to the Supreme Court, the answer is "no." The leading civil rights organizations— the NAACP, the Urban League, and the Congressional Black Caucus—all opposed the Thomas nomination (Silkcourts, 1991), despite the fact that 70 percent of African Americans polled supported it (Kelly, 1991). When G. H. W. Bush ran for reelection in 1992, these same black elites did not support his candidacy. For Republicans to gain the electoral support of the leading black elites engaged in judicial appointment politics, they would have to compromise the conservative ideological litmus tests that conservative activists insist on, and instead nominate liberal black judges. This Republican presidents have flatly refused to do.

Why did female judges fare somewhat better under Reagan and G. H. W. Bush? First, a sizable number of pro-life interest groups are composed of conservative women. Indeed, the pro-life interest group Concerned Women for America is one of the key players involved today in judicial confirmation politics (see Chapter 5). Thus, these Republican presidents were able to court conservative female activists by appointing conservative women to the federal bench. But these Republican presidents have not been able to win over liberal female activists—for example, those affiliated with NOW or NARAL—by appointing conservative women to the federal bench (Ireland interview, 2003). In short, pro-life female judges are deemed unacceptable to these liberal activists (see Chapter 5). Consider that NOW and NARAL have led the fight against three pro-life women nominated by G. W. Bush: Priscilla R. Owen (Fifth Circuit), Carolyn B. Kuhl (Ninth Circuit), and Janice Rogers Brown (D.C. Circuit) (see Chapter 5).

CLINTON RESUMES CARTER'S DIVERSIFICATION STRATEGY

Just as Jimmy Carter had done sixteen years before him, Clinton pledged in his 1992 presidential campaign to appoint significant numbers of minorities and women to the federal courts, proclaiming diversity on the bench to be one of the great legacies of the Carter presidency and the "New South." In fact, Clinton expressly promised to outdo Carter's record number of minority and female appointments and to make the courts "look like America" (Mannies, 1992).

However, the Democratic Party of the 1990s was much different from the party of the 1970s during Carter's presidency. Under the stewardship of Clinton during the 1990s, the Democratic Party underwent an important shift in its policy stands on two issues that had come to define Democrats as the party of the ideological left for the previous thirty years: race and crime (Carmines and Stimson, 1989). Of the two issue positions, the most dramatic shift was the Democratic Party's co-option of the Republican Party's tough "law and order" agenda, abandoning the party's previous emphasis on the protections of a criminal defendant's civil liberties (Chernoff, Kelly, and Kroger, 1996). Similarly, although not quite as severe a shift as with the crime issue, the Democratic Party also moved to the right regarding race relations. Most notable were the party's abandonment of support for affirmative action quotas and its rejection of statutory entitlements for the poor, a policy whose impact is particularly devastating to black populations in the inner city (Wilson, 1987).

This strategic political move to the right of the ideological spectrum on Clinton's part proved quite savvy. In short, since the 1970s, white voters have grown increasingly conservative on the issues of crime and race (Edsall and Edsall, 1992). Thus, experts agree that Clinton's "new" Democratic ideology essentially brought many disaffected white urban males—the so-called "Reagan Democrats"—back into the Democratic fold and ultimately propelled the Democratic Party back into the White House after Republican domination of the Executive Branch for the previous twenty-four years (Chernoff, Kelly, and Kroger, 1996). In fact, Clinton's strategy was so successful that he was the first Democratic president since FDR to serve eight years in office.

There is one notable voting bloc, however, whose ideology has *not* seen a dramatic ideological shift to the right on race and crime: African Americans. In short, while many white voters may embrace Clinton's "new" Democratic ideology, black elites and black voters firmly remain "old" Democrats. In other words, blacks continue to support the "liberal" ideology that came to define the Democratic Party—white and black—in the 1960s and 1970s. In the area of criminal law enforcement, blacks continue to favor strong protections of the civil liberties of criminal defendants; in the area of race relations, African Americans still strongly advocate the use of race preferences to ensure an equal playing field for minorities after centuries of government-sanctioned racial discrimination (Browning and Cao, 1992; National Institute of Justice, 2001, Tables 2.16, 2.25). This is true of black elites, as well as the mass black electorate (Bolce, De Maio, and Muzzio, 1992).[7] Indeed, in a survey of black judges conducted in the early 1980s, Michael Smith found that 63 percent of African American jurists described themselves as politically "liberal" and another 30 percent described themselves as "moderates" (M. Smith, 1983).

Not surprisingly, with black Democrats advocating a more "liberal" brand of ideology than Clinton's, Clinton was careful to frame his affirmative action strategy for the federal bench in terms of *descriptive* representation, rather than *substantive* representation—purposely deemphasizing the liberal political views that his black appointees were likely to bring to the bench. This stands in sharp contrast to Carter's stated purpose for diversifying the federal courts: to give minorities and women not just faces, but voices, on the federal bench. Days before his election in 1992, Clinton delivered a position paper to the *National Law Journal* in which he stated:

> A most troubling aspect of judicial appointments during the Reagan-Bush era has been the sharp decline in the selection of women and minority judges, at the very time when more and more qualified women and minority candidates were reaching the time of their lives where they could serve as judges. While there are many fine women and minority attorneys all over the country who would potentially be superb federal judges, Mr. Bush's appointments fail to reflect the breadth and diversity of the bar, much less that of our nation.
>
> The narrow judicial appointments of George Bush have resulted in the emergence of a judiciary that is less reflective of our diverse society than at any other time in recent memory. I strongly believe that the judiciary thus runs the risk of losing its legitimacy in the eyes of many Americans. (Clinton, 1992)

Clinton continued framing the diversity issue in these descriptive terms throughout his presidency. For instance, at a speech to the American Bar Association in 1999, he said: "Anybody who has ever been in a courtroom, either as an advocate or a client, knows that if you are in court, the judge is the most important person in the world. And to have a judiciary that reflects the diversity of America, as well as its commitment to equal justice under law, and to professional excellence is a profoundly important national goal" (Clinton, 1999, at 36).

In addition to his emphasis on descriptive rather than substantive representation, Clinton's diversification strategy differed from Carter's in several other key respects. Unlike the Carter administration, the Clinton administration had no written policy concerning the recruitment of minority candidates for the federal bench. Nor did the Clinton administration revive the judicial nominating commission used during the Carter presidency, which was expressly ordered to seek out qualified minorities and women for judicial appointments. Instead, nominations were jointly handled by the White House Counsel's Office and the Justice Department's Office of Policy Development—jointly referred to as the Judicial Selection Group (Goldman and Slotnick, 1999). Finally, having backed off of many traditional Democratic stands concerning affirmative action, Clinton certainly was not advocating the use of quotas to achieve the desired goal of diversity on the federal bench, as did the Carter administration. Yet in the final analysis, Clinton did deliver on his campaign promise to achieve greater diversity in the federal courts.

In his eight years in office, Clinton appointed eight blacks (11.6 percent of all Clinton appellate court appointments) and twenty women (32.8 percent) to the courts of appeals and fifty-three blacks (17. 4 percent of all Clinton district court appointments) and eighty-seven women (28.5 percent) to the district courts (see Table 4-1). At the court of appeals level, Clinton appointed the first African Americans to the Fourth Circuit (Roger L. Gregory)[8] and the Seventh Circuit (Ann C. Williams) but did not appoint the first woman to any appellate court. Clinton was also the first president in history to appoint more "nontraditional" judges—women and minorities—than white male judges to the federal courts.

But given Clinton's moderate "new" Democratic ideology, an affirmative action appointment strategy served him quite well. In short, Clinton desperately needed to satisfy the policy demands of black and female Democratic activists; their support at the polls would become increasingly more crucial in mobilizing African American and female voters—two of the Democratic Party's most loyal constituencies—as electoral competition between the two major parties became increasingly tight in the 1990s. As Clinton turned his back on many liberal stands of the "old" Democratic Party, however—particularly in the areas affecting blacks—he had to worry about alienating these groups. By using an affirmative action strategy to fill lower federal court judgeships, Clinton could redeem himself with these crucial party activists and interest groups so that they would mobilize the Democratic Party's base on Election Day.

But minority and female activists kept a close eye on Clinton's diversification efforts immediately after he was elected and throughout his presidency. Having delivered key votes to Clinton in the 1992 election, these activists fully intended to hold him to his campaign promise to make the cabinet and the judiciary "look like America."

The Call for More Black Judges

Longing for the substantive and descriptive representation on the federal bench that they had been denied during the twelve years of the Reagan/ G. H. W. Bush era, African Americans wasted no time after Clinton's election to demand that the newly elected Democratic president—whom blacks were instrumental in getting elected—diversify the federal bench. New York's *Amsterdam News* urged Clinton, along with New York Senators Daniel P. Moynihan (D) and Alphonse D'Amato (R), to select African Americans for lower federal court judgeships, calling it the "most profound message" the new president could send to African Americans:

The truth is that Whites, led by politicians and business people with a sprinkling of academicians thrown in . . . absolutely refuse to acknowledge or even examine the fact that they have created an abysmally corrupt criminal justice system. This is especially true on the local and state levels.

Yet, this reality flows from the top. It flows from a series of presidents who cared little for law and nothing for justice when it came time for appointments to the federal bench.

In the Reagan, Bush, Ford and Nixon years, these coveted lifetime appointments to the very top rung of the ladder of criminal justice; the province, the bastion, if you will, of the white conservative male, and a Black ultra-conservative male, Clarence Thomas, created a federal judiciary that is on its very face unfair.

In the 50 states, there are only 43 active Article III judges who happen to be Black . . .

As startling as this may be, it does not tell the whole story . . . [I]n areas such as the District of Columbia, First, Second, Third and Fourth Circuits, where there are Black populations exceeding 12 percent in the general population of the U.S., black judges are hardly to be found. There are only 11 out of 222 available positions. These figures service neither justice nor even the appearance thereof.

While all the above represents bad news, there is some good news just so long as President-elect Clinton reads these comments and goes about fulfilling one of the promises of his presidency . . .

President Clinton cannot send a more profound message to Blacks in America than by correcting immediately the outrageous imbalance in the federal judiciary. (Editorial, *Amsterdam News*, 1992)

What is also interesting to note about this editorial is the author's belief that increasing diversity, rather than employing an ideological litmus test, is the best way to ensure that African Americans' more liberal positions on crime policy are represented on the federal bench. Again, this demonstrates why Clinton was able to appoint more moderate whites—those at odds with black elites on issues such as the death penalty—to the federal bench and still satisfy minority elites with his aggressive diversity agenda.

Perhaps the cry for increased diversity on the bench was greatest in Chicago where, despite a significant black population, there were no African Americans on the Seventh Circuit Court of Appeals. For example, three black elites argued that Clinton needed to seat an African American on the Seventh Circuit to ensure that the millions of blacks living in that jurisdiction had adequate substantive and descriptive representation in the federal judicial system. More importantly, they urged readers of the *Chicago Defender* to contact the president and his staff and urge him to appoint a black to the Seventh Circuit:[9]

Clinton has done an outstanding job of promoting diversity within the federal courts through his appointments of minority and women to the federal bench. The president now has a unique opportunity to continue down this progressive path by integrating the Seventh Circuit with the appointment of an African American to one or both of the vacant seats that have been created by two current judges taking senior status.

The time to act is now. There are hundreds of thousands of African Americans and other persons of color residing in this jurisdiction who have no voice or representation on this important court—yet we are bound by its rulings.

We urge you to join us in our pursuit of a worthy and important goal by contacting the president and his staff to express your support for diverse appointments to the Seventh Circuit.

Having a federal court of appeals that "looks more like America" is important to litigants, to the public's understanding of this nation's justice system and to helping to destroy damaging stereotypes about minorities.

More importantly, the appointment of an African American to the Seventh Circuit Court of Appeals will send an important message of hope to those who have too long been excluded from participating in this country. (Willis, Britt, and Powell, 1994)

Although Clinton's first appointment to the Seventh Circuit went to a white woman—Diane P. Wood—eventually, the demands of the black activists in Chicago were met when Clinton filled a second vacancy on that court with a black woman, Judge Williams. Clinton won great praise for this appointment from the editorial board of the *Chicago Defender*, which wrote that Clinton "will certainly be revered as the most proficient chief executive ever" as regards presidential appointments of African American Title III judges:

One of the truest measures of William Jefferson Clinton, the man and the president, may be that he has truly helped racially balance the scales of justice in America by appointing more than one-third of all the African American judges named in the past half-century.

Hats off to you, Mr. Clinton for nearly five dozen appointments of African American judges since 1993. May history judge you well, at least on this matter. (Editorial, *Chicago Defender*, 1999)

The Call for Blacks in the Justice Department

Black elites were equally vocal in demanding that Clinton appoint African Americans to high-ranking positions in the Justice Department—that is, either attorney general or assistant attorney general for civil rights. The chairman of the Congressional Black Caucus when Clinton was elected, Congressman Edolphus Towns (D-NY), urged Clinton to consider a black for the position of attorney general because that position is most important to the black community. Congressman Towns went so far as to suggest possible nominees: Congressman John Conyers Jr. (D-MI), New York federal district court judge Robert L. Carter, Professor Drew Days III of the Yale Law

School, and New York district court judge Constance B. Motley. None too subtly, Towns also reminded Clinton of black voters' support in electing him to office:

> We write to express our profound belief that your [Bill Clinton's] nomination for attorney general is, for the African American community, the most important one that you can make . . . Since the beginning of the republic, the evolving state of the American legal system has defined the hopes and possibilities of African Americans. As the chief law enforcement officer of the United States in your administration, it is critical than the attorney general understand the profound importance of this . . .
>
> African Americans voted in record numbers, and overwhelmingly, for the hope and change that your candidacy represented, and such a gesture indicates, as your other post-election actions have, that such change is real. We are completely confident that under your leadership, your administration will move further towards healing the historic wounds of racial and ethnic division than any other president. (Towns, 1993)

Although Clinton did not meet African American expectations by naming an African American to the post of attorney general, he did name a prominent African American woman, Lani Guinier, to be the assistant attorney general for civil rights. However, when Guinier's writings as a law professor concerning the rights of minorities under the Voting Rights Act came under sharp attack from the political right, Clinton immediately backed down and withdrew Guinier's nomination. This led to a host of editorials and commentaries from black elites criticizing Clinton for not standing behind his nominee, with constant reminders that African Americans stood firmly behind Clinton in the 1992 election. In the *Chicago Defender*, Lewis Martin wrote that "anger among Black Americans swept this nation like a thunderstorm" after the withdrawal of Guinier's name. "At bottom in this dispute are racism and bigotry," he continued, "which are as American as apple pie. I was personally wounded by the action of this president, for whom I had campaigned and voted" (Martin, 1993).

A similar complaint was lodged by the editorial board of the *Michigan Chronicle*:

> The response to President Bill Clinton's official kicking of Lani Guinier to the curb has ranged in the African American community from angry to very angry.
>
> We add our angry voice to the choir.
>
> The president—perched again on a tightrope attempting to appease moderates, conservatives and limited categories of so-called liberals—quickly offered an explanation to this withdrawal of Guinier's nomination to head the civil rights division of the Justice Department.
>
> "Over time it became obvious to me [Clinton] that Ms. Guinier's confirmation hearing would engender a sustained and bitter debate over civil rights: a de-

bate that would have been divisive and polarizing at 'a time when our nation needs healing . . ."

Divisive and polarizing? For whom?

. . . Perhaps those who are militantly skeptical in our community—who preach we must never, ever believe our salvation lay outside our own collective efforts—have hit the nail squarely on the $200 haircut. (Editorial, *Michigan Chronicle*, 1993)

Another black commentator emphasized that by backing down on the Guinier nomination, Clinton had raised concerns within the black community as to his commitment to combat discrimination:

The outrage in the Black community goes beyond the indignities visited upon Guinier, although denying her the opportunity to defend her record in confirmation hearings and to rebut the opposition's attempt to demonize her were important factors.

I believe much of the outrage reflects shaken confidence in the administration's willingness to aggressively combat discrimination.

Just as the Guinier appointment signaled an activist role for the Justice Department's Civil Rights Division, withdrawal of the appointment signals the right wing that they can pressure the administration to go slow on civil rights . . .

. . . the president should stand tall against those who would weaken civil rights by appointing people, both for the Justice Department and for the Supreme Court and lower courts, who are wholeheartedly committed to advancing the protection of the civil rights laws. (Jacobs, 1993)

Notwithstanding the fact that Clinton subsequently nominated another African American, Patrick L. Deval, for the civil rights post, the ill will surrounding the Guinier affair would be tempered only when Clinton countered conservative senators' refusal to confirm Deval's replacement, Bill Lann Lee, by single-handedly installing Lee into the position first, as an "acting" appointee, and then as a recess appointee.

Clinton's Exploitation of Controversial Black Nominees

Clinton also gained widespread support from the black community by exploiting several situations in which minority candidates for positions on the bench or at the Justice Department were having tough confirmation fights at the hands of the Republican majority in the Senate. In short, Clinton seized these opportunities to score points with black leaders by signaling them that he, like they, believed Republicans to be racists. Most notable among these controversial nominations was Lee, to whom Clinton gave a recess appointment after the Senate refused to confirm him on the ground that he supported the use of racial quotas in government-sponsored programs; Gregory, to whom Clinton gave a recess appointment after the Senate refused to confirm him on the ground that the Fourth Circuit Court of Appeals allegedly needed no more judges; and Ronnie White, whom the Senate rejected for a seat on the U.S. District Court for the Eastern District of Missouri on the ground that he was "pro-death penalty." Although arguably none of these nominations was thwarted because of race, as opposed to ideology, Clinton took every opportunity to paint the Republican leadership as racist and the Democratic Party as standing up for the rights of minorities.

THE BILL LANN LEE NOMINATION

Like his first nominee to head the Civil Rights Division at the Justice Department, Guinier, Clinton's third and final nominee, Lee, was the subject of much attack by conservative activists. As they did with Guinier (and to a lesser extent with the second nominee, Deval), conservatives once again played the race and crime cards with Lee, warning that he was yet another Clinton nominee from the NAACP Legal Defense Fund and another proponent of racial quotas and opponent of the death penalty. But contrary to his refusal to stand by Guinier in the face of Republican opposition, with the Lee nomination, Clinton did more than just defend his nominee. In fact, when the Republican-led Senate refused to confirm Lee because of his support for affirmative action, Clinton effectively overrode the "advice and consent" power of the Senate on presidential nominations, first by naming Lee "acting" head of the Civil Rights Division and then by giving him a recess appointment as assistant attorney general for civil rights. Accordingly, African American activists in the Democratic Party were now cheering President Clinton, citing the Lee case as proof of the president's commitment to civil rights and support for the African American community:

> When President Clinton recently made a rare move to appoint Bill Lann Lee as "acting" assistant attorney general for civil rights, the chief executive made the right decision. Clinton showed the nation that sometimes a president must move aggressively to do the right thing.
>
> Although Clinton bypassed the Senate confirmation process in this case, such a detour can be justified. Why? Because the person who fills the job is traditionally considered to be the United States' top civil rights enforcer and unfortunately, the position has remained unfilled for far too long.
>
> That is especially true when one considers the serious problems caused by racism, sexism, ageism, prejudice against the disabled and other poisonous prejudices in this country. (Editorial, *Chicago Defender*, 1997)[10]

Black elites again lauded President Clinton when, in August 2000, he bypassed the Senate once more and made Lee not "acting" assistant attorney general for civil rights but "actual" head of the Civil Rights Division, using his constitutional power to make recess appointments when Congress is not in session:

> It was a very smooth move recently by President Clinton—appointing Bill Lann Lee to be the nation's top civil rights officer—despite rabid opposition by Republicans.
>
> Lee . . . had seen his full approval to the post languish in the Senate at the behest of sniping Republicans who have objected to what they see as Lee's left-wing stance in support of affirmative action and other racially-tinged issues.
>
> Good move, Mr. President and good luck, Mr. Lee. You may need it amidst the confounding cartel of conservatives who stymied the appointment for so long. (Editorial, *Chicago Defender*, 2000)

By using aggressive tactics to seat Lee in the civil rights position at the Justice Department, Clinton was able to effectively undo the damage he had done to his standing with black elites during his first term over the Guinier affair.

THE ROGER GREGORY NOMINATION

When Clinton took office, the Fourth Circuit Court of Appeals was one of three circuits to have no African American judges (the First and Tenth Circuits were the other two). Particularly troubling to the president was the fact that the Fourth Circuit, which includes the states of Virginia, West Virginia, Maryland, North Carolina, and South Carolina, contained the largest African American population of any U.S. appellate court jurisdiction (Lewis, 2000a). Claiming to want to rectify this injustice, in 1995 Clinton nominated James A. Beaty Jr. of North Carolina to fill one of four vacancies on the Fourth Circuit—a seat that had traditionally been set aside specifically for a North Carolina resident. Only one year earlier, Beaty had been easily confirmed as a U.S. District Court judge in North Carolina. Now facing an opposition Republican Congress, however, Beaty's appeals court nomination ran into immediate trouble. Republican Senate leaders, including Senate Judiciary Committee chairman Hatch, accused Beaty of being "soft" on crime, citing one of his district court opinions in which he overturned a murder conviction on procedural grounds.[11] Accordingly, as part of their strategy to delay hearings and confirmation votes on all Clinton appointees who were ideologically objectionable to the Republican majority, the Senate Judiciary Committee never held hearings on Beaty's Fourth Circuit nomination, and by 1998 the nomination was returned without action (Savage, 2000).

Clinton, however, was still determined to seat a black jurist on the Fourth Circuit. Thus, in August 1999, he nominated James A. Wynn Jr., also of North Carolina, to fill the North Carolina judicial slot on the Fourth Circuit. However, Senator Jesse Helms of North Carolina, as the home state senator, was single-handedly able to block Wynn's confirmation (Jackson, 2000). Helms's stated reason for this action was that the chief judge of the Fourth Circuit, J. Harvie Wilkinson, had told Helms that no more judges were needed on the Fourth Circuit (Masters, 2000). This was despite the fact that the U.S. Judicial Conference had declared this seat a "judicial emergency" because it had been vacant for more than a decade (Masters, 2000).

Still determined to see a black judge seated on the Fourth Circuit during his presidency, Clinton decided to side-step Helms, and so, while the Wynn nomination languished, Clinton sought a black Virginia resident to fill another vacancy on the Fourth Circuit—thereby taking away Helms's veto power as he would no longer be the home state senator. In June 2000, Clinton nominated Gregory of Virginia for a seat on the Fourth Circuit designated for a Virginia resident (Masters, 2000). Both senators from Virginia—one a Democrat (Charles S. Robb) and one a Republican (John W. Warner)—pledged their support for Gregory's nomination (Masters, 2000). Despite the support this time from both home state senators, the Senate Judiciary Committee took no steps to hold confirmation hearings on the Gregory nomination, just as they had done with the Wynn nomination. Clinton followed up the Gregory and Wynn nominations by selecting yet another black for a vacancy on the Fourth Circuit in October 2000, Andre M. Davis of Maryland (Gibson, 2000). However, with a hotly contested presidential election in the balance, all three nominations (Wynn, Gregory, and Davis) would die at the close of the congressional session, and Clinton's efforts to appoint the first black to the Fourth Circuit Court of Appeals would fail. With the election of Republican G. W. Bush to the White House in 2000, the chances for a black Fourth Circuit judge being appointed in the next presidential administration were uncertain at best.

Clinton then took the extraordinary, though not unprecedented, step of making a recess appointment to the Fourth Circuit.[12] With Congress not in session, Clinton was able to do what he had failed repeatedly to do over the previous five years: seat the first black person on the Fourth Circuit. On December 27, 2000, Clinton unilaterally appointed Gregory to the Fourth Circuit (Lewis, 2000a). In a ceremony in the Oval Office, the president declared: "It is unconscionable that the Fourth Circuit has never had an African American appellate judge. It is long past time to right that wrong. Justice may be blind, but we all know that diversity in the courts, as in all aspects of society, sharpens our vision and makes us a stronger nation" (quoted in Lewis, 2000a).

Not surprisingly, Republican leaders were outraged by the president's disregard of the Senate. Senator James M. Inhofe (R-OK) publicly vowed to keep Gregory from ever receiving a lifetime judicial appointment when he would come before the Senate for a confirmation vote in the next congressional session (Lewis, 2000b). Ultimately, these threats proved groundless. In his first batch of federal court nominations, G. W. Bush resubmitted Gregory's name for a lifetime appointment to the Fourth Circuit, and that nomination sailed through the Senate in July 2001.

THE RONNIE WHITE NOMINATION

On October 7, 1999, the Senate rejected the nomination of White, the first black to serve on the Missouri Supreme Court, for a judgeship on the U.S. Federal District Court for the Eastern District of Missouri. Although days before the roll-call vote it had looked like White would be confirmed—after being reported favorably out of the Judiciary Committee not once but twice, and receiving the backing of Republican Missouri senator Christopher S. Bond—several key Republican senators, including Bond and Judiciary Committee chairman Hatch (R-UT), switched their votes at the behest of the other Republican Missouri senator, John Ashcroft. Ultimately, the vote on the White nomination went strictly along party lines, and he was defeated 54–45 (Babbington and Biskupic, 1999).[13]

Although White's nomination was reported out of the Judiciary Committee favorably by a 15–3 vote, conservative Republican leaders—led by former senator Ashcroft—charged that White "has a serious bias against the death penalty" (quoted in Babbington and Biskupic, 1999). Ashcroft went so far as to contact leading law enforcement groups to muster public support for this position—an unheard-of move in a fight over a lower federal court nominee (Babbington and Biskupic, 1999). It should be noted that as a home state senator in the White controversy, Ashcroft held the power under Senate custom to block White's nomination at the Judiciary Committee stage—commonly referred to as *senatorial courtesy*. Yet because of the close Senate race in which he was then engaged with former Democratic Missouri governor Mel Carnahan (Ayres, 1999)—a race in which the death penalty, for reasons wholly unrelated to White, had come to play a significant factor[14]—Ashcroft chose to take his objections over White's confirmation to the floor of the Senate where his opposition would gain much more public attention. After losing his bid for reelection to the Senate in 2000—and while serving as attorney general under President G. W. Bush—Ashcroft did an about-face on Ronnie White and vowed not to oppose him should Bush renominate him; this gesture was widely seen as Ashcroft's attempt to ease tensions with the Congressional Black Caucus—a relationship seriously injured by the White confirmation fight (Alvarez, 2001).

As we will see in Chapter 7, at the time of the vote, Ashcroft no doubt believed that engaging in a high-profile floor debate against an allegedly "pro-criminal" judicial nominee would send an important "signal" to conservative activists—constituents whom Ashcroft desperately needed to mobilize given his hotly contested reelection race with Carnahan. But what Ashcroft and fellow Senate Republicans did not foresee was the role their actions would ultimately play in causing Ashcroft's defeat in the 2000 senatorial election. In short, what Ashcroft and his colleagues did not anticipate was the impact their public actions would have in mobilizing Missouri's black activists against Ashcroft, leading to a record number of black voters turning out for Carnahan (see Chapter 7).

Clinton wasted no time in exploiting the Republicans' miscalculation. Immediately after the defeat of White's nomination, he publicly declared: "Today's defeat of Ronnie White's nomination . . . was a disgraceful act of partisan politics . . . Unfortunately, by voting down the first African American judge to serve on the Missouri state Supreme Court, the Republican-controlled Senate is adding credence to the perception that they treat minority and women judicial nominees unfairly and unequally" (quoted in Brogan, 1999).

Vice President Al Gore, by then a Democratic presidential candidate, told the *Amsterdam News* in an exclusive interview later that month:

> I think it was a clear injustice on the part of the Republicans in the Senate. They made him [White] a political target to curry favor with right wing extremist groups, and in the process they did a great injustice to a fine person with a distinguished record who was eminently qualified to be a judge. They rejected him in a way that I think really was insult . . . African American nominees have had a much tougher time before the Senate. Still, you can't know for sure the motivation of each individual senator; you can't look into their hearts. The record speaks for itself. (quoted in Boyd, 1999)

The Call for Female Leadership in the Justice Department

By the time Clinton was elected in 1992, women had made real strides in American society—largely through a litigation campaign conducted in the federal courts aimed at securing the same protections under the 1964 Civil Rights Act as had been afforded minorities. But with Clinton's election, the activists wanted to turn their attention in a different direction. As the former president of NOW, Patricia Ireland, explained: "There is a real shift and a real possibility for successfully advancing rather than just defending women's rights. We will no longer be on the outside, but also on the inside" (quoted in Neuffer, 1992). In fact, many political observers believed that women were more politically mobilized during Clinton's 1992 campaign than ever before, in part because of anger over Justice Thomas's confirmation proceedings[15] and fear that G. H. W. Bush would appoint justices to the Supreme Court who would try to turn back abortion rights (Enda, 1992).

Having helped turn women out strongly for Clinton at the polls, female activists, like African American activists, were prepared to hold Clinton to his campaign promise to make the cabinet and the judiciary "look like America." As the former president of NARAL explained: "Getting the right people elected is only the beginning. Vigilance and making sure the right people do the right thing is a continuous process" (Faye Wattleton quoted in Frolick, 1992). Accordingly, female activists wasted no time in demanding that Clinton appoint a significant number of women to his cabinet. Women's rights groups pressed their agenda in a meeting with Clinton's transition team in early December 1992 (Lewis, 1992a), demanding that Clinton appoint a woman to the post of attorney general. This was critical to female activists, as this cabinet post was considered one of the four most important spots in the administration, along with the departments of the treasury, state, and defense (Lewis, 1992a).

But Clinton's first round of cabinet appointments were disappointing for leading female activists:

> In the [Clinton] transition team there were some people who would periodically call Ellie Smeal [head of the Fund for a Feminist Majority] or call somebody else [active in the women's movement] and [keep us informed of what was] happening, and one of the calls that came through [to the leading women activists] was about the cabinet, saying that there were lots of women's names being submitted [to Clinton for consideration], [but that] they weren't ending up on the short list. And that's when we [female activists] made a big public push [for female appointees to the cabinet] . . . And so that was part of our idea, that you hold your friends accountable . . . because they are only as good as you push them to be. Political people do respond to pressure. (Ireland interview, 2003)

Leading female activists—including NOW president Ireland; Eleanor Smeal, head of the Fund for a Feminist Majority; Harriet Woods, chairwoman of the National Women's Political Caucus; and Jane Danowitz, executive director of the Women's Campaign Fund—thus publicly complained, with Danowitz saying, "This train is pulling out of the station and not enough women are on board" (quoted in Neuffer, 1992). In a letter to the president-elect, Smeal called on Clinton to "shatter the glass ceiling" (Ifill, 1992). She also suggested that she would like to see no fewer than six of fourteen cabinet positions go to women (Editorial, *The Record*, 1992). This prompted Clinton to accuse female activists of being "bean counters," more interested in quotas than qualifications (Ifill, 1992). But only days later, Clinton acceded to the female activists' demands and nominated Zoe Baird to be the first woman attorney general in history. Although short of their goal of gaining six cabinet posts, in the final analysis, female activists were nonetheless pleased with Clinton's selection of three women to top cabinet posts. As Ireland said, it was "time to be congratulating ourselves and the women of this country and President Clinton, frankly. He has appointed a very diverse Cabinet, especially on racial and ethnic diversity lines. We're still looking for an equal share of power. And, at the same time, going from 11 to 22 percent women in the Cabinet is a substantial gain." [16]

When it was later revealed that Baird had hired two illegal immigrants as nannies, she was forced to withdraw her nomination. Women's groups, however, pressured Clinton to nominate another woman as attorney general because "we think the best qualified person will be a woman for the same reasons that a woman was selected . . . the first time." [17] To do otherwise, female activists warned, would mean an "end of the honeymoon" between Clinton and his female political base (Ireland, quoted in Shogren, 1993). Wanting to satisfy the demands of critical female activists, Clinton was prepared to nominate another woman, Kimba M. Wood, a judge in the Southern District of New York. However, her name was dropped from consideration when it was revealed that she, too, had hired an immigrant to care for her young children, although her failure to pay social security taxes at the time was not technically illegal. Perhaps fearing that Clinton would now refuse to nominate a woman as attorney general, women's groups were quick to organize a grass-roots campaign to pressure the White House to choose a third woman to head the Justice Department, turning this issue into one of a double standard for women. As Patricia Ireland said: "I think he [Clinton] wants a woman in this job and I think we're going to have a woman in this job. The double standard that we're dealing with is in the culture, it's across the country. It's that double burden that women carry of being the caregivers of the very young and the very old." [18] In the end, Clinton satisfied the demands of female activists by naming Janet Reno as attorney general. Reno had no children and was easily confirmed by the Senate.

Demands for Women on the Federal Bench

When it came to increasing the number of women on the lower federal courts, female activists had little to complain about; Clinton appointed eighty-seven women to the district courts and twenty women to the courts of appeals (Table 4-1). Woman activists admit, however, that they kept tallies throughout Clinton's presidency on the number of minority and female judicial appointments being made. Ireland noted that NOW and other groups "tried very hard" to hold Clinton accountable for his campaign promise:

> The political director on our staff was one of the ones who kept her finger on that pulse. But I don't think that it was as conscious an effort or as comprehensive an effort as it should have been. And in part [this is] because we [NOW] tended to respond to the areas where we would get a call from the Clinton team saying, "Hey this is not going to happen." And we never really heard much on that count because [judicial] appointments [for women] seemed to be coming out with some good results. (Ireland interview, 2003)

And so, to the extent that Clinton maintained his commitment to appointing women to the courts, female activists remained pleased with the president and tended not to push too hard for lower court appointments.[19]

The Issue of Substantive Representation

Carter's and Clinton's affirmative action appointment strategy, without question, increased descriptive representation on the federal bench. But what we still do not know is whether the Democrats' black and female judicial appointees also provided the substantive representation that black and female activists hoped they would. In other words, do black and female judges adjudicate cases consistent with the ideology of black and female activists affiliated with the Democratic Party? This is critical, as minority and female activists demand substantive as well as descriptive representation on the bench. In order to answer this question, I will analyze the voting behavior of black judges and female judges on the courts of appeals.

EXPECTATIONS OF JUDICIAL VOTING BEHAVIOR

Black Versus White Judges

Prior research comparing the voting behavior of black and white judges in the 1970s—specifically, in cases involving crime and race discrimination—show no statistically significant differences between the two racial groups (Gottschall, 1983; Uhlman, 1978; Walker and Barrow, 1985). But these studies were done before the influx of very conservative white judges appointed by Reagan and G. H. W. Bush. Accordingly, when comparing black and white judges of all presidential cohorts, I would expect there to be a statistically significant difference between the decision-making behavior of black and white judges.

When comparing black and white judges appointed by the same president, I would not expect any significant difference in the way Carter's black and white appointees vote, but I would expect a difference in the way Clinton's black and white appointees vote. This is because, as previously stated, white Democrats became more conservative between Carter's and Clinton's presidencies while black Democrats did not. Thus, I would expect Clinton's black and white cohorts to lie farther from each other on the ideological spectrum.

We also want to compare the ideology of black judges appointed under Clinton versus those appointed under Carter. Because the political ideology of black Democratic elites did not shift significantly between the Carter and Clinton years, it is reasonable to expect Clinton's and Carter's black appointees to lie close together on the ideological spectrum.

Female Versus Male Judges

Prior studies comparing decision-making based on gender have found mixed results. For example, Songer, Davis, and Haire (1994) found no statistically significant difference in voting between male and female judges in search and seizure cases and obscenity cases, but they did find a significant difference in voting between men and women in gender discrimination cases. Thus, whether there are gender differences would seem to depend on the legal issue at hand. In this chapter, I will examine differences in voting based on gender in abortion cases, as this issue is paramount to female activists involved in judicial confirmation politics. When comparing all presidential cohorts, I would expect to find a statistically significant difference in how men and women decide abortion cases. When comparing Democratic appointees only, however, I would not expect to see a statistically significant difference in decision-making because Democratic nominees—male and female—were closely scrutinized for their positions on abortion.

In this chapter, I will focus on only three categories of cases. To assess differences in voting between white and black judges, I look at (1) search and seizure decisions and (2) race discrimination decisions. To assess differences in voting between male and female judges, I look at abortion cases. I look only at these categories of decisions because these are the types of legal/political issues in which we would most likely see differences based on race and gender. In contrast, in the states' rights cases, there is no theoretical basis to believe that blacks and whites, or men and women, see these issues differently. Explanation and coding for the variables is set forth in Appendices B (search and seizure cases), C (race discrimination cases), and E (abortion cases). The models are the same as used in Chapter 3, with one exception in each model. In the search and seizure and race discrimination models, I add a variable to control for the race of the judge, and in the abortion models, I add a variable to control for the gender of the judge.

TABLE 4-2

Logit Coefficients for the Likelihood of a Vote to Uphold a Search or Seizure, Nonconsensual Search and Seizure Cases, January 1, 1996 to December 31, 2001

	MLE	Robust SE	Δ Probability[a]
Constant	−.37★	.20	NA
Background-Based Variables			
Black Judge	−.68★	.27	−.16
Appointing Presidential Cohort			
Clinton Appointee	Baseline	NA	.00
G. H. W. Bush Appointee	.65★★★	.18	.16
Reagan Appointee	.70★★★	.16	.17
Carter Appointee	−.64★★★	.18	−.14
Nixon Appointee	.64★	.28	.16
Regional Background of Judge			
Compared with Southern Judge			
Southern Judge	Baseline	NA	.00
Eastern Judge	−.55★★	.22	−.12
Midwestern Judge	−.41★★	.16	−.09
Ninth Circuit Judge	−.90★★★	.18	−.19
Tenth Circuit Judge	−.15	.19	−.03
Fact-Based Variables			
Location of Search Compared			
with Home			
Search of Home	Baseline	NA	.00
Search of Automobile	.33★	.17	.08
Search of Person	.24	.17	.06
Search of Luggage	.52★	.21	.13
Presence of Warrant	1.02★★★	.18	.23
Limited Search	.25★	.13	.06
Border Search	.14	.22	.03

(Vote against criminal defendant coded 1; vote for criminal defendant coded 0)

$N = 1,469$
Likelihood Ratio Test (15 df) = 164.86★★★
% correctly predicted = 66.01
% observed in null model = 50.30
Proportional Reduction in Error = 31.60

★$p \leq .10$; ★★$p \leq .01$; ★★★$p \leq .001$ (two-tailed test)

[a]Change in probability is measured as the distance from a probability of .5 assuming the presence of that variable.

RESULTS

Black Versus White Judges

The results of the logistic regression analyses for all presidential cohorts are shown in Tables 4-2 (search and seizure) and Table 4-5 (race discrimination). Consistent with the above-stated hypotheses, there is a statistically

TABLE 4-3

Logit Coefficients for the Likelihood of a Vote Against a Criminal Defendant, Nonconsensual Search and Seizure Cases, U.S. Courts of Appeals, January 1, 1996 to December 31, 2001

	CLINTON AND CARTER APPOINTEES		
	MLE	Robust SE	Δ Probability[a]
Constant	−.23	.28	NA
Background-Based Variables			
Appointing President and Race			
White Clinton Judge	Baseline	NA	.00
Black Clinton Judge	−1.02★	.41	−.22
White Carter Judge	−.71★★★	.19	−.16
Black Carter Judge	−1.11★★	.38	−.23
Regional Background of Judge			
Compared with Southern Judge			
Southern Judge	Baseline	NA	.00
Eastern Judge	−.44	.41	−.10
Midwestern Judge	−.31	.26	−.07
Ninth Circuit Judge	−.85★★★	.26	−.19
Tenth Circuit Judge	−.41	.29	−.09
Fact-Based Independent Variables			
Location of Search			
Search of Home	Baseline	NA	.00
Search of Automobile	.17	.26	.04
Search of Person	.45★	.26	.11
Search of Luggage	.36	.34	.09
Presence of Warrant	.76★★	.26	.18
Limited Search	.13	.20	.03
Border Search	.07	.37	.02

(Vote against criminal defendant coded 1;
vote for criminal defendant coded 0)

$N = 630$
Likelihood Ratio Test (11 *df*) = 42.09★★★
% correctly predicted = 67.34
% observed in null model = 65.40
Proportional Reduction in Error = 5.61

★$p \leq .10$; ★★$p \leq .01$; ★★★$p \leq .001$ (two-tailed test)

[a]Change in probability is measured as the distance from a probability of .5 assuming the presence of that variable.

significant difference in the voting behavior between black and white judges in both the search and seizure model and the race discrimination model.

As expected, white judges are more likely than their African American counterparts to vote in a "conservative" manner when it comes to issues of criminal law enforcement and race discrimination. With respect to the search and seizure cases, with everything else held constant, the probability of a vote to uphold search and seizure decreases 16 percentage points with a

TABLE 4-4

Comparison of Voting Across Presidential and Racial Cohorts, Probability That a Judge Will Vote to Uphold a Search or Seizure, Nonconsensual Search and Seizure Cases, U.S. Courts of Appeals, January 1, 1996 to December 31, 2001, Carter and Clinton Appointees

	White Clinton Judge	Black Clinton Judge	White Carter Judge	Black Carter Judge
Compare a White Clinton Judge with a:	—	+.22*	+.16***	+.23**
Compare a Black Clinton Judge with a:	−.18**	—	−.06	+.02
Compare a White Carter Judge with a:	−.16***	+.06	—	+.07
Compare a Black Carter Judge with a:	−.23**	−.02	−.07	—
N = 630				

$*p \leq .10; **p \leq .01; ***p \leq .001$ (two-tailed test)

black judge (Table 4-2). With respect to the race discrimination cases, with everything else held constant, the probability of a vote against a minority's claim of race discrimination decreases by 17 percentage points were a black judge to hear the same case (Table 4-5).

We now turn to the models that analyze voting by Democratic judges only. Tables 4-3 and 4-4 show the results of the search and seizure models, and Tables 4-6 and 4-7 show the results of the race discrimination models. As predicted, we see that race is a statistically significant predictor of voting behavior in search and seizure cases as well as race discrimination cases for Clinton appointees, but there is no statistically significant difference in the voting behavior of Carter's black and white appointees in these two types of cases.

Turning to Table 4-4, the probability of a white Clinton appointee voting against a criminal defendant on a search and seizure motion increases by 22 percentage points compared with a black Clinton appointee. Table 4-7 shows that the probability of a white Clinton appointee voting against a race discrimination plaintiff increases by 24 percentage points compared with a black Clinton appointee. Comparing black and white judges appointed by Carter, we see a much different picture. In neither model are the differences between black and white Carter appointees statistically significant, although the signs of the coefficients suggest that white Carter appointees are more likely to vote in a "conservative" manner than black Carter appointees.

Finally, we compare black Carter judges and black Clinton judges. Table 4-4 shows us that in search and seizure cases, there is no statistically

TABLE 4-5

Logit Coefficients for the Likelihood of a Vote Against a Plaintiff, Nonconsensual Race Discrimination Cases, U.S. Courts of Appeals, January 1, 1994 to December 31, 2001

	MLE	Robust SE	Δ Probability[a]
Constant	−1.22***	.24	NA
Background-Based Variables			
Black Judge	−.71**	.27	−.17
Female Judge	−.08	.18	−.02
Appointing President			
Clinton Appointee	Baseline	NA	.00
G. H. W. Bush Appointee	1.18***	.22	.26
Reagan Appointee	1.13***	.20	.26
Carter Appointee	.18	.22	.04
Nixon Appointee	.80*	.32	.19
Regional Background of Judge			
Compared with Southern Judge			
Southern Judge	Baseline	NA	.00
Eastern Judge	−.32*	.18	−.08
Midwestern Judge	−.51***	.16	−.12
Ninth Circuit Judge	−.62**	.20	−.15
Tenth Circuit Judge	−.76**	.30	−.18
Fact-Based Independent Variables			
Equal Protection Claim	.86**	.20	.20
Class Action	1.16***	.30	.37
White Plaintiff	.77**	.15	.18
Race Plus Other Claim	.53**	.19	.13
Pro Se Plaintiff	−1.43**	.35	−.31

(Vote against plaintiff coded 1;
vote for plaintiff coded 0)

$N = 1,408$
Likelihood Ratio Test (15 *df*) = 200.74***
% correctly predicted = 70.53
% observed in null model = 66.01
Proportional Reduction in Error = 15.09

*p ≤ .10; **p ≤ .01; ***p ≤ .001 (two-tailed test)

[a]Change in probability is measured as the distance from a probability of .5 assuming the presence of that variable.

significant difference in voting between the two black cohorts; Table 4-7 shows us that in race discrimination cases, there is also no statistically significant difference between the two black cohorts.

These results lead to three important findings. First, there would appear to be support for the notion that Clinton's black judges are significantly more "liberal" than their white counterparts on the federal bench. This could also be interpreted as support for the notion that the Republican-led majority exhibited stronger opposition to Clinton's African American ap-

TABLE 4-6

Logit Coefficients for the Likelihood of a Vote Against a Criminal Defendant, Nonconsensual Race Discrimination Cases, U.S. Courts of Appeals, January 1, 1996 to December 31, 2001, Clinton and Carter Appointees

	MLE	Robust SE	Δ Probability[a]
Constant	−.99★★★	.24	NA
Background-Based Variables			
Appointing President and Race			
White Clinton Judge	Baseline	NA	.00
Black Clinton Judge	−1.05★	.47	−.24
White Carter Judge	.10	.22	−.02
Black Carter Judge	−.53	.38	−.13
Regional Background of Judge			
Compared with Southern Judge			
Southern Judge	Baseline	NA	.00
Eastern Judge	−.41	.31	−.10
Midwestern Judge	−.27	.26	−.07
Ninth Circuit Judge	−.70★	.33	−.17
Tenth Circuit Judge	−.20	.32	−.05
Fact-Based Independent Variables			
Equal Protection Claim	−.18	.35	−.04
Class Action	.61	.46	.15
White Plaintiff	.62★★	.26	.15
Race Plus Other Claim	.63★★	.28	.15
Pro Se Plaintiff	−1.44★★	.59	−.30

(Vote against criminal defendant coded 1; vote for criminal defendant coded 0)

$N = 590$
Likelihood Ratio Test (12 *df*) = 34.53★★★
% correctly predicted = 77.00
% observed in null model = 76.27
Proportional Reduction in Error = 3.07

★$p \leq .10$; ★★$p \leq .01$; ★★★$p \leq .001$ (two-tailed test)
[a]Change in probability is measured as the distance from a probability of .5 assuming the presence of that variable.

pointees than his white appointees on the basis of ideology rather than race, as Clinton's black judges lay farther away on the ideological spectrum from the Republican Senate's preference point than did Clinton's white judges.

Second, the fact that Clinton's black judges, but not his white judges, espoused a much more "liberal" ideology than Clinton did—at least regarding criminal law enforcement and race issues—lends support for the notion that Clinton used diversity appointments not to further his own policy agenda, but rather to shore up support among African American activists—

TABLE 4-7

Comparison of Voting Across Presidential and Racial Cohorts, Probability That a Judge Will Vote for a Plaintiff, Nonconsensual Race Discrimination Cases, U.S. Courts of Appeals, January 1, 1994 to December 31, 2001, Clinton and Carter Appointees

	White Clinton Judge	Black Clinton Judge	White Carter Judge	Black Carter Judge
Compare a White Clinton Judge with a:	—	+.24**	−.02	+.13
Compare a Black Clinton Judge with a:	−.24**	—	−.26**	−.13
Compare a White Carter Judge with a:	+.02	+.26**	—	+.15*
Compare a Black Carter Judge with a:	−.13	+.13	−.15*	—
N = 590				

*$p \leq .10$; **$p \leq .01$ (two-tailed test)

critical players in the Democratic Party's efforts to prevail on Election Day. In other words, Clinton appointed liberal black judges notwithstanding the fact that these judges were likely to decide cases in a manner more liberal than Clinton's own preferences.

Third, in contrast to Clinton's judges, Carter's black and white judges shared the same judicial ideology as did Carter, thus allowing Carter to achieve greater diversity on the federal bench without compromising his policy agenda. This may suggest that Carter and Clinton had different motives for pursuing an affirmative action strategy for the federal courts.

Female Versus Male Judges

The results of the logistic regression analyses for the abortion models are shown in Tables 4-8 and 4-9. Consistent with my hypothesis, there is a statistically significant difference in voting behavior of male and female judges in abortion cases when comparing all presidential cohorts. With everything else held constant, female judges are less likely to uphold an abortion regulation by 30 percentage points than are male judges (Table 4-8).

Table 4-9 breaks down the data by party.[20] While there is no statistically significant difference in voting based on gender when looking at Clinton and Carter appointees, there is a statistically significant difference in voting based on gender comparing Reagan and G. H. W. Bush appointees. With everything else held constant, female Republican appointees are less likely to vote to uphold an abortion restriction by 40 percentage points compared with male Republican appointees.

TABLE 4-8

Logit Coefficients for the Likelihood of a Vote to Restrict Abortion, Nonconsensual Abortion Cases, U.S. Courts of Appeals, January 1, 1978 to December 31, 2002

	MLE	Robust SE	Δ Probability[a]
Constant	−2.70**	.85	NA
Background-Based Variables			
Female Judge	−1.41*	.78	−.30
Appointing President			
Clinton Appointee	Baseline	NA	.00
G. H. W. Bush Appointee	3.15**	.91	.54
Reagan Appointee	3.44**	.80	.61
Carter Appointee	.76	.82	.06
Nixon Appointee	1.82*	.92	.23
Southern Judge	1.12*	.46	.25
Fact-Based Variables			
Statute Restricting	1.17*	.47	.26
Abortion for Minors			
Post-*Casey* Decision	.03	.85	.01

$N = 179$

Likelihood Ratio Test (7 *df*) = 68.20; significant at .000

% correctly predicted = 79.10

% observed in null model = 51.39

Proportional Reduction in Error = 57.00

*$p ≤ .10$; **$p ≤ .001$ (two-tailed test)

[a]Change in probability is measured as the distance from a probability of .5 assuming the presence of that variable.

Conclusion

The second elite mobilization strategy to emerge in the modern political era is the president's use of affirmative action to shore up support among minority and female activists. Because minority and female activists affiliated with the Democratic Party are overwhelmingly liberal, this elite mobilization strategy is largely confined to Democratic presidents. Although Carter was the first president to employ this strategy, an affirmative action judicial selection policy was particularly useful to Clinton because it allowed him to soften the hostile feelings of African American activists engendered by many of Clinton's "new" Democratic policies that were viewed as contrary to the interests of lower-class blacks (e.g., welfare reform and "tough" crime policies).

Decision-making data also confirm that activists' expectations about these "nontraditional" appointees were met. Black appointees do, in fact, tend to be more supportive of criminal defendants' civil liberty rights and

TABLE 4-9

Probability of a Judge Voting to Restrict Abortion by Appointing President and Gender, Nonconsensual Abortion Cases, U.S. Courts of Appeals, January 1, 1978 to December 31, 2002

	REAGAN AND BUSH APPOINTEES			CLINTON AND CARTER APPOINTEES		
	MLE	Robust SE	Δ Probability[a]	MLE	Robust SE	Δ Probability[a]
Constant	.18	.42	NA	-1.48**	.50	NA
Female Judge	-2.22**	.75	-.40	-.74	1.28	-.18
Southern Judge	.62	.60	.15	1.50*	.70	.32
Statute Restricting Abortion for Minors	2.44*	1.10	.42	.38	.77	-.09
Post-Casey Decision	.89	.65	-.21	-1.27*	.73	-.28

N = 86	N = 68
Likelihood Ratio Test (4 df) = 18.77***	Likelihood Ratio Test (4 df) = 10.51*
% correctly predicted = 77.77	% correctly predicted = 83.60
% observed in null model = 74.41	% in null model = 79.11
Proportional Reduction in Error = 15.04	Proportional Reduction in Error = 21.49

*$p \leq .10$; **$p \leq .01$; ***$p \leq .001$ (two-tailed test)

[a]Change in probability is measured as the distance from a probability of .5 assuming the presence of that variable.

minorities' civil rights than white appointees; and women appointees do, in fact, tend to be more supportive of a woman's right to choose abortion. These findings lend strong support for the theory that diversification on the federal bench is necessary to provide not only descriptive representation of litigants, but substantive representation as well.

Political Activists Turn Their Attention to the Confirmation Phase of the Appointment Process

TWO INSTITUTIONAL IMPEDIMENTS made involvement by outsiders in the judicial confirmation process—even at the Supreme Court level—very difficult before the early part of the 20th century. First, until 1929, judicial nominations were debated and voted on behind closed doors in executive sessions (Harris, 1953). Nor were confirmation hearings open to the public (Maltese, 1995). Second, senators were not popularly elected until passage of the Seventeenth Amendment in 1913, insulating them from an electoral backlash were they to vote to confirm a controversial nomination. Accordingly, it was rare for activists—party activists or special interest groups—to be involved in judicial confirmation proceedings before 1913, and to the extent that they were, their involvement was focused on exerting influence on the confirmation of Supreme Court nominees.[1] As for lower court judgeships, party activists, as we know, were singularly focused on influencing home state senators and the president during the nomination process—the awarding of patronage—rather than the confirmation process.

Despite removal of both these impediments by the 1930s, John A. Maltese (1995) states that it was not until the 1960s that interest groups became a permanent fixture in Supreme Court confirmation politics. Activists, however, did not begin to turn their attention to lower federal court confirmations with any regularity until the 1980s with the formation of the Alliance for Justice—a coalition of liberal interest groups (Aron interview, 2002). Before the 1980s, then, confirmation battles over lower court nominations were waged at the behest of a senator, rather than activists.[2] But once groups like the Alliance for Justice and its conservative counterpart, the Judicial Selection Monitoring Project (JSMP), began to monitor all lower court nominations, and once other grass-roots interest groups began to flood into the appointment process, a third elite mobilization strategy would emerge: the use of strategic tactics by senators designed to obstruct the confirmation of a designated lower court nominee—one opposed by activists aligned with the senator's party. While our two previous elite mobilization strategies were aimed at broad nomination goals of the president, this elite mobilization strategy is aimed at a specific nominee's confirmation proceedings in the Senate. What allows interest groups to be so much more directly involved in this elite mobilization strategy is the greater access they have to senators than to the president. As the president of NOW explains, its local chapter presidents "tend to know their members of Congress on a first-name basis . . . . In most chapters, if not the president, then the matriarch of the chapter is politically connected from years and years of activism in the community and can pick up the phone and call if not the [congressional] member, then the chief of staff" (Gandy interview).

As we will see in Chapter 6, senatorial obstructionist tactics include requiring a roll-call vote (rather than the traditionally used voice vote) on a nomination, voting "no" in roll call against a nomination, making provocative statements on the floor of the Senate against a nominee, delaying a vote on a nomination, vetoing a nomination through senatorial courtesy, filibustering a nomination, and refusing to engage in a judicial log-roll on a nomination. But before moving to these specific tactics, we will review why senators began using such procedural tactics in the first place.

The Emergence of Judicial Selection Watchdogs During the Reagan Administration

As promised in the 1980 election, upon his inauguration in 1981, Reagan began a concerted campaign to "pack" the federal courts with conservative judges—that is, those who believed in the "sanctity of life" and, by implication, in overturning *Roe v. Wade*. Equally critical, in 1982, the Federalist Society was formed by a group of "conservatives and libertarians dedicated to reforming the current legal order." Among other things, members of the Federalist Society advocated changing the criteria about judicial selection from the issue-oriented approach then prevalent in the Reagan White House (pro-life judges versus pro-choice judges) to a philosophical approach centered around finding judges who will "say what the law is, not what it should be."[3] The Federalist Society would soon wield a lot of influence in judicial selection as its members became key players in the Reagan Justice Department, including all twelve assistant attorneys general (Special to the

New York Times, 1986). Not surprisingly, with control of the Justice Department, many of Reagan's judicial nominees would also come from the ranks of the Federalist Society, including Robert H. Bork (D.C. Circuit), Richard A. Posner (Seventh Circuit), Ralph K. Winter Jr. (Second Circuit), Stephen F. Williams (D.C. Circuit), John T. Noonan (Ninth Circuit), and the most famous Federalist Society member, Antonin Scalia (first appointed to the D.C. Circuit and later to the Supreme Court) (Schwartz, 1988; Special to the *New York Times,* 1986).

For the most part, Reagan's efforts to "pack" the federal courts with conservative ideologues went unchecked for his entire first term (Aron interview, 2002). But upon his reelection in 1984, liberal activists began to become concerned with the long-term impact Reagan's court-packing efforts would have given another four years of unfettered control in shaping the federal judiciary (Aron interview, 2002). Accordingly, soon after Reagan's reelection, a group of liberal activists joined forces to form the Judicial Monitoring Project under the auspices of the Alliance for Justice; its primary goal was to monitor all of Reagan's judicial nominees and try to defeat those deemed most objectionable to member organizations of the Alliance (Aron interview, 2002). The Alliance for Justice describes itself as a "national association of environmental, civil rights, mental health, women's, children's and consumer advocacy organizations."[4] The formation of the Alliance for Justice also led to the influx of additional special interest groups working independently to fight controversial Reagan nominees, including NOW, also a member of the Alliance for Justice; People for the American Way; Common Cause; the Leadership Conference on Civil Rights; and the NAACP.

By the end of 1985, with a host of conservative courts of appeals nominees sailing through the confirmation process that year;[5] the newly mobilized coalition of liberal interest groups began to exert political pressure on Democrats on the Senate Judiciary Committee to stop rubber-stamping Reagan's judicial nominees (Schwartz, 1988). While at first their calls to rehaul the confirmation process so as to take a closer look at Reagan's nominees met with some resistance from Democratic senators, the nomination that finally made Democrats pay heed to the liberal activists was that of Alex Kozinski. Kozinski, only thirty-four years old when Reagan nominated him to the Ninth Circuit Court of Appeals, would become the youngest judge to serve on the federal appellate bench (Smith and Kamen, 1985). After Kozinski's initial hearing before the Judiciary Committee turned up nothing controversial on the candidate, it appeared that his nomination would easily win the approval of the committee (Clarity and Weaver, 1985).

One week before the vote was to occur in the committee, however, the newly formed coalition of liberal activists and interest groups, led by the Alliance for Justice, charged Kozinski, during his tenure as the Merit Systems Board's special counsel, with being hostile to federal "whistle blowers"— federal employees who report government waste, fraud, and mismanagement. Liberal activists demanded that the committee hearings be reopened to hear testimony on the new charges (Clarity and Weaver, 1985), but the committee ignored that demand and voted unanimously to report the nomination favorably to the full Senate chamber (Staff Writer, *Washington Post*, 1985). The only recognition of the seriousness of the liberal activists' allegations came from Senators Paul Simon (D-IL) and Dennis W. DeConcini (D-AZ), who, though voting for the nominee, expressed reservations in so doing. Simon explained, "frankly, I feel some unease with the nomination, but I do not have a basis to vote against it." DeConcini added, "I hope that Kozinski will hear these words and that he will moderate his temperament and manners that he has exhibited in the past" (Simon and DeConcini, quoted in Hager, 1985a).

Later, however, when affidavits from former employees at the Merit Systems Board suggested that the nominee had misled the committee during the first hearing, the nomination was yanked from the Senate floor and sent back to the committee for further investigation. Specifically, two witnesses alleged in sworn affidavits that Kozinski had failed to defend such employees and instead helped federal managers get rid of workers without being charged with improper personnel practices (Kurtz, 1985a).

At the second hearing, Democratic senators Howard M. Metzenbaum (OH) and Carl Levin (MI) accused Kozinski of misleading the committee about a lawsuit brought against him by a former employee and a monetary settlement he had paid her. Kozinski had testified previously that he had an "excellent relationship with his staff" (Kurtz, 1985b). These exchanges prompted Republican senator Hatch to come to Kozinski's defense and demand that a final vote be taken (Hager, 1985b). Chairman Strom Thurmond (R-SC) called the Democrats' tactics "the puniest, most nit-picking charges" (Franklin, 1985). Such acrimony at a confirmation hearing of a lower court judge was unheard of at that time; today, it is considered de rigueur.

Despite Democrats' reopening of the hearing, Kozinski's nomination was again reported favorably by the committee to the full Senate chamber. There, after a floor fight and roll-call vote—considered unusually harsh tactics against a lower court nominee at that time, as voice votes were the norm for lower court nominations—Kozinski was confirmed, 53–43 (Jackson and Hager, 1985). However, not missing an opportunity to curry favor with liberal interest groups, Senator Levin commented that the "close vote sends a message that the American people want judges who, whatever their other qualifications, can be counted on to treat people fairly, decently and forth-rightly" (Kurtz, 1985c). And so, we see the beginning of a new elite mobi-lization strategy.

Empowered by its ability to bring the Kozinski nomination to a roll-call vote, even though it ultimately lost, the Alliance for Justice immediately an-nounced that its next targets would be conservative lower court nominees Sidney A. Fitzwater (Northern District of Texas) and Jefferson B. Sessions (Northern District of Alabama). Under mounting pressure from liberal ac-tivists to cease simply rubber-stamping Reagan's lower court nominees, Democrats on the Judiciary Committee responded by announcing that they wanted to slow down the confirmation process so as to allow for more time to investigate these candidates (Kurtz, 1985d).

With more time to strategize with Democratic senators about how to de-feat these two nominations, this round of confirmation battles proved more fruitful for liberal activists than the Kozinski fight. Regarding the Fitzwater nomination, civil rights groups claimed that Fitzwater had posted election signs outside of minority precincts designed to mislead black and Hispanic voters. These charges of racism led five Democrats on the committee to vote against Fitzwater; only one Democrat voted in favor of the conservative nominee (Schwartz, 1988). Democrats then mounted an unsuccessful fili-buster against the Fitzwater nomination and insisted on a roll-call vote, re-sulting in another large number of votes against a Reagan nominee; the final tally was 52–42 (Kurtz, 1986a).

Liberal groups were much more successful with the Sessions fight. Ses-sions was defeated by the Judiciary Committee 10–8 after charges of racism were lodged by the NAACP Legal Defense Fund. Specifically, the NAACP alleged that Sessions had made racially insensitive comments while serving as the U.S. attorney for the Southern District of Alabama during the Rea-gan administration (Williams, 1986c). Sessions acknowledged while testify-ing before the Judiciary Committee that he had called the NAACP, the ACLU, the Southern Leadership Conference, and the National Council of Churches "un-American organizations" (Editorial, *New York Times*, 1986). Sessions was also reported to have called a white civil rights lawyer "a dis-grace to his race" (Kurtz, 1986b). Republicans on the Judiciary Committee tried to have the nomination sent on to the full Senate for consideration de-spite the committee's rejection, but such maneuvering ultimately failed, and Sessions was never confirmed. Ironically, he was subsequently elected to the Senate (R-AL) and today sits on the Judiciary Committee.

More contentious than either the Sessions or Fitzwater nominations was the battle liberal activists waged against Daniel A. Manion for a seat on the Seventh Circuit Court of Appeals. During the 1960s, Manion was the co-host of a television and radio program with his father, Clarence Manion, who was a leading member of the conservative John Birch Society (Williams, 1986a). In various programs, the nominee was critical of Supreme Court decisions handed down by the Warren Court on desegregation, religion, and obscenity (Editorial, *New York Times*, 1986). A lawyer-based group in Chicago also charged that Manion was unqualified for the post in that his law practice in Indiana involved personal injury litigation and small cases, rather than the types of cases heard by federal courts (Williams, 1986a). On the basis of these attacks, the Judiciary Committee denied approval to Manion by a vote of 9–9 (Williams, 1986b). All seven Democrats and two Republicans on the committee voted against Manion; however, through a parliamentary maneuver (the same one that proved unsuccessful during the Sessions fight), the nomination was sent on to the Senate floor for consideration (Williams, 1986b). Senate Democrats on the Judiciary Committee promised a heated floor fight. Senator Biden (D-DE) stated that the vote would be "close, but I will do everything possible to defeat the nomination." Edward M. Kennedy (D-MA) added, "Clearly, if Mr. Manion were to implement his personal views on the Federal bench, he would be completely unacceptable" (Biden and Kennedy, quoted in Williams, 1986b).

Fearing the defeat of its second nominee in one year—and a crucial year at that, as control of the Senate was at stake in the midterm elections of 1986—the Reagan administration decided to implement a full-force campaign to win confirmation of Manion on the Senate floor. White House officials believed that without a top-level lobbying campaign, the Manion nomination would be defeated (Shenon, 1986a). Reagan was willing to go so far as to call key Republican senators to ensure he had their vote (Shenon, 1986b), prompting liberal interest groups to step up their attacks against Manion. In June 1986, People for the American Way launched a radio advertising campaign that called Manion "unfit by any standard" for the federal bench (Special to the *New York Times*, 1986). In addition, the group sponsored two advertisements on the Cable News Network urging viewers to write their senators to oppose Manion's confirmation (Special to the *New York Times*, 1986).

With control of the Senate still in the hands of Republicans, Democrats knew they had an uphill battle to defeat Manion. On June 26, 1986, the Senate voted to confirm Manion by a vote of 48–46. However, by virtue of an unusual parliamentary maneuver by Senate Democratic leader Robert C. Byrd, Manion's appointment was still not assured. In short, had Byrd voted his true preference—to not confirm Manion—the vote would have been a tie, and Vice President G. H. W. Bush would have broken the tie in favor of confirmation. By voting for Manion, Byrd put himself on the winning side of the vote, and this gave him the right to call for reconsideration of the vote, which he did immediately (Shenon, 1986c). The vote was postponed until after the two-week July 4th recess, which gave the Democrats more time to search for the one extra vote they needed to defeat Manion. During this delay, a report surfaced that Republican senator Slade Gorton (R-WA) had made a deal with Attorney General Meese: In exchange for Gorton's promise at the last minute to switch his vote approving Manion, the White House promised to nominate a favored nominee of Gorton's to the federal court in Washington State (Shenon, 1986d). This prompted Gorton's Democratic challenger in the Senate race to accuse Gorton of "selling out" (Turner, 1986).[6]

Just before the second vote on the Manion nomination, Reagan told Senate Republican leaders that confirmation of Manion was a major test of his presidential power (Special to the *New York Times*, 1986). Republican senators who had been wavering on their votes ultimately did not cross the president; on July 24, 1986, Manion was confirmed by a vote of 50–49, with Vice President Bush breaking a 49–49 deadlock in the Senate (Shenon, 1986e). After Republicans lost control of the Senate in the 1986 midterm elections, one Washington official was reported to have remarked, "it's a good thing we got Manion through this year" (Editorial, *Washington Post*, 1986).

The last confirmation battle of the Reagan administration involved the nomination of Bernard Siegan to the Ninth Circuit Court of Appeals. Like those directed at Sessions, Fitzwater, and Manion, objections to Siegan also centered around allegations that he was hostile to the civil rights of minorities. In short, liberal activists gathered evidence that Siegan advocated a return to pre–New Deal constitutional interpretation protecting "economic liberties" (Greenhouse, 1988). What Siegan was really arguing, according to the liberal judicial watchdogs, was that the federal and state governments lack the ability to legislate social welfare policy. Moreover, Siegan had argued that the Court's major rulings outlawing desegregation had no legitimate constitutional basis, saying, "There is no fundamental or natural right to education, nor to an integrated education; each is a political right created by government and is accordingly not within the guarantees of the 14th Amendment" (Siegan, quoted in Levin, 1987, at 114). Siegan's views were so controversial that even some conservatives labeled him a judicial "activist" (Greenhouse, 1988). His nomination died at the committee level.

Conservative Activists Organize
to Support Reagan Nominees

During the Reagan and G. H. W. Bush presidencies, with an ideologically compatible president in the White House, conservative organizations mostly sat on the sidelines when it came to lower court judicial selection. The most activity that the conservative interest groups might engage in was defending a Reagan nominee in the press once targeted by the left (Jipping interview, 2002). That passive strategy would change, however, with the confirmation battle over Thomas for a seat on the Supreme Court. Already stinging from the left's defeat of the nomination of Bork, conservatives were determined not to permit liberal activists a second victory regarding Bush's 1991 Supreme Court nomination. Accordingly, conservative forces copied a page from the liberals' playbook and began engaging in the same type of confirmation tactics that had been successful for the left during the Bork fight. Most critically, this entailed rallying the conservative base behind the Thomas nomination and using this clout to threaten Republican senators and conservative Democrats with a political backlash should they vote against the nominee. This time, the conservative forces would win the confirmation battle.

Determined not to repeat the mistakes of the Bork battle, conservative activist Jipping was able to unite previously fractious conservative groups for a united conservative front determined to see the conservative Supreme Court nominee confirmed this time around (Moore, 1993). The following year, Jipping turned this now coalesced group into JSMP.

Jipping founded JSMP in August 1992 as part of the Center for Law and Democracy, which was affiliated with the conservative think tank Free Congress Foundation (Moore, 1993). JSMP speaks for a coalition of conservative grass-roots organizations nationwide and, according to its website, "seeks to promote a restrained judiciary by discouraging the nomination and preventing the confirmation of judicial activists." Among other things, JSMP evaluates judicial nominees on the basis of ideology, tracks federal judicial vacancies, participates in debate over the proper scope of judicial power, and "monitors Senate action in the judicial confirmation process."[7] As its former director, Jipping, has acknowledged, JSMP also closely "tracks Senators' votes on nominations, with an eye toward making judicial appointments an issue in future presidential and Senate elections" (Moore, 1993). In short, JSMP would serve as the conservatives' counterpart to the liberals' Alliance for Justice.

JSMP's monitoring activities are not, however, limited exclusively to judicial nominees; the group also tracks nominees to the Justice Department. In this capacity, JSMP was particularly vocal in its opposition to Guinier, Clinton's first nominee to head the Civil Rights Division at the Justice Department, bringing to Republican senators' attention her controversial scholarly writings about the Voting Rights Act (Lewis, 1993b). Armed with these writings, Republicans in the Senate were ultimately able to force Clinton to withdraw her nomination.[8] JSMP also opposed another Clinton nominee, Lee, to the position of deputy general of civil rights (Feder, 1997).

With a nationwide network of conservative grass-roots groups at its disposal, JSMP has proved to be a force in national politics by engaging in major political mobilization efforts designed to aid Republican senators who, at JSMP's behest, rallied against Clinton nominees found particularly objectionable to JSMP. Indeed, one of the group's first mobilization efforts involved sending out more than 1 million direct-mail fund-raising letters— signed by none other than Bork, the nominee who is largely responsible for mobilizing conservative activists to engage in judicial confirmation politics in the first place (Moore, 1993).

In sum, by the end of the G. H. W. Bush administration, the forces were in place to wage political campaigns against lower court nominees identified by groups on the right or the left to be unfit to sit on the federal bench— unfit only to the extent that they were not sympathetic to the political views and legal positions espoused by those litigation-oriented interest groups and political activists. Table 5-1 shows all the lower court nominations subject to interest group objections in the modern political era (1969–2004). As this table demonstrates, although once it was unheard of to challenge a president's lower court judicial selection, today it is routine practice.

Since our third elite mobilization strategy comes into play only once political activists decide to target a specific nominee, we now turn to the decision-making process of activists over which nominations to challenge.

How Do Interest Groups Decide Which Nominations to Fight?

As previously stated, unlike the other elite mobilization strategies, the urging of senators to block specific judicial nominees requires much more direct and specific communications between activists and politicians. It is incumbent upon those political activists concerned with the composition of the federal courts to make it known to key politicians in their own party—most notably, senators who sit on the Judiciary Committee—which nominees they find unsuited for the federal bench. In order to gain a

TABLE 5-1

Outcomes of Lower Court Nominations Contested by Interest Groups, Nominations Made 1969–2004

	Newspaper Editorial[a]	Hearing	Committee Vote	Roll-Call Vote
Nixon Administration (0 total)				
No objections	—	—	—	—
Ford Administration (1 total)				
94th Congress				
Harry Wellford (Sixth Circuit)	Yes	No	No	No
Carter Administration (2 total)				
96th Congress				
Abner Mikva (D.C. Circuit)	Yes	Yes	Approved	58–31
Patricia Wald (D.C. Circuit)	Yes	Yes	Approved	77–21
Reagan Administration (14 total)				
97th Congress				
Judith Whittaker (Eighth Circuit)****	Yes	No	No	No
98th Congress				
J. Harvie Wilkinson (Fourth Circuit)	No	Yes	Approved	58–39
99th Congress				
Alex Kozinski (Ninth Circuit)	No	Yes	Approved	53–43
Daniel Manion (Seventh Circuit)	Yes	Yes	Not Approved	49–49
John Noonan (Ninth Circuit)	No	Yes	Approved	Unanimous Consent
Sidney Fitzwater (Northern District TX)	No	Yes	Approved	52–42
Jefferson Sessions (Northern District AL)	Yes	Yes	Defeated	No
Andrew Frey (D.C. Circuit)****	No	No	No	No
Michael Horowitz (D.C. Circuit)****	No	No	No	No
100th Congress				
Susan Liebeler (Federal Circuit)	Yes	Yes	No	No
David Sentelle (D.C. Circuit)	Yes	Yes	Approved	87–0
Bernard Siegan (Ninth Circuit)	Yes	Yes	Defeated	No

(continued)

TABLE 5-1 *(continued)*

	Newspaper Editorial[a]	Hearing	Committee Vote	Roll-Call Vote
David Treen (Fifth Circuit)	No	No	No (Withdrawn)	—
Charles Butler (Southern District AL)	No	Yes	Approved	Unanimous Consent
G. H. W. Bush Administration (8 total)				
101st Congress				
Clarence Thomas (D.C. Circuit)	Yes	Yes	Approved	100–0
Kenneth Carr (Western District TX)	No	No	No	No
102nd Congress				
Lillian BeVier (Fourth Circuit)	Yes	Yes	Yes	No
Edward Carnes (Eleventh Circuit)	Yes	Yes	Approved	62–36
Francis Keating (Tenth Circuit)	No	Yes	No	No
Andrew Keinfeld (Ninth Circuit)	No	Yes	Approved	Unanimous Consent
Kenneth Ryskamp (Eleventh Circuit)	Yes	Yes	Defeated	No
Vaughn Walker (Northern District CA)	Yes	Yes	Approved	Unanimous Consent
Clinton Administration (23 total)				
103rd Congress				
Rosemary Barkett (Eleventh Circuit)	Yes	Yes	Approved	61–37
Martha Daughtrey (Sixth Circuit)	No	Yes	Approved	Voice Vote
Lee Sarokin (Third Circuit)	Yes	Yes	Approved	63–35
104th Congress				
James Beaty (Fourth Circuit)	No	No	No (Blue Slip)	No
William Fletcher (Ninth Circuit)	No	Yes	Approved	58–41
Merrick Garland (D.C. Circuit)	Yes	Yes	Approved	76–23
Margaret McKeown (Ninth Circuit)	No	Yes	Approved	80–11
Charles Stack (Eleventh Circuit)	No	Yes	No (Withdrawn)	No
Judith McConnell (Southern District CA)	Yes	Yes	No (Withdrawn)	No
R. Samuel Paz (Central District CA)	Yes	Yes	No (Withdrawn)	No
Peter Edelman (D.C. Circuit) ★★★★	Yes	No	No	No

105th Congress				
Marsha Berzon (Ninth Circuit)	No	Yes	Approved	64–34
Barbara Durham (Ninth Circuit)*****	No	No (Withdrawn)	No	No
Timothy Dyk (Federal Circuit)	No	Yes	Approved	74–25
Richard Paez (Ninth Circuit)	Yes	Yes	Approved	59–39
Sonia Sotomayor (Second Circuit)	Yes	Yes	Approved	68–28
Frederica Massiah-Jackson (Eastern District PA)	Yes	No	No (Withdrawn)	No
106th Congress				
Susan Oki Mollway (D HI)	No	Yes	Approved	56–34
Margaret Morrow (Central District CA)	No	Yes	Approved	67–28
Clarence Sundram (Western District NY)	No	Yes	No (Withdrawn)	No
Bonnie Campbell (Eighth Circuit)	No	Yes	No	No
Raymond Fisher (Ninth Circuit)	No	Yes	Approved	68–29
Ted Stewart (D UT)****	No	Yes	Approved	93–5
G. W. Bush Administration (2001–2004) (32 total)				
107th Congress				
Terrence Boyle (Fourth Circuit)	Yes	No/No*	No/No	No (Blue Slip)
Jay Bybee (Ninth Circuit)	No	No/Yes*	No/Approved	75–18
Deborah Cook (Sixth Circuit)	Yes	No/Yes*	No/Approved	66–25
Miguel Estrada (D.C. Circuit)	Yes	No/Yes*	No/Approved	Filibustered
Richard Griffin (Sixth Circuit)	Yes	No/Yes*	No/Approved	Filibustered
Carolyn Kuhl (Ninth Circuit)	Yes	No/Yes*	No/Approved	Filibustered
Michael McConnell (Tenth Circuit)	Yes	Yes***	Approved	Voice Vote
David McKeague (Sixth Circuit)	Yes	No/Yes*	No/Approved	Filibustered
Priscilla Owen (Fifth Circuit)	Yes	Yes/Yes**	Defeated/Approved	Filibustered
Charles Pickering (Fifth Circuit)	Yes	Yes/Yes**	Defeated/Approved	Filibustered (received recess appt)
John Roberts (D.C. Circuit)	Yes	No/Yes*	No/Approved	100–0
Henry Saad (Sixth Circuit)	Yes	No/Yes*	Approved	Filibustered
Dennis Shedd (Fourth Circuit)	Yes	Yes***	Approved	Voice Vote

(continued)

TABLE 5-1 (continued)

	Newspaper Editorial[a]	Hearing	Committee Vote	Roll-Call Vote
D. Brooks Smith (Third Circuit)	Yes	Yes	Approved	64–35
Lavenski Smith (Eighth Circuit)	No	Yes	Approved	Voice Vote
William Steele (Eleventh Circuit)	No	No (Withdrawn)	No	No
Jeffrey Sutton (Sixth Circuit)	Yes	No/Yes*	No/Approved	52–41
Larry Block (Ct Fed Claims)	No	Yes	Approved	Voice Vote
Paul Cassell (DUT)	No	Yes	Approved	67–20
Christopher Cox (Ninth Circuit)****	Yes	No	No	No
108th Congress				
Claude Allen (Fourth Circuit)	No	Yes		No
Janice Brown (D.C. Circuit)	Yes	Yes	Approved	Filibustered
D. Michael Fisher (Third Circuit)	No	Yes	Approved	Voice Vote
Thomas Griffith (D.C. Circuit)	Yes	Yes	Approved	No
William Haynes (Fourth Circuit)	No	Yes	Approved	No
Brett Kavanaugh (D.C. Circuit)	Yes	Yes	Approved	Filibustered
William Myers (Ninth Circuit)	Yes	Yes	Approved	Filibustered
William Pryor (Eleventh Circuit)	Yes	Yes	Approved	Filibustered (received recess appt)
Diane Sykes (Seventh Circuit)	No	Yes	Approved	70–27
James Leon Holmes (D AR)	Yes	Yes	Approved	51–46
Michael Mosman (D OR)	No	Yes	Approved	93–0
Victor Wolski (Ct Fed Claims)	No	Yes	Approved	54–43

*No hearing under Democratic control in 107th Congress; hearing under Republican control in 108th Congress.

**Hearing under Democratic control in 107th Congress; hearing under Republican control in 108th Congress.

***Hearing and Senate vote occurred only after Democrats lost control of the Senate in November 2002.

****Nomination never officially made by president because of interest group opposition.

*****Objections to Clinton nominee made by liberal interest groups.

[a]Editorials in the *Wall Street Journal*, *Washington Times*, *New York Times*, or *Washington Post*.

comprehensive understanding about how activists go about targeting specific lower court nominees, I conducted interviews with leading elites on both the right and the left of the ideological spectrum who head organizations that actively participate in judicial confirmation politics. On the left, I interviewed Nan Aron, president of the Alliance for Justice; Kim Gandy, current president of NOW; Elizabeth Cavendish, former legal director of NARAL; and Ralph Neas, director of People for the American Way (PFAW). The sample includes representatives of different types of interest groups. PFAW and NOW are multi-issue civil rights organizations; NARAL is a single-issue organization addressing a woman's right to choose abortion; and the Alliance for Justice is an umbrella organization that represents other interest groups and specifically monitors the federal judiciary on behalf of those groups.

On the right, I interviewed Thomas Jipping, former director of JSMP and former senior fellow in legal studies at Concerned Women for America; Roger Pilon, director of the Cato Institute's Center for Constitutional Studies (Cato); Eugene Meyer, executive director of the Federalist Society; and a senior fellow for a conservative coalition of interest groups who asked not to be identified by name (referred to as Senior Conservative Spokesman). Like the liberals, the sample of conservatives interviewed also represents different types of groups. JSMP is an umbrella organization monitoring the federal judiciary on behalf of hundreds of conservative interest groups; Concerned Women is a multi-issue family values interest group; and the Federalist Society and Cato Institute are policy think tanks that study, among other things, the judicial selection process.

What is striking about the message that elites and activists involved in judicial selection monitoring convey is the intensity of their feelings about who sits on the lower federal courts. Indeed, this intensity of elite opinion on both the left and the right serves as the foundation for the theory of elite mobilization, for without such intense feelings, grass-roots organizations would not bother to mobilize the party's respective bases over a politician's position on a lower court judgeship.

Targeting Nominees

As an initial matter, I asked the interest group and think tank leaders what activities they engage in when a president they support is in the White House and is presumably nominating judicial candidates they support. In other words, what do conservative groups do while G. W. Bush is president, and what did liberal groups do when Clinton was president?

Conservative think tank leaders all stressed that they do not take positions on individual nominees during Democratic administrations or Republican administrations (Pilon interview, 2002; Meyer interview, 2002). Thus, a change of administration, they claim, has little to no impact on their activities concerning judicial appointments. This is true even of the Federalist Society, which was reportedly going to assume the American Bar Association's (ABA) traditional role of rating all judicial nominees early in G. W. Bush's presidency (Lewis and Johnston, 2001):

> [Before G. W. Bush was elected] we had been trying to present information and facts about the ABA. And then the ABA was going to be taken out of the process by this administration. I suppose [people thought the Federal Society would assume the ABA's role of rating judges] because we had been writing about this function, and in Washington everyone wants to be involved in things like selecting judges, but we just felt that . . . we're not a position-taking organization. It's a totally different thing than the sort of things that we do and it's not something we aspired to. (Meyer interview, 2002)

In contrast, interest groups on the left and right drastically reverse roles when the party changes in the White House. During the Clinton administration, conservatives were on the attack, seeking to defeat Democratic judicial nominees while liberal groups played defense, defending the records of Clinton nominees under siege and keeping "score" of how many minority and female judges Clinton had appointed (Aron interview, 2002). With few exceptions, Clinton nominees were deemed acceptable to liberal interest groups. Those deemed unacceptable usually involved log-rolling on Clinton's behalf—that is, he would nominate a Republican senator's favored candidate in exchange for the Republican majority's promise to confirm one of Clinton's favored nominees (Aron interview, 2002; Cavendish interview, 2002).[9] Once G. W. Bush was elected, conservative watchdogs moved into the defensive position, while liberals went on the offensive (Jipping interview, 2002). As the Senior Conservative Spokesman explained:

> In the Clinton administration we would have [sent information about nominees to senators] more often [than we do during the G. W. Bush administration] . . . Now, [during the G. W. Bush presidency, Republican senators] . . . are getting information about nominees from either [the] Justice [Department] or [the White House] Counsel . . . We still communicate with certain [Senate] staff quite often and senators to some degree quite often, but its not the same kind of thing where we are sending them [information about nominees]. Instead, with a sympathetic president in office, conservative activists push for fair treatment for embattled nominees. (Senior Conservative Spokesman interview, 2002)

In short, if there is to be a confirmation battle, the out-of-power interest groups put the nominee in play, and the in-power groups then respond.

Contrary to the way Supreme Court nominations work, the in-power groups do not engage in activity on behalf of a nominee unless that nominee is being targeted by opposing groups (Aron interview, 2002; Gandy interview, 2002; Jipping interview, 2002).

How do the out-of-power groups ultimately make a decision about whom to target? Not surprisingly, with hundreds of judicial vacancies on the lower federal courts in each presidential term, several activists conceded that they lack the resources to try to defeat every lower court nominee named by a president of the opposing party. Instead, they agree unanimously that they must choose their battles carefully.

In order to make that decision, groups must first conduct research on the nominees' backgrounds. While some groups—NOW, for example—conduct research on every nominee, including district court nominees, most of the liberal groups initiate research only on court of appeals nominees and those district court nominees who are brought to their attention as being particularly troublesome. Similarly, grass-roots members of these organizations might bring information to the group's leadership in Washington, D.C. (Gandy interview, 2002).[10] As a practical matter, then, confirmation battles are fought almost exclusively on court of appeals nominees because of a lack of resources; district court nominees are investigated and targeted only in extreme cases (Aron interview, 2002; Gandy interview, 2002).

Conservative groups did not appear to be quite as systematic about their research efforts. Jipping, when he was with JSMP, claimed to initiate investigations of Clinton nominees only when a problematic candidate was brought to his attention—a more passive strategy than that practiced by the liberal interest groups: "How those nominees were brought to our attention [happens] in a variety of ways. Sometimes by the Senate staffers. They would call and say '[check out] so and so.' Sometimes it would be a grass-roots activist in a state, where there was an active discussion that a prominent lawyer was being considered for a judgeship and they had a lot of information" (Jipping interview, 2002).

Once having done the research on a nominee, the organizations must then decide whether to initiate a campaign against that judicial candidate. That decision, on both the left and the right, seems to turn on several factors.

What ultimately makes a nominee so objectionable as to warrant a costly confirmation battle will depend on whether one talks to elites at umbrella organizations and think tanks—such as JSMP, the Alliance for Justice, Cato, and the Federalist Society—or elites at issue-oriented membership groups—such as NARAL, NOW, and Concerned Women for America. In other words, is judicial selection all that this activist must be concerned with—certainly the case at JSMP and the Alliance—or is there a greater cause beyond judicial selection with which the political elite must be concerned—for instance, the right to choose abortion at NARAL or the right to life at Concerned Women for America?

Conservative elites at umbrella groups or think tanks want to focus the judicial selection debate on a nominee's philosophical view of the role of the judiciary in American government. Specifically, this involves the debate about "judicial activism" versus "judicial restraint." As Jipping explained the debate, the difference between an activist and a restrained judge is that "one is driven by issues and one is not":

> The two fundamental categories of judges is what they do with the law: [Whether] they [are] restrained by the law, or whether they can shape and form the law. It's a direct outgrowth of our separation of powers. An activist judge is one who believes he has the authority to change or make the law. Either change its meaning, or discover enumerated provisions. A restrained judge takes the law, either a statute or constitutional provision, as he finds it with the meaning it already has. Meaning is given to law by the lawmaker, not by judges. Interpretation . . . ascertains meaning, it doesn't determine or create meaning. (Jipping interview, 2002)

To conservatives, an "activist" judge is one who not only recognizes rights allegedly not contained in the Constitution but also "refuse[s] to hold the federal government to its enumerated powers" (Pilon interview, 2002). In other words, these conservatives want the federal courts neither to find rights not found in the Constitution nor to find powers not found in the Constitution.

The director of the Federalist Society stated the debate yet another way. Fearing that the term "activist" can be—and indeed has been—used by the left to attack the Rehnquist Court's penchant for overturning congressional legislation deemed to violate principles of federalism, Meyer frames the debate about judicial philosophy as whether a judge will employ a "textualist" interpretation of the Constitution—that is, seeking only to interpret the meaning of the actual text of the document as written:

> The proper question to ask in our view is not "is this judicial activism," because that is vague. The proper question would be, "is the Court interpreting the text and meaning of the Constitution?" If it is, and they're doing the best they can do . . . their judgment might be off, but there's not a structural problem. If the Court is saying, "gee, we don't like the direction policy is going in this country" [or] "we want to change the direction of policy" . . . that's not a proper role for the courts. (Meyer interview, 2002)

The framing of the debate about judicial activism actually began to surface during the Reagan administration, when conservative academics and elites formed the Federalist Society.[11] This approach, however, has come into its own only during the G. W. Bush administration. Today, liberal activists contend that G. W. Bush has transformed what was once a purely academic debate into a full-blown litmus test for lower federal court appointees. As Gandy says:

> The current crisis [over judicial ideology] . . . started back in 1982 with a small group of people, some of whom are now in important positions . . . called the Federalist Society. And their goal was to change the way that the law is made and enforced in this country. To make a change in the way everything was done. And they did it little by little . . . And in the last twenty years, I think they've already accomplished an enormous amount of what they wanted to do, and it has gone completely under the radar . . . *Now, [membership in the Federalist Society] is a litmus test . . . If you haven't been a long time [Federalist Society] member, you have to hurry up and sign up fast. Because it's quite literally a litmus test* . . . Anything we've [progressives] ever done, they can simply pronounce that Congress didn't have the authority to do that . . . They're setting up a line of reasoning that . . . has the potential to completely undo all of the civil rights statutes. (Gandy interview, 2002; emphasis added)

But many liberals contend that this focus on "activism" is merely intended to mask what remains the Republican Party's true litmus test for lower federal court judges—that is, wanting to undo *Roe* and *Casey* (Cavendish interview, 2002; Gandy interview, 2002).

On the left, Aron's umbrella group, the Alliance for Justice, also tries to steer the debate away from specific political issues. Aron says that she tries to focus the issue on whether the president is nominating candidates who will be "open minded" once taking the bench, and who view the courts as accessible to all groups:

> We want fair judges with an open mind . . . We don't expect that they'll agree with us every time. We do expect that judges will at least listen to the evidence presented to them with an open mind and give an aggrieved plaintiff, a group of discriminated women or people of color, the same opportunity that they will the corporations . . . We want judges who will bring experience from having done pro bono work, not your corporate [lawyer] type. [We want] lawyers who know what it's like to be poor or represent someone who is poor and who has a difficult time getting to the court. (Aron interview, 2002)

Aron believes that the most important question to ask of a nominee is what that nominee's view is of the role the courts play in American society: "Is it a view of the courts that they should be open and accessible to underrepresented people . . . That issue for me is the critical one because it is that very important jurisprudential vision of what a judge should be doing" (Aron interview, 2002).[12]

However, these political elites readily concede that their desire for a broader philosophical approach to judicial selection is at odds not only with that advocated by leaders of membership organizations, such as NARAL and Concerned Women for America—indeed, these two groups are almost singularly interested in whether a judge supports or opposes *Roe*—but more important, the membership organizations' grass-roots activists at the local level. The issue-oriented elites in Washington and their grass-roots members "outside the Beltway" want to focus not on broad philosophical debates, but on the positions judges hold on political issues. For example, for NARAL, the only issue is whether the nominee is pro-choice or pro-life:

> There isn't an exact algorithm [in deciding whom to target]. There are times when a nominee is so outrageous right out of the box that it's not a lengthy process to decide to oppose. Though he wasn't a judicial nominee, when Ashcroft was nominated to be attorney general, that was a no-brainer because anyone who's worked in choice [the pro-choice movement] knows that he was a real leader in the Senate; and as attorney general, the whole time back in Missouri, this was the sine qua non of what he was fighting for. And likewise as a senator. That was simple. Then there are other people, like Michael McConnell coming up [for consideration by the Senate], who's an academic, with a very long record against *Roe v. Wade*, written. Academics tend to write more about it [the *Roe* case]. Those are really simple. Then there are several [G. W. Bush nominees] who have done political work like John Roberts in prior Republican administrations when they were taking positions that were hard-line anti-choice. That hearing [for Roberts] was scheduled before Jeffords switched [party allegiances], and there was quick opposition to him, too. (Cavendish interview, 2002)

Members of the conservative interest groups that Jipping used to represent while at JSMP tended not to think about the issue of judicial activism but merely about whether the nominee was "anti-this" or "pro-that." "What that means," Jipping said, "is that some constituency groups that are focused on certain issues . . . say the abortion issue or the gun issue," will be interested only from "that issue kind of perspective. Victims' rights organizations, for example. Property rights groups. These areas where their issue is as much driven by legal decisions as it is by legislatures. They'll be interested, but only, or most often only, from their particular angle." If a nominee doesn't have a position on that particular issue, such people won't want to get involved. "It's a bedeviling problem," Jipping said, pointing out that "our education effort is way behind in terms of trying to impact [this problem]" (Jipping interview, 2002).

It is impossible, however, for the umbrella groups to ignore the issue-oriented approach advocated by the grass-roots organizations. This is because, in order for their message to have any real impact in influencing the appointment process, it is not enough for elites "inside the Beltway" to voice objections to nominees—by posting information on their websites, publishing op-ed pieces in leading conservative or liberal media outlets, or lobbying politicians directly. Rather, as everyone interviewed readily conceded, it is absolutely critical that they also get *grass-roots activists* involved in the process—by writing letters, sending e-mails, telephoning their elected representatives, and in some extreme cases, organizing rallies against specific lower court nominees (Jipping interview, 2002; Cavendish interview, 2002; Aron interview, 2002; and Gandy interview, 2002). These grass-roots activities are critical because they send messages to senators that thousands of the most mobilized constituents in their party object to a particular nominee, and that their critical support of that politician in the next election may turn on a senator's public stance on that nominee. For example, on the conservative side, Jipping said:

> We [JSMP] don't do a lot of direct lobbying from us to the senators [in order to get them to vote against a particular nominee]. It wouldn't be effective . . . I long ago disabused myself of the notion that because Republican senators articulate the right principles that there would be spontaneous combustion. That they'd do what they said they would do. It just doesn't work. It's too much of an insider game to just work [at defeating a nominee from] . . . inside the Beltway. You have to get your constituents involved . . . The structure we were building was a grass-roots [structure]. That's the approach JSMP took from the beginning. (Jipping interview, 2002)

And in discussing his move from JSMP, the umbrella group affiliated with a network of conservative grass-roots organization, to Concerned Women for America, a membership group with its own grass-roots activists dedicated to conservative family values, Jipping highlighted the enormous benefits to working more directly with people at the grass-roots level:

> [Concerned Women for America] is a membership organization, as opposed to just a think tank like [JSMP]. You don't want to do things just hoping people will use them. Here, you can do things and put them directly to your members. For example, we had, in Des Moines and Chicago . . . , our members participating in rallies supporting Miguel Estrada's nomination [to the District of Columbia Circuit]. We can go directly to our state leaders, give them some information, and in a couple of days, they can get rallied . . . The impact that grass-roots citizens can have on the political process, whether that be through lobbying or elections, is more direct than [that of] any organization. (Jipping interview, 2002)

Similarly, on the Democratic side, Gandy explained that "there are only so many pressure points you have with members of Congress, and it mostly boils down to the people who can vote for them or who can give them money" (Gandy interview, 2002). Cavendish of NARAL concurred, saying that "NARAL brings the grass-roots component to the table"; that is, "when we're there, [there is] the threat of grass-roots backlash, the positive carrot of possible grass-roots contributors . . . Just the political oomph. Because they know we mobilize people at election time" (Cavendish interview, 2002).

How, then, are these two very different approaches to framing the judicial selection debate ultimately reconciled? "Grass-top" elites must walk a fine line; their rhetoric cannot be solely focused on lofty ideals about judicial philosophy or they will risk alienating their grass-roots activists, who are so critical to the process. Accordingly, the Washington elites' public pronouncements on specific nominees almost always reference judicial candidates' political ideologies and the way these nominees can be expected to vote in controversial cases before them. But not *all* issues important to the extreme factions of the two parties will get played out in the judicial confirmation process. To the extent that grass-top elites must focus on political issues to satisfy their grass-roots members, they do so in a very strategic manner—focusing predominantly on those "hot button" issues that will also resonate with the *mass electorate*. In other words, a senator is likely to vote against a particular judicial nominee, or the president is likely to withdraw a nomination, *only* if it will ultimately help the senator or president get reelected. And so, the objectionable political stand of the judicial candidate must also be one at odds with a majority of potential voters for that party.

In fact, this is exactly why "inside the Beltway" elites would prefer to keep the debate about judicial nominees on the philosophical level, so as not to alienate potential votes in the Senate. For example, Jipping very much wanted to avoid turning all judicial confirmation debates on G. W. Bush nominees into ones about abortion so as not to lose pro-choice Republican senators' votes in close confirmation battles:

> Let's say that you have a Supreme Court nominee, and all the pro-life groups are demanding that he be a pro-life person and commit to overruling *Roe v. Wade*, and the left is saying exactly the opposite. So that the only thing that's being talked about is abortion. And let's say you know from all kinds of evidence that he will vote to overturn *Roe v. Wade*, so he is somebody that the right would really like. Can you tell me how you get to fifty-one votes [for confirmation] if the only issue being talked about is abortion? You don't get any Democrats. You don't get half a dozen Republicans. Tell me how you win if you're not giving even all the Republican senators something else to talk about. Is the left going to talk only about abortion? Of course, that's all they care about. But, I'd like to frame the issue in a way that gives the Kay Bailey Hutchinsons [Republican senator from Texas] of the world, for example—who care about issues beyond abortion, but on the issue of abortion [she] is pro-choice—something to . . . hang their decision on . . . If you go to the Senate and you want to get the fifty-one votes on somebody who the conservatives believe is very, very good, you have to frame it [the issue] . . . from a crass, political, how-do-you-win scenario . . . you've got to broaden your message. You've got to have other things to talk about. (Jipping interview, 2002)

For activists on the left, the dichotomy between the right's stated focus in the judicial selection debate—that is, judicial activism—and what they believe to be the right's true agenda—turning back the clock on abortion, civil liberties, and civil rights—is particularly frustrating:

> There's a real divide between the way Republicans play with ideology and the way Democrats do. Republicans talk about how they want judges who interpret the law, not make the law. And there should be no ideological litmus tests. They use that term ["litmus test" as one] of aspersion. When you watch their feet and look at their documents, [however,] like their own Justice Department documents from the '80s where they are trying to chart where the Court should go, they want the judicial nominees to be very well aware of where all the division points are in the law, and how the law could go in so many different ways, in so many areas, and why judicial nominees should be so sensitive to this, and why judicial nominees matter. They really care. (Cavendish interview, 2002)

Keeping in mind the necessity to synthesize the grass-roots groups' issue-oriented concerns with the concerns of activists and policy experts like Jipping, Meyer, and Pilon, what, then, were the right's stated objections to Clinton nominees? Conservatives proclaimed these individuals to be judicial activists while sitting on other courts, and in support of these charges, they almost always relied on prior rulings in criminal cases and civil rights cases as evidence of their judicial activism.[13] This permitted the right to frame the debate in terms of judicial philosophy, while at the same time allowing senators to take issue positions that satisfied grass-roots activists. For example, many Clinton nominees faced confirmation fights because they were allegedly "soft on crime" or they supported race "quotas."

It is also telling that crime and quotas were the issues on which conservatives primarily chose to focus, while placing much less emphasis on the abortion issue. Since the 1960s, the Republican Party has been successful in using the issues of race and crime to defeat Democratic Party candidates by portraying those candidates as out of step with the American mainstream (e.g., Chernoff, Kelly, and Kroger, 1996; Carmines and Stimson, 1989). Accordingly, if the objective is to persuade Republican senators to reject a Democratic nominee, the conservative interest groups are well served if they give the Republican senators positions widely popular with the American electorate on which to fight these Clinton nominees. In contrast, as Jipping expressly stated in his interview, because there are several Republicans who are pro-choice—and a majority of voters support abortion rights—if a confirmation debate is to center on the abortion issue, there is no way for conservatives to persuade fifty-one senators to vote against a nominee. Accordingly, when making their case in the press, conservative elites make sure to tie in their claims of judicial activism to specific instances, usually related to crime or race. For example, in objecting to Rosemary Barkett, nominated to the Eleventh Circuit, Jipping said: "Judge Barkett's record reveals views far outside the mainstream as well as aggressive judicial activism . . . Judge Barkett's empathy for convicted killers often leads her to vote to keep them from receiving the just punishment for their crimes" (Jipping and Lombardi, 1994).

In a similar move, the *Wall Street Journal* editorial board accused Ninth Circuit nominee Richard Paez of being a "judicial activist" on the basis of his previous opposition to two California referenda designed to ban affirmative action in the state's public universities (Editorial, *Wall Street Journal*, 2000).

What have objections by left-wing activists centered on during the G. W. Bush administration? Unlike those of conservative activists, liberals' objections have been strictly over issues, rather than judicial philosophy. They have predominantly, though not exclusively, turned on three very salient issues with both grass-roots activists and potential Democratic voters: racism (as opposed to affirmative action quotas), sexism, and abortion.[14] These are issues that the Democratic Party has traditionally been successful in using to defeat Republican political candidates by portraying them as too "conservative" for the American mainstream. For example, Bob Herbert, in the *New York Times*, opposed confirmation of Pickering to the Fifth Circuit on the basis of his support of segregation during the 1950s, and not because of his presumed opposition to affirmative action in the 1990s and 2000s (Herbert, 2002). Similarly, the *New York Times* editorial board opposed Pickering's confirmation on the basis of his district court judicial voting record against minority voting rights and women's abortion rights and in support of corporate defendants in employment discrimination cases—all issues that work against Republican candidates and for Democratic candidates with voters in many regions of the country (Editorial, *New York Times*, 2002). There have thus far been no objections lodged based on a nominee's opposition to affirmative action or support of the death penalty—issues on which a majority of voters do not agree with the far left of the Democratic Party.

A first consideration in choosing whom to fight is whether the groups can come up with a sufficient written record that supports their decision to fight the nominee. As one of the liberal activists put it, "Interest groups with limited resources need to try and find those battles where there are enough persuadables that you can actually win" (Cavendish interview, 2002). On the conservative side, Jipping explained the decision to oppose a Clinton nominee as follows:

> We had to be able to articulate the case. To actually be able to put it on paper. To give real examples. Explain it, not just go on intuition or what someone said. Even if it was a widespread perception, if we couldn't make the case, particularly

in written form, then we wouldn't be credible in coming to that conclusion . . . Basically, it had to be not just on the basis of one [legal] decision. Not one single activist decision. It had to be a pattern. We had to be able to make the case about their judicial philosophy or anticipated judicial philosophy if they were not already a judge. (Jipping interview, 2002)

A second consideration in choosing whom to fight, at least for liberal groups, is how recently they were successful at winning another confirmation battle. This is because liberal activists firmly believe that Democratic senators on the Judiciary Committee will only vote against so many judicial nominees in deference to the president. How many "no" votes each senator has is a huge question mark for these groups. Accordingly, for liberals, yesterday's confirmation fight directly affects tomorrow's confirmation fight. Liberal activists do not expect to win two high-profile battles in a row. And so, they must carefully time when they will fight and when they will remain silent:

I think it's an obstacle that [Democratic] senators think and know these guys [G. W. Bush nominees] are bad but won't vote against them because they believe there is no political price to be paid for [deferring to G. W. Bush]. Yet, our polling shows [that] people support a strong role for the Senate [in the appointment process]. They don't want their senators to be potted plants by 75 percent margins roughly. They say that senators are elected as checks on the president. They think that senators should vote "no" if a nominee is going to roll back rights. It's sort of weird that senators haven't assimilated that thinking into their own role. (Cavendish interview, 2002)

Finally, some groups look to the ideological balance on a given circuit court of appeals or the ideology of the states in those circuits when trying to reach a decision on whether to fight a nominee. For NARAL, the question is how many judges on a circuit currently oppose choice and how many states in that circuit are controlled by anti-choice legislatures:

You'd say, "How bad is this person's record and how much of a difference does it make?" Like the Fifth Circuit is swinging right now—from being a circuit that was the real protector of rights, knock[ing] down many of the Jim Crow barriers and [being] a hugely progressive force . . . And you look at the composition of the states. Are the states gong to be spewing up anti-choice legislation for those judges to rule on? In politics you're always thinking about persuadables. Where you can make a difference. What's in play? What's swinging? The Fifth Circuit is swinging, and if it has Louisiana down there, they've tried to ban abortion since *Roe v. Wade* in '90 or '91. Mississippi is absolutely calamitous for choice and [so is] . . . Texas (Cavendish interview, 2002).

Other groups, like NOW, say they will not engage in such strategic considerations when they believe that none of a president's judicial nominees are acceptable. Instead, they have, in varying degrees, objected to all of W. Bush's nominees (Gandy interview, 2002).

So now that the "inside the Beltway" elites have chosen a judicial nominee to target, have educated their grass-roots activists on those views, and have had the grass-roots activists make their views known to their senators, it becomes incumbent for senators "to take a position" (using Mayhew's term) and respond to their elite constituents. In other words, a confirmation fight provides a useful opportunity for senators to "score points" with their elite constituents who are closely following the senators' responses to their objections.

Conclusion

Through in-depth interviews with members of liberal and conservative interest groups and policy elites most actively involved in the judicial confirmation process, we gleaned important new insights into the close relationship between political activists and senators over judicial appointments. We also learned how interest groups decide which lower court nominees to target. In the next chapter, we will examine how senators respond once activists on the left and right indicate that a particular nomination is objectionable. In short, senators engage in a variety of tactics designed to ameliorate the activists aligned with their party and obstruct the judicial confirmation process—our third elite mobilization strategy.

CHAPTER 6

The Rise of Senate Obstructionism
in the Judicial Confirmation Process

IN THE LAST CHAPTER, we learned how activists make their demands known to senators concerning objectionable judicial nominees. Now we want to learn how senators go about responding to these demands, which they must if they wish to secure support from these activists in their next election. Senators respond to activists by engaging in our third type of elite mobilization strategy: obstructing confirmation of objectionable nominees. Senators obstruct confirmation through a variety of tactics: forcing roll-call votes on all nominations; delaying committee hearings, committee votes, and roll-call votes; blue-slipping nominees; filibustering nominees; and refusing to engage in judicial log-rolls. In short, through use of these tactics Republican senators send cues to conservative activists who support the Republican Party, and Democratic senators send cues to liberal activists who support the Democratic Party. The cues tell the activists expressly, "I stand with you in opposition to a specific nominee," and implicitly, "I consider that nominee's political views to be unacceptable." We now examine each of these tactics.

Roll-Call Votes

When interest groups object to a nominee, their most optimal outcome would be to defeat a nominee at the level of the Judiciary Committee (Gandy interview, 2002; Jipping interview, 2002). Thus, interest groups on the left spend most of their efforts trying to persuade Democratic members of the Judiciary Committee to vote against objectionable nominees, and groups on the right try to persuade Republican members to vote against judicial candidates to which they object. Groups do not try to persuade senators of the opposite party at the committee level. Accordingly, the clearest cues of opposition to a judicial nominee are "no" votes by Judiciary Committee members. But in order to defeat a nominee at the committee level, the party with which the interest group is affiliated must control the Judiciary Committee because senators on the committee are not likely to vote "no" to nominees made by a president of his or her own party; Democrats unanimously voted for Clinton's nominees, and Republicans thus far have unanimously voted for G. W. Bush's nominees.

Assuming that the activists fail in defeating a nomination at the committee level, there is another way for senators to cast a vote against an objectionable nominee, thereby sending favorable cues back to activists. All of the activists interviewed made it clear that even when the outcome of a confirmation battle is virtually certain—that is, there are more than fifty votes to confirm the nominee (or sixty votes assuming a filibuster will be mounted)—they nevertheless still push for the nomination to go to the floor of the Senate for a full floor debate and roll-call vote. This forces senators to stand up and make their views known and allows activists to be certain where these politicians stand. This is critical information that activists can use against a politician when he or she is up for reelection. Moreover, it sends a signal to senators on the opposite side of the aisle that future candidates may also be facing similarly tough confirmation battles. In other words, there will no longer be a free ride for anyone seeking a lifetime appointment to the lower federal courts.

For example, during the Clinton administration, Jipping did not often agree with the Republican Senate majority leadership's decisions simply not to hold hearings or roll-call votes on many Clinton nominees:

> I did not support the decision to put them [objectionable nominees] on the shelf and hope they die. I wanted them [the Republican leadership] to hold votes. I wanted them to have debates. When [nominee] Frederica Massiah Jackson came up and there was a vote scheduled for the floor, we were outraged that Trent Lott [then Senate majority leader] canceled the vote to allow the president to withdraw the nomination. We wanted that vote to take place. We wanted the hearings to be held. We wanted the debates to be on C-Span. (Jipping interview, 2002)

When a roll-call vote was held on a controversial nominee to the District of Hawaii, Susan Oki Mollway, Jipping praised Republican senators, even though they were unable to defeat her: "The 34 No votes show that the Senate heard the cry of Grassroots America to stop this nominee" (quoted in Bell, 2002b, at 81).

The leader of another conservative organization also believes that roll-call votes are a way to get Republican senators to take the judicial selection issue more seriously:

> One of the biggest things we changed in Clinton's administration was emphasizing that nominees should not be rubber-stamped. What I mean is that you should have a roll-call vote on them instead of unanimous consent. It shows you are taking this seriously. I don't think there is anything wrong with putting [a nomination] to a roll-call vote . . . It puts everybody [in the Senate] on the record and shows that it is a considered decision rather than "no objection, so ordered." We got Republicans to begin taking this [lower court judgeships] more seriously, particularly when they looked at some of the Clinton judges and how they were ruling on particular issues and what it showed about their judicial philosophies. I think that might have raised an awareness. (Senior Conservative Spokesman interview, 2002)

Liberal activists also like this tactic. For example, when interviewed in the midst of the D. Brooks Smith confirmation fight, Aron, Gandy, and Cavendish all conceded that a full vote by the Senate was likely to result in Smith's confirmation even though these groups forcefully opposed him because he belonged to an all-male gun club. Nevertheless, these activists all concurred that a vote still should take place. According to Aron, "In politics . . . you never predict the outcome . . . [And in addition] I want to know where every senator stands" (Aron interview, 2002). Gandy echoed this sentiment regarding the Smith vote: "We have many [senators] who are going to ask for floor time [to oppose the D. B. Smith nomination], which is a major [accomplishment] . . . We have people asking for floor time because we want to make it [the senators' positions on the Smith nomination] public, we want to make it [his confirmation] a fight. We want to say [to the senators who vote "yes"] that if you screw women, you're going to have to deal with this [strong backlash from NOW]" (Gandy interview, 2002). The same is true for Cavendish: "The numbers [to defeat D. Brooks Smith] aren't there. But a strong vote can send a signal that the [Democratic] senators take seriously . . . the norm of not participating in discriminatory clubs" (Cavendish interview, 2002).

Herein lies the core explanation as to why, in the 1990s, we began to see so many lower court nominees confirmed not by unanimous consent—the traditional method used to confirm lower court nominees for two hundred years—but by roll-call vote after a full floor debate: political activists were demanding these votes. Consider that in 1997, eleven district court nominees (38 percent of all district court nominees confirmed that year) were confirmed by roll-call vote, but between 1979 and 1996, only one district court nomination was confirmed by roll-call vote (Cohen, 1998).

Delay Tactics

Another tactic that allows senators to obstruct confirmation—thereby sending a cue indicating that they are sympathetic to the activists' objections—involves delaying a Judiciary Committee vote. Most often, such delays are initiated by the chair, and as long as his or her party remains in control of the Senate, that nominee will not get a hearing.[1] This tactic was used successfully by Hatch when he chaired the Judiciary Committee during the Clinton administration and by Patrick J. Leahy (D-VT) when he chaired the committee during the G. W. Bush administration. Ironically, despite extensive delays on many lower court nominees, conservative activists complained that Hatch let too many Clinton nominations proceed to hearings, and liberal activists complained that Leahy let too many G. W. Bush nominations proceed to hearings (Gandy interview, 2002; Aron interview, 2002; Jipping interview, 2002). Turning once again to Figure I-2, we see that at the beginning of the modern political era, delay in the number of days to confirmation ebbed and flowed on the basis of whether a presidential election was looming. For example, it took only 33.3 days for Carter nominees to the courts of appeals to be confirmed in the first two years of his presidency, but it took 78.1 days during the last two years of his presidency. Then, beginning in Reagan's second term, the number of days to confirmations begins to increase for periods with election years and periods without election years. The non–election year period of Reagan's first term was 33.9 days, and the non–election year period in his second term nearly doubled—to 66.3 days. For elections periods, during Reagan's first term, there was a delay of 65.8 days for 1983–84; during his second term, there was a delay of 153.9 days for 1987–88. But perhaps most striking in Figure I-2 is the extraordinary increase in the number of days it takes to be confirmed beginning in Clinton's second term in office—a non–election year period (1997–98)—and the fact that confirmation delays are no longer tied to presidential election years, but rather, delays persist in non-presidential election years as well. In the 105th, 106th, and 107th Congresses, the average court of appeals judge waited more than 300 days to be confirmed—ten times as long as when Carter was president.

JUDICIAL GRIDLOCK BEGINS DURING
THE CLINTON ADMINISTRATION

Having wrested majority control from the Democrats in the 1994 national elections, the Republicans found themselves in control of the Senate with a Democratic president for the first time since the Truman administration. The new Republican majority wasted no time in invoking its "advice and consent" power as a weapon to force Clinton to cede unprecedented power to Republican leaders over lower federal court appointments. In 1995, the Republican leadership (Chairman Hatch and Majority Leader Lott) embarked on a campaign to stall confirmation of *all* Clinton judicial nominees to the lower federal courts. This created such a shortage of judges on these courts that conservative Chief Justice Rehnquist urged the Republican majority to lift its moratorium on federal court confirmation votes in his annual State of the Judiciary Report. At the very least, Rehnquist scolded the Senate, these Clinton nominees should be accorded the up or down roll-call votes to which they are constitutionally entitled (Greenhouse, 1996a).

The Republican leadership justified this delay tactic on a single ground: ideology. They claimed that Clinton, under a Democrat-controlled Senate, had been appointing "judicial activists" to the lower federal courts and that, absent action by the now Republican-controlled Senate under their constitutional right of "advice and consent," Clinton would continue to do so throughout his presidency (Lewis, 1995). In other words, Republicans were engaging in a classic elite mobilization strategy as they used delay tactics to send cues to their activists indicating their sympathy for the conservative activists' positions regarding Clinton nominees. The chair also likely knew that if these nominees were put up for votes, they would be confirmed. Here, Senator Hatch sends a signal to conservative activists about Clinton's judges:

> I believe you could probably point out deficiencies in judges of every President. But I am really concerned, in this day of rampant criminal activity, with the flood of drugs into our society, that we have judges who are being appointed [by Clinton] on a daily basis who have a philosophy like [Clinton appointee] Judge Barkett's, who do not blame the acts of these criminals on themselves but blame them on society, blame them on their environment, on anything but their own volition and their own desire to do wrong . . .
>
> [W]hen people who are not insane commit heinous murders and heinous crimes and are spreading drugs among our young people and are destroying the youth of this Nation and doing it with full intent to do so and to profit from their decisions, or because they are murderers, then I think we ought to come down pretty doggoned hard on them; that is, if we want to have a civil, humane, free, and fair society.
>
> I will have more to say about these judges in the future, but I have become so alarmed about some of these decisions that I just felt I had to come to the floor today and make this point, since we on the Judiciary Committee have this very important honor of working with these judges. I do not think anybody can say that I have not done my very best to try to accommodate this administration, to try to help them in the appointment of judges. I am going to continue to do that as long as I can. I want to be fair to this President. On the other hand, these type of judges are giving me the chills.[2]

Similarly, Senator Charles E. Grassley (R-IA), who sat on the Judiciary Committee, argued:

> I think it is fair to say that President Clinton's judicial appointments communicate the President's vision of the kind of America that the President would like to have. I do not share his soft-on-crime vision. I do not think most Americans do. Mr. President, you can say that you are putting all the cops on the streets all you want, but unless you appoint federal judges who will enforce the law and protect victims over criminals, all the cops in the world will not make any difference.[3]

The following year, trying to justify the Judiciary Committee's continued refusal—*after* Clinton's reelection in 1996—to hold hearings on many of Clinton's nominees, Senator Hatch stated, "too many of the president's judicial appointees have misused their judicial authority to implement a liberal agenda that President Clinton has been unwilling or unable to implement through the political process."[4] Clinton, too, weighed in on the issue, claiming that partisan politics was jeopardizing the judicial system: "We can't let partisan politics shut down our courts and gut our judicial system. The intimidation, the delay, the shrill voices must stop so the unbroken legacy of our strong, independent judiciary can continue for generations to come" (quoted in Baker, 1997).

Some of the Republican leaders opposed quickening the pace unless they could extract further concessions from the Clinton administration. For example, at a Republican leadership conference, Senator Phil Gramm (R-TX) offered a resolution that would have given a small number of Republican senators a veto power over nominees to the federal appeals courts; such privilege had previously been confined to district court nominations (Lewis, 1997). A second proposal, by Senator Gorton (R-WA), would have required Republican senators to reject judicial nominees whose philosophies had not been cleared by the Republican leadership (Lewis, 1997). Trying another tactic, some Republican senators sought to decrease the number of judgeships on the District of Columbia Court of Appeals, rather than give Clinton the opportunity to fill two vacancies on this pivotal federal appeals court.[5] In response to these various proposals, Democrats charged that such tactics were designed to intimidate the president into ceding significant power to the Republican majority in choosing federal court nominees—and, in turn, replace the president as the driving force in shaping judicial ideology on the lower federal courts.[6] In the end, none of these proposals was adopted. However, in order to break the deadlock over judicial confirmations, Clinton ultimately was forced to accede to the demands of certain key senators, who were in effect saying, "Nominate my favored Republican candidate to a judgeship, and I will confirm your favored candidate for a judgeship." This type of judicial "log-roll" is discussed below in this chapter.

In the end, although it took Clinton's nominees longer to be confirmed, most of them were nevertheless confirmed. Thus, both the president and conservative Republican senators gained political mileage from this very public fight—Republicans by slowing down the process and the president by staying his course and refusing to withdraw most of his objectionable nominations, particularly the minority and female candidates.

JUDICIAL GRIDLOCK CONTINUES DURING
THE G. W. BUSH ADMINISTRATION

When G. W. Bush took office, Republicans controlled both houses of Congress. In the Senate, the majority was slim—fifty Republicans and fifty Democrats, with the Republican vice president breaking all tie votes. Accordingly, when Bush named his first batch of lower court nominees in May 2001, it looked as if these nominees would have no problem being confirmed, notwithstanding the fact that many were identified by liberal activists as very conservative. However, in a stunning reversal of fortune, a Republican senator, James Jeffords of Vermont, announced that he would become an Independent and thereafter caucus with the Democratic Party, thus giving the Democrats a fifty-one to forty-nine majority in the Senate. Again, a regime of divided government prevailed.

Despite this turn of events, however, G. W. Bush continued to appoint conservative candidates for the federal bench. For example, in June 2001, the president nominated Kuhl to the Ninth Circuit; pro-choice groups deemed her to be extremely hostile to abortion rights (Cavendish interview, 2002). Sensing that the president was not about to back down on his ideological agenda to appoint conservatives to the bench, Democratic leaders in the Senate quickly adopted a course of action similar to that taken by Republicans during the Clinton presidency: delay the president's most controversial nominees—that is, those flagged by interest groups as the most conservative—and quickly confirm all uncontroversial nominees—those not flagged by interest groups as problematic. Thus, Democratic leaders could tout the speed and number of confirmation votes taken by the end of 2001:

> The average time between nomination and confirmation for court of appeals judges this year has been approximately 100 days, which includes the delay and reorganization of the Senate [due to the change in leadership] and the wait for the ABA peer reviews . . . The average length of time between nomination and confirmation of those circuit court nominees approved during President Clinton's most recent term was 343 days . . . Accordingly, even with all the delays caused by Republicans, this Senate is acting on court of appeals nominees, on

average, 8 months faster than the Republican Senate acted on Clinton nominations during the last 4 years.[7]

But as even liberal voices noted, what the Democratic leadership failed to acknowledge was that these "swiftly" confirmed nominees represented only the uncontroversial of the bunch. When, if ever, were G. W. Bush's controversial nominees to be given hearings and floor votes? As the normally liberal editorial board of the *Washington Post* stated:

> The Judiciary Committee chairman, Democratic Senator Patrick Leahy, has offered no reasonable justification for stalling on these nominations. The Senate, so far this year, has confirmed 18 nominees—most of them uncontroversial and most of them district judges. Mr. Leahy's spokesman says that focusing on the least controversial nominations to lower-ranking courts enables the Senate to get the most done the quickest. This approach, which mimics the one that Mr. Leahy's predecessor as committee chairman—Republican Senator Orrin Hatch—employed during the Clinton administration, also allows the Senate to confirm a respectable number of nominees while going slow on any that might raise the hackles of liberal senators or interest groups. But, controversial nominees are no less entitled to hearings. (Editorial, *Washington Post*, 2001)

Indeed, of the original fifteen nominations G. W. Bush made in May 2001, only five had been confirmed by year's end, and two of the five confirmed were Democrats. Of those ten appellate nominees not confirmed, only one, Pickering, had even had a hearing by December 2001, and the Judiciary Committee decided to delay its vote on him in order to collect more information about his judicial record while a district court judge. Not surprisingly, leading liberal interest groups objected to all ten of the stalled nominees and did not oppose the five nominees confirmed. This led the conservative newspaper the *Washington Times* to call the stalled nominations a "hostage crisis" (Editorial, *Washington Times*, 2001).

The situation only worsened in 2002 for Bush's most conservative nominees. At the beginning of the year, Chairman Leahy pleaded with the president to work with Democratic leaders to select more moderate judges, thus easing the delay in filling judicial vacancies: "I have already laid out a constructive program of suggestions that would help . . . return the confirmation process to one that is a cooperative, bipartisan effort. I have included suggestions for the White House, that it work with Democrats as well as Republicans, that it encourage rather than forestall the use of bipartisan selection commissions, and that it consider carefully the views of home state senators."[8] The president, however, rebuffed all suggestions of bipartisanship, even after the Judiciary Committee voted down two of his nominees (Pickering and Owen, which effectively killed their nominations). Republicans only became more adamant that the president not make concessions.

As Republican National Committee strategist John J. Pitney Jr. explained: "A failure [by the president] to support him [Pickering] could send a signal to future nominees that the White House will back down in the face of opposition. Pickering is a Black Hawk helicopter, and the White House is the Ranger team operating on the motto, 'No one gets left behind'" (quoted in Shepherd, 2002). And so, by the midterm elections in 2002, when Republicans regained control of the Senate, only one of the ten controversial nominations made in G. W. Bush's first batch in May 2001 (Lavenski Smith) had been given a floor vote by Democratic leaders.

When Democratic control of the Senate came to an end in January 2003, delay tactics for Democratic leaders also came to an end. As discussed in Chapter 8, Democratic senators would adapt their elite mobilization strategy in light of having lost control of the Senate. Rather than relying on delay tactics to signal their activists, they would instead use the filibuster to obstruct confirmation of nominees flagged by interest groups as hostile to liberal causes.

Blue-Slipping Nominees

Another elite mobilization tactic available to home state senators of a particular nominee who wish to please sympathetic interest groups is the "blue slip," a practice sometimes referred to as senatorial courtesy.

Although the terms *blue slip* and *senatorial courtesy* today are often used interchangeably, senatorial courtesy actually has a much longer and richer history. Senatorial courtesy is a Senate custom dating back more than two hundred years, to when George Washington had his nomination for naval office of the Port of Savannah rejected by the Senate "as a courtesy" to the nominee's home state senators because they preferred another candidate (Bell, 2002b). According to Michael J. Gerhardt (2001), there are really three forms of senatorial courtesy: the deference a president owes a home state senator's choice for a lower court judgeship, the deference one member of the Senate owes another regarding his or her choice for a lower court judgeship in the home state, and the expectation that the president will consult with a senator before nominating someone from his or her home state to a confirmable post.

The blue slip procedure is simply the Senate Judiciary Committee's institutionalization of the first type of senatorial courtesy mentioned above, believed to have been initiated in the early 1950s (Denning, 2001). As the custom evolved in the 20th century, when the president nominates someone for a lower court judgeship—district court or court of appeals—the chair of the Judiciary Committee sends each home state senator a slip of blue paper asking for his or her approval of the nominee. Traditionally, if either of the home state senators failed to return the blue slip approving the nominee, it died at the committee level, and the nominee was never given an up or down vote by the full Senate. With a home state senator effectively having the ability to veto a president's lower court nominee, it behooves the president to consult with senators before making a nomination to a court in a senator's state.

Before the modern political era, the blue-slip privilege was exercised infrequently. Moreover, home state senators used the privilege not for policy purposes, but rather to secure patronage for their elite constituents (Slotnick, 1980). In other words, if the president nominated someone for a judgeship and a senator wanted one of his or her political allies for that judicial seat in the home state, a blue slip would force the president to the bargaining table. As long as presidents continued to cooperate with home state senators, blue slips were rare.

As presidents in the modern political era began to use judicial selection as a means to promote a political agenda—thereby satisfying their party's policy-oriented activists—home state senators saw that they could use blue slips to promote their own policy goals as well. In other words, if the president nominates someone for a lower court judgeship—and the home state senators' key elite constituents express objections to the nominee on ideological grounds—an effective means of showing support for those elite constituents is for the home state senator to "blue-slip" the nomination. The blue slip then becomes another one of the obstructionist tactics senators use during the confirmation process for purposes of mobilizing elites in their party.

SENATOR KENNEDY'S ATTEMPT TO
REFORM THE BLUE-SLIP PRIVILEGE
DURING THE CARTER ADMINISTRATION

In 1978, Congress passed the Omnibus Judgeship Act,[9] which created more than one hundred new judgeships for Democratic president Carter to fill. Because Carter saw this as an opportunity to fill the lower federal courts with diversity appointments, he announced that the nominees for these new seats to the courts of appeals would be selected by a nominating commission, in place since he had taken office in 1977 (see Chapter 4).

The following year, the chairman of the Judiciary Committee, Senator Kennedy (D-MA), held hearings to establish the procedures that would be used for the hearings and confirmations of so many new appointments. As part of those hearings, Kennedy wanted to investigate the historical underpinnings of the blue-slip privilege and whether the committee should continue honoring blue slips. Kennedy made his views known. Concerned that Republican senators might try to block Carter's historic efforts to diversify the federal bench—a policy Kennedy strongly supported—Kennedy said in his opening statement of the hearings that he would not "unilaterally table a nomination simply because a blue slip is not returned by a colleague." [10] But he did not go so far as to suggest complete abandonment of the privilege, recognizing the long tradition of senatorial courtesy. Instead, he proposed that should a blue slip not be returned by a home state senator (indicating the senator's disapproval of the nominee), the Judiciary Committee would vote on whether to proceed with the nomination. [11]

Since senators rarely used blue slips at this time—the policy-oriented use of the procedure not yet fully realized—the new judgeships were filled throughout 1979 and most of 1980 without any home state senator exercising senatorial courtesy. However, with only two months left before the 1980 presidential election, Republican senators tried to hold off thirteen confirmation hearings by exercising their blue-slip privileges (Lyons, 1980). This proved to be the first test of Kennedy's reform efforts on the blue-slip privilege. When Senator Helms (R-NC) sought to block Judiciary Committee hearings on North Carolina district court nominee Richard Erwin, whom he had blue-slipped—and Kennedy refused to halt the proceedings—a shouting match ensued between Republicans and Democrats on the committee (Lyons, 1980). Democrats accused Helms of using his blue-slip privilege for improper purposes—that is, because he did not like the ideology of the judge. Although the hearings were put off that day, eventually, Erwin was confirmed.

SENATOR THURMOND IGNORES THE BLUE SLIP DURING THE REAGAN ADMINISTRATION

When Republicans captured control of the White House and the Senate in the 1980 elections, Senator Thurmond (R-SC) would become chairman of the Judiciary Committee. Thurmond was a faithful conservative ally of the Reagan administration, aiding the president in his efforts to pack the federal courts with conservative judges. At the beginning of his tenure, Thurmond vowed to restore the blue-slip system that Kennedy had tried to undermine (Pike, 1983). However, in order to further the president's political agenda, the first time that a senator tried to exercise a blue slip against one of Reagan's nominees, Thurmond simply ignored it and let the nomination proceed to a hearing. Specifically, a liberal California senator, Alan M. Cranston, blue-slipped a nominee for a district court judgeship in California—state court judge John P. Vukasin. Cranston justified his blue slip on policy grounds—that he had received numerous complaints about Vukasin's treatment of women and minority lawyers in his courtroom (Pike, 1983). Thurmond proceeded to hold hearings on the nominee, and the committee approved Vukasin along party lines. Senator Cranston then tried, again unsuccessfully, to block Vukasin's confirmation on the floor of the Senate.

But Thurmond's treatment of blue slips seemed to turn on the party of the senator exercising them. When Republican senator John W. Warner of Virginia exercised his blue-slip privilege to block Fourth Circuit nominee Kenneth Starr (who would later become the Whitewater independent prosecutor)—on the ground that the circuit seat for which he was nominated was intended for a Virginian, which Starr was not—Thurmond agreed to kill the nomination (Nelson, 1983). Reagan was able to seat Starr on the federal bench by nominating him to the D.C. Circuit Court of Appeals where there are no home state senators with blue-slip privileges.

BLUE-SLIP PRIVILEGES REINSTATED UNDER JUDICIARY CHAIRMEN BIDEN AND HATCH

When the Democrats regained control of the Senate in the 1986 midterm elections, Senator Biden (D-DE) assumed the chairmanship of the Judiciary Committee. Biden restored the Kennedy rule—whereby one blue slip would not be allowed to kill a nomination. In some instances, Biden would let a Republican nominee proceed to a hearing even though both home state senators returned negative blue slips, provided the "president begged the senator's permission in advance" (Safire, 2001). Accordingly, Biden was quite deferential to Republican presidents Reagan and G. H. W. Bush in allowing their lower court nominees to receive floor votes. However, when the tables were turned—a Democratic president and a Republican-controlled Senate—the new chairman, Hatch, would not be as generous to President Clinton as Biden had been to Presidents Reagan and G. H. W. Bush. Hatch assured his fellow Republican senators that individual blue slips would be given "great weight" under his chairmanship (quoted in Gordon, 1995). So much weight, in fact, that he reinstituted the pre-Kennedy rule whereby one blue slip killed a nomination (Associated Press, 2001). As a result of this significant rule change, Republican senators wielded much more power in blocking Clinton's nominees to the federal courts, and several senators took full advantage of this enhanced veto power.

For example, the Republican senator from Michigan, Spencer Abraham, blue-slipped three nominees for two different Michigan-designated seats on the Sixth Circuit Court of Appeals (Helene White and Kathleen McCree Lewis). A single Republican senator from Colorado, Wayne Allard, used his blue-slip privilege to block two consecutive Clinton nominees to the Tenth Circuit Court of Appeals; Allard's objection to the first of those nominees,

James M. Lyons, stemmed from a report Lyons had issued exonerating the Clintons in the Whitewater affair (the other was a district court nominee, Patricia Coan). Perhaps the most high profile of these blue-slip battles was waged in the Fourth Circuit Court of Appeals. There, Republican Senator Helms blue-slipped three African American nominees to that circuit. So frustrated was the president with Helms's efforts to block his nominations to the Fourth Circuit—Clinton wanted to name the first African American to that circuit—he gave one of the black nominees, Gregory, a recess appointment in the last days of this presidency (see Chapter 4).

Hatch did not, however, go so far as to support a Republican-backed proposal aimed at giving Republicans *more* power to block Clinton nominees to the court of appeals—that is, to grant all senators blue-slip privileges over all courts of appeals nominees in the circuit in which their home states were located. This would have allowed, for example, a Michigan senator to veto a Sixth Circuit nominee to an Ohio-designated seat on that circuit. Republicans once again justified their tactics strictly on ideological grounds: that Clinton was appointing too many judicial "activists" to the federal courts. But Hatch warned Republicans that such a policy could spell disaster down the road were there a Republican president nominating candidates for the bench: "When a Republican administration puts forth a Fourth Circuit Court of Appeals nomination for a North Carolina or South Carolina seat, are Republicans in the Senate really going to be content to permit [Democratic] Senators Mikulski [of Maryland], Sarbanes [of Maryland] and Robb [of Virginia] to exercise a veto over that nominee?" (quoted in Henry, 1997).

SENATOR HATCH CHANGES THE BLUE-SLIP RULE
WHEN G. W. BUSH IS ELECTED

When Senator Hatch found himself the chairman of the Judiciary Committee under unified government in January 2001, he did an about face on the blue-slip privilege. As a result of the Republican Party's efforts to block Clinton nominees en masse in some circuits, most notably the Fourth and Sixth Circuits, Hatch no doubt feared that Democratic senators would retaliate against the newly elected Republican president when he tried to fill the seats left vacant at the end of Clinton's second term. With at least one Democratic senator in thirty-one states, a large number of the one hundred judicial vacancies existing at the beginning of G. W. Bush's presidency could potentially be in jeopardy were the one-blue-slip rule to govern. Accordingly, gearing up for G. W. Bush's first round of lower court appointments, Senator Hatch announced that he would now proceed with a committee hearing, provided one of the two home state senators approved of the nomination (Associated Press, 2001). So incensed were Democrats with this partisan rule change that they walked out of a Judiciary Committee meeting before votes could be taken on four top Justice Department nominees made by Bush (Johnson, 2001). Although he was willing to allow a single senator to deny a Clinton nominee a federal court judgeship, Hatch attacked Democrats for wanting the same rules to apply when a Republican held the White House: "They [Democrats] want an absolute right to kill a nominee and we can't give them that" (quoted in Associated Press, 2001).

THE BLUE-SLIP PRIVILEGE UNDER SENATOR LEAHY

After the president's first batch of lower court nominations was announced in May 2001—and included what many liberal activists deemed conservative ideologues—it looked like the Democrats were headed for a huge fight with Republicans on the new blue-slip rule allowing hearings with the support of only one home state senator. But all of this became moot when Senator Jeffords defected from the Republican Party, giving the Democrats back control of the Senate. The new chairman of the Judiciary Committee, Leahy of Vermont, instituted his own policy concerning blue slips: One negative blue slip from a home state senator would impede a nomination, and two negative blue slips would automatically kill the nomination (Holland, 2001).

With Democrats back in control of the judicial confirmation process, Democratic home state senators began to use their blue-slip privileges liberally to block nominees of President G. W. Bush for vacancies in the Fourth and Sixth Circuits; they claimed such efforts were justified as those judgeships would have been filled by Clinton but for the Republicans' unfair blue-slip tactics in those states. No Bush nominees to these two circuits were given hearings in 2001 and 2002 while the Democrats controlled the Senate. Moreover, Democratic senator Barbara Boxer of California was able to kill the nomination of a controversial nominee to the Ninth Circuit—Kuhl—whose positions on abortion made her a target of pro-choice interest groups (Cavendish interview, 2002). Boxer's mere threat of exercising her blue-slip privilege against another possible G. W. Bush nominee to the Ninth Circuit, California representative Christopher Cox, was sufficient to force that nominee to withdraw his name from consideration (Safire, 2001).

HATCH RESUMES CONTROL OF
THE JUDICIARY COMMITTEE

The Senate would change hands again in 2003, and Senator Hatch would again resume the chairmanship of the Judiciary Committee. Given the Democrats' liberal use of the blue-slip privilege to block G. W. Bush's nominees from getting confirmed in the 107th Congress, Hatch quickly announced that he would not let Democrats abuse that privilege in the 108th Congress: "Negative blue slips will be given substantial consideration, but they will not be dispositive" (quoted in Lewis, 2002). Moreover, Hatch made clear that one home state senator alone could not kill a nominee. Defending this position, Hatch pointed out that when Senators Kennedy and Biden chaired the committee in the 1970s and 1980s, they did not allow a single blue slip to tie up a nominee (Brune, 2003). In practice, under the new Hatch blue-slip rule, blue-slipped nominees—even in instances in which both home state senators objected to a nominee—were given committee hearings and committee votes and, when approved, were sent to the floor of the Senate. Despite loss of this elite mobilization tactic, however, Democratic senators were still able to obstruct confirmation of these blue-slipped nominees by resorting to the filibuster.

Filibustering Nominees

The filibuster is a legislative tactic unique to the Senate. It effectively allows one senator to impose a super-majority requirement on the passage of legislation or the confirmation of any executive nomination requiring the "advice and consent" of the Senate, votes that would otherwise be subject to a simply majority rule. A filibuster permits unlimited debate on the issue at hand; today, unless there are sixty senators (although this number has fluctuated over time) who vote to cut off the debate (known as a *cloture motion*), the legislation or nomination is not put to a substantive vote and effectively dies. The first known use of the filibuster dates to 1790, when senators from Virginia and South Carolina used extended debate in an attempt to kill a bill relocating the first Congress to Philadelphia (Burdette, 1940). The Senate first adopted a cloture rule in 1917; however, until 1949, cloture could be used only to end filibusters on legislative matters (Beth, 2002).

In modern times, the filibuster became the principal tactic of southern Democrats to thwart civil rights legislation. The filibuster against the Civil Rights Act of 1964 lasted seventy-four days until enough votes were finally mustered to pass a cloture motion (Whalen and Whalen, 1985). However, because Senate business came to a complete halt when a filibuster was launched, the procedure was rarely used (Matthews, 1973) until it underwent a significant change in the modern political era. In 1972, a two-track system was put in place whereby Senate business would continue as usual on all issues besides the objectionable legislation or nomination; with this two-track system, filibusters became a much more frequent occurrence (Fisk and Chemerinsky, 1997).

The first use of a filibuster on the Senate floor to block confirmation of a judicial nominee was in 1968, when President Lyndon Johnson nominated Associate Justice Abraham Fortas to replace retiring Chief Justice Warren.[12] Using this nomination as a means to attack the activism of the Warren Court, Republicans joined forces with southern Democrats to block the nomination (Kalman, 2000). As Johnson had already announced his intention not to run for reelection, he could do little for the troubled nomination. Lacking the necessary votes for cloture, Fortas was never confirmed as chief justice.

The procedure was not invoked again in the context of a judicial confirmation battle until the waning days of the Carter administration over the nomination of Stephen Breyer for the First Circuit Court of Appeals (and now an associate justice on the Supreme Court), though not on ideological grounds. The filibuster was instituted by a lame-duck Democratic senator from North Carolina, Robert B. Morgan, who held a personal grudge against Breyer for his work, as counsel to the Judiciary Committee, in helping defeat Morgan's choice for a North Carolina judgeship (Charles Winberry) (Editorial, *New York Times*, 1980). But with the support of Judiciary Committee chairman Senator Kennedy (also Breyer's home state senator) and other Judiciary Committee members, including Republican member Senator Thurmond, the Senate first approved a cloture motion 68–28, and subsequently confirmed Breyer.

FILIBUSTERING DURING THE REAGAN ADMINISTRATION

The use of filibusters to keep lower court judges off the bench on ideological grounds did not begin until the Reagan presidency. First was Wilkinson, nominated to the Fourth Circuit Court of Appeals. Civil rights groups objected to the Wilkinson nomination, claiming that Wilkinson's lack of legal experience (he had never even practiced law) made him unacceptable for the bench, much the same way that lack of legal experience had been used to reject similarly situated minority candidates for the bench during the Carter administration. In other words, white candidates for the bench were being given preferential treatment over minority candidates. Although knowing they lacked the fifty-one votes to defeat Wilkinson, some Democrats, led by Senator Kennedy, joined the civil rights activists and mounted a filibuster. In the cloture debate, Kennedy called Wilkinson "the least qualified nominee ever submitted for an appellate court vacancy" (quoted in Greenhouse, 1984). Eventually, Republicans were able to get sixty votes to cut off debate, and Wilkinson was subsequently confirmed by a simple majority. Democrats would try, but fail, to block three more Reagan appointees with filibusters: Rehnquist for chief justice of the United States Supreme Court, Manion for the Seventh Circuit, and Fitzwater for the Northern District of Texas (see Chapter 5).

Since the Democrats controlled the Senate during the G. H. W. Bush administration, they were in a position to block Bush nominees through simple majority votes. But there was one controversial Bush nominee against whom a filibuster was used because of the unusual situation that Democrats in the Senate were split over the nomination: Edward K. Carnes for the Eleventh Circuit. Major civil rights groups, including the NAACP and the Southern Christian Leadership Conference, opposed Carnes claiming that as a state assistant attorney general in Alabama, he had exhibited an insensitivity to racial issues in death penalty cases (Lewis, 1992b). However, with the support of one prominent liberal activist, Morris Dees, director of the Southern Poverty Law Center, several Democrats backed Carnes (Tolchin, 1992). Those Democrats opposed to the nomination thus needed a filibuster to block confirmation because they lacked the fifty-one votes to defeat the nominee. However, with Dees's support, Carnes prevailed on a cloture motion 66–30, and he was subsequently confirmed 62–36. Four Democrats, including Judiciary Committee member Simon (D-IL), actually voted to end debate on the Carnes nomination but then voted against confirmation of Carnes. These senators were beginning to fear that should Clinton win the 1992 election, Republican senators might try using the filibuster tactic against Democratic nominees (Lewis, 1992b).

FILIBUSTERS DURING THE CLINTON ADMINISTRATION

Three Clinton lower court nominations were the subjects of filibusters. Ironically, it was the Democrats, not the Republicans, who first filibustered a Clinton judge: Stewart, nominated to the District of Utah. The reason that some Democrats opposed a nominee of their own president was due to the fact that Stewart was a conservative Republican, nominated by Clinton as part of a deal with Judiciary Committee Chairman Hatch. As discussed below, Clinton felt compelled to engage in this log-roll so as to break partisan gridlock that had tied up many of his other nominees, most notably Marsha Berzon and Richard Paez, both nominated to the Ninth Circuit Court of Appeals and both objected to by conservative activists (Lewis, 1999a). In practical terms, then, Stewart was not a Democratic nominee, but a Republican one.

When a coalition of environmental interest groups, including the Wilderness Society, the Sierra Club, and the Natural Resources Defense Council, voiced serious objections to the Stewart nomination, environment-friendly Democrats signaled their support by deciding to challenge the

Stewart nomination. Most notable among this group was Vice President Albert A. Gore Jr. (Lewis, 1999a). Lacking the votes necessary to defeat this Republican nominee, Democrats threatened a filibuster (Lewis, 1999b). The first vote for cloture was 55–44, strictly along party lines, and so the Stewart nomination could not proceed to a confirmation vote. Incensed by the Democrats' tactics, Judiciary Chairman Hatch refused to allow any other confirmation votes to go to the floor until Stewart was confirmed. Thus, what was supposed to be a deal to end gridlock, had only produced more gridlock. Finally, Democratic and Republican leaders reached an accord, allowing the votes of Stewart, Berzon, and Paez to all proceed on the same day (Lewis, 1999c). However, when the time came to vote on these three judicial candidates, Republicans went forward only with the Stewart vote, and he was confirmed.

It would be another six months before the Berzon and Paez nominations would be put up for a floor vote. But their confirmations hit another road block when Senator Robert C. Smith (R-NH) filibustered these two nominations on the grounds that they were too liberal. But with little support for prolonged debate among Republican leaders, including Majority Leader Lott (R-MS) and Hatch, the cloture motions were passed 86–13. The following day, the two Ninth Circuit nominees were confirmed by votes of 63–34 for Berzon and 59–39 for Paez (Chiang, 2000).

THE FILIBUSTER WARS OF THE G. W. BUSH ADMINISTRATION

With Democrats controlling the confirmation process in the 107th Congress—and very much united in the goal to keep President G. W. Bush's most conservative nominees off the federal bench—there were no ideologically driven filibusters for the first two years of the Bush presidency; Democrats simply kept objectionable nominees from getting a floor vote. However, Republican senators filibustered three nominees (Lavenski Smith, Richard Clifton, and Julia Smith Gibbons) not on ideological grounds but to force a vote on a nominee for the Federal Election Commission; all three cloture motions passed, and G. W. Bush's nominees were easily confirmed with bipartisan support.

But with unified Republican control returning in the 108th Congress, liberal activists intensified the pressure to fight confirmation of conservative judicial candidates nominated by the president in the 108th Congress, many of whom were unconfirmed nominees from the 107th Congress. But now, as the minority party, Democrats no longer could defeat judicial candidates at the committee level or floor level. Further, they could neither delay hearings and floor votes as they had done so effectively in the 107th Congress nor rely on home state senator blue slips, as Hatch had wrested that power. That left Democrats with only one tactic for obstructing confirmation of extremely conservative nominees: the filibuster.

Many political pundits questioned the Democrats' resolve to carry off this strategy. Could they hold together a coalition of forty votes over a prolonged period of time? And could they filibuster more than one nomination at one time? So far, it appears that the answer to both of these questions is a resounding "yes."

In February 2003, the Democrats mounted their first filibuster against Miguel A. Estrada, nominated to the D.C. Circuit. When Republicans were unable to muster more than fifty-five votes for cloture on numerous occasions, Estrada finally asked that his nomination be withdrawn (Lewis, 2003). Nine more filibusters would be used against G. W. Bush nominees to the courts of appeals in the 108th Congress: Owen and Pickering, nominated to the Fifth Circuit; William H. Pryor, nominated to the Eleventh Circuit; Kuhl and William Myers, nominated to the Ninth Circuit; Brown, nominated to the D.C. Circuit; and David McKeague, Richard Griffin, and Henry Saad, nominated to the Sixth Circuit.[13] When repeated cloture motions failed, G. W. Bush seated two of these nominees (Pickering and Pryor) on the bench through recess appointments. Senate Democrats retaliated by threatening to filibuster all of G. W. Bush's federal court appointments unless the president promised to cease unilaterally seating judges on the bench while the Senate was in recess (Stolberg, 2004). The two sides remained at an impasse for six weeks until finally the president capitulated and promised not to make recess appointments to the federal courts for the remainder of his first term in office (Lewis, 2004).

The End of Judicial Log-Rolls

Presidents throughout the 20th century often have found themselves at odds with powerful senators of the opposite party over a judicial nomination because of senatorial courtesy. Accordingly, in the spirit of compromise, every president since FDR has named between two and four people of the opposite party to the courts of appeals; a much larger number of cross-party appointments were made to the district courts (Goldman, 1997). When Nixon was elected without his party controlling the Senate, he was obviously going to have to deal with many home state senators of the opposite party. Thus, the Nixon administration understood that it would have to cut deals with Democratic senators in order to secure confirmation of Nixon's preferred judicial candidates. Out of political necessity, classic log-rolling became a common tactic the Nixon administration used in the selection of lower court judges (see generally Goldman, 1997, at 209–10).

Another type of log-rolling that was once common involved the exchange of a critical vote on an important piece of legislation the president wanted in exchange for the president's appointment of a judicial candidate preferred by a home state senator. For example, President Johnson was said to have appointed a South Carolinian to the federal bench in exchange for Senator Thurmond's support of civil rights legislation, as well as electoral support at the Democratic National Convention (McFeeley, 1987). Hatch similarly reports that Reagan was forced to enter into such legislative-judicial exchanges with Democratic senators: "The tactic of log-rolling became the norm. Today, votes on nominees are often traded like commodities—ten judges in exchange for a vote on this, two commissioners for a vote on that. This objectionable practice is so common and accepted that it has become as important in keeping the Senate functioning as unanimous consent and other key parliamentary rules" (Hatch, 2002, at 123).

But bipartisan compromise regarding judicial selection poses serious political problems for the president. In short, conservative and liberal activists alike regard compromising on ideological criteria as an anathema. As leading conservative activist Jipping explains: "I don't like deals. I don't think that's a good way to pick judges because it ends up distracting from the central criterion [of judicial philosophy]. But also, the Republicans are notoriously bad dealers" (Jipping interview, 2002).

Liberal activists express a similar distaste for ideological compromise in judicial selection, though they seem more willing to acknowledge that political realities sometimes dictate log-rolling to move the process along. As Alliance for Justice director Aron states:

> We at the Alliance . . . have always taken the view that federal judgeships are of such critical importance and judges have such huge power over people's lives that each and every person has to be a person who meets the highest standards. Having said that, we're also not out to prevent the opportunity for some wonderfully qualified candidates to move through the process for a trade. But . . . we've got to look at each and every nominee carefully. Which means that we will oppose a candidate [who is part of a trade, but we understand] . . . the fact that reality dictates [trades] . . . We're not naive either . . . Oftentimes we'll oppose [a Republican nominated by a Democrat as part of a trade] because that's what people count on us as doing. But we also know that we won't be an obstacle to the possibility of a trade taking place. In fact, people might be relying on us to oppose a candidate to set up the trade. (Aron interview, 2002)

Because the key party and issue activists today place ideological purity over political compromise—indeed, this was what separated the new breed of party activists from old-line party members beginning in the 1960s (see Chapters 1 and 2)—presidents are much more loath to enter into judicial log-rolls. And when presidents and senators do enter into these log-rolls, it usually spells trouble for at least one of the two sides.

LOG-ROLLING UNDER REAGAN AND G. H. W. BUSH

The most notable judicial log-rolls during the Reagan administration involved trades not with Democratic senators, but with Republicans. As discussed in Chapter 5, the confirmation fight over Seventh Circuit nominee Manion came right on the heels of an embarrassing defeat for the Reagan administration regarding the Sessions nomination to an Alabama district court. Accordingly, wanting to avoid another setback, and with several Republicans publicly announcing their opposition to Manion, Reagan was forced to do some horse-trading with members of his own party. Specifically, Reagan proposed a deal to Washington senator Slade Gorton. In exchange for Gorton's promise to vote for Manion, Reagan agreed to clear the way for Gorton's choice for a district court judgeship in the Western District of Washington. That nominee, William L. Dwyer, was opposed by conservatives in the Reagan administration and in Washington State because he had previously represented a man suing a leading conservative for libel. Indeed, a conservative state senator from Washington labeled Dwyer "ultra-liberal" and "not even a Republican" (Turner, 1986). Reagan also cut a deal with Senator David Durenberger (R-MN) to nominate his favored candidate for a district court judgeship in Minneapolis in exchange for Durenberger's vote for Manion. Both senators ultimately voted for Manion, sealing his confirmation with a vote of 49–49 and Vice President George H. Bush breaking the tie. These deals prompted Judiciary Committee member Biden to remark: "judicial pork barreling is dead wrong. It was clear that a majority of the Senate did not favor the Manion confirmation. But when it came time to vote, the White House made a deal with some senators by agreeing to appoint individuals to the federal bench that the President or [Attorney General] Ed Meese had opposed only hours ago" (quoted in Gailey, 1986). As payback, Democrats in the Senate blocked confirmation of Gorton's candidate for the district court, and so ironically, Gorton's part of the judicial log-roll was never realized (Kurtz, 1986c).

Gorton's trade would also soon prove to be a political disaster for him. As discussed in Chapter 7, his opponent in the 1986 senate race, Brock Adams, made the Manion trade a central issue in his bid to unseat Gorton. This campaign strategy proved quite successful, and Adams went on to defeat Gorton in the November election. Not only did Gorton's eleventh-hour backroom deal displease Democrats in his home state, but because he made a trade to secure a judgeship for a Democrat, Gorton also wound up alienating leading conservatives in Washington.

CLINTON LOG-ROLLS

Unlike Reagan and G. H. W. Bush, Clinton was more inclined to resort to the judicial log-roll despite the possible backlash from liberal activists. Two things made it easier for Clinton to resort to this strategy than Republican presidents. First, Clinton was not as committed to packing the courts with liberals as Republican presidents were committed to packing the courts with conservatives; at the first sign of trouble, Clinton would often withdraw a troubled nomination (Johnson, 2000). As we saw in Chapter 4, Clinton's appointment strategy stressed diversity more than ideology. Second, liberal activists simply were not as hostile to the possibility of a trade as their conservative counterparts; they were willing to accept compromise as long as it meant easing judicial confirmation gridlock. However, in the end, Clinton proposed only three trades in his eight years in office, notwithstanding the long delays many of his judicial nominations faced.

First was a trade between Clinton and Republican Senator Gorton—the same senator who had entered into the disastrous trade with Reagan in 1986. Although Gorton's trade with Reagan led to his defeat for reelection in 1986, he was elected to the other senate seat from the state of Washington in 1988. During Clinton's presidency, Gorton had placed a hold on Clinton's old Oxford roommate and chairman of his California presidential campaign, William Fletcher, who had been nominated to the Ninth Circuit Court of Appeals. In exchange for moving along the Fletcher nomination, Gorton demanded that Clinton nominate a conservative Washington Supreme Court judge, Barbara Durham, to the Ninth Circuit. With the Fletcher nomination sitting in limbo for three years, Clinton agreed to the trade. Liberal activists immediately voiced objections to the Durham nomination, with Aron calling it a "Faustian bargain" (quoted in Carter, 1999). Aron went on to state that Durham's "elevation to the Ninth Circuit would harm individual rights. The Clinton administration gets high marks for appointing many highly qualified and excellent judges to the federal bench. Justice Durham does not meet the high standard set for federal judges" (quoted in Carter, 1999). Ironically, Gorton would once again not receive his end of the judicial bargain. After Fletcher was confirmed and seated on the Ninth Circuit, Durham withdrew her nomination, citing personal reasons. However, Aron believes Durham withdrew because she feared that liberal activists would defeat her nomination (Aron interview, 2002). Although Gorton demanded that he be given another chance to nominate a Republican to the Ninth Circuit after Durham's withdrawal, Clinton refused.

The second log-roll of note during the Clinton administration involved a trade between the president and Judiciary Committee Chairman Hatch. After the Republicans had all but shut down judicial confirmations to the circuit courts of appeals for two years after Clinton's reelection in 1996, Democrats were desperate to get the process back on track. One nominee to the Ninth Circuit, Paez, had waited more than three years to be confirmed, and another nominee to that circuit, Berzon, had awaited a confirmation hearing for more than a year. Hatch promised Clinton to move along the Paez and Berzon nominations in exchange for Clinton's nomination of Ted Stewart, a Republican ally of Hatch's, to the District Court of Utah. Clinton again agreed to the trade, despite much opposition from liberal interest groups, particularly the environmental lobby. But with Stewart's nomination came an end to years of gridlock in the judicial confirmation process.

A third, although never consummated, log-roll occurred when Clinton and Senator Helms (R–NC) discussed a deal that would have allowed Clinton to name the first African American to the Fourth Circuit Court of Appeals—an issue that became of great symbolic significance to Clinton because of his desire to diversify the federal bench (see Chapter 4). In exchange, Clinton would appoint Terrence Boyle to a second Fourth Circuit seat reserved for a North Carolinian; Boyle had been nominated by President G. H. W. Bush, but his nomination died when the elder Bush was not reelected in 1992. Senator Helms proposed this trade during Clinton's first term in office, but the White House declined the offer (Wilson, 2003). However, as judicial gridlock intensified during Clinton's second term in office—including four vacancies on the Fourth Circuit alone—Clinton's team approached Helms about entering into the same trade he had proposed earlier; this time, it was Helms who rejected the trade (Wilson, 2003). As detailed in Chapter 4, Clinton eventually resorted to making a recess appointment after the 2000 election in order to name the first African American to the Fourth Circuit.

Finally, Clinton tried unsuccessfully to strike a deal with Republican Senator Allard of Colorado that would have resolved an impasse over the nomination of Patricia A. Coan, a federal magistrate judge in Colorado. Coan was originally nominated by Clinton in May 1999 to fill a vacancy on the District of Colorado. However, Allard refused to return his blue slip on the nomination because he wanted Colorado deputy attorney general Christine Arguello to receive that nomination. Allard was unhappy that the district court nomination was made without his being consulted, Clinton instead turning to a panel of Democrats in the state who had chosen Coan. As the Clinton presidency was drawing to a close, and Senator Allard appeared unwilling to lift his hold on the Coan nomination, the White House offered to nominate Allard's favored candidate, Arguello, for the district court seat in exchange for Allard's support of Coan for a seat on the Tenth Circuit Court of Appeals. However, Allard rejected this trade, saying that although he was pleased Clinton was now considering Arguello for the district court, he could not support Coan for the higher court (McAllister, 2000). At the urging of Colorado Democrats, who strongly supported Arguello for either of the two judgeships, Clinton eventually nominated her for the seat on the Tenth Circuit, but with the 2000 election looming, the full Senate never acted on her nomination (Romano, 2000).

G. W. BUSH LOG-ROLLS

G. W. Bush's first set of nominations had the appearance of reaching across the aisle as he nominated two black Democrats for appellate court judgeships. One of them, Gregory, was the same judge to whom Clinton had given a recess appointment at the very end of his term in office. G. W. Bush also named Boyle—who had once been discussed as part of a trade with the Clinton White House in exchange for Helms's agreement to back an African American nominee—to fill one of the Fourth Circuit vacancies. Although Gregory was confirmed only two months after being nominated, North Carolina senator John Edwards blue-slipped Boyle, and thus, his nomination remained in limbo throughout the 107th and 108th Congresses. At the beginning of the 109th Congress he finally received a committee hearing.

For the most part, and much to the consternation of liberal activists, G. W. Bush has shunned the practice of log-rolling with senators over judicial nominations. This is true notwithstanding the fact that his party lost control of the Senate early in his presidency. It was liberal activists' hope that by having Democrats hold up G. W. Bush's most conservative nominees, the president would be forced to come to the bargaining table, just as Republicans had forced Clinton to do:

> For every decent Clinton nominee who was deep-sixed, not because they were liberal nut bars, but because they [Republican leadership] wanted to "show" Clinton (which is what I think was going on), there [now] need[s] to be tit for tat [in the G. W. Bush administration]. Say, "No offense guy [judicial nominee of W. Bush], but you're the trade for Ronnie White. And you're the trade for Peter Edelman. And you're the trade for so and so." A fairly short period of hard-

ball would've brought Bush to the table to say, "we can work this out." Give us Ronnie White, give us Peter Edelman. Give us Bonnie Campbell [nominated, but never confirmed, to the Eighth Circuit]. Give us all of the Democrats who stayed on the table who rightfully had these judgeships. These were not George [W.] Bush's judgeships to fill.... They were Bill Clinton's. To say that it's George [W.] Bush's right to fill those [lower court] positions [left vacant upon Clinton's leaving office], it was not. Those were Democratic appointees, and there is supposed to be a balance of power. That's how you get any kind of reasonable balance on the courts. (Gandy interview, 2000)

Aron, of the Alliance for Justice, echoes this sentiment. She believes, like Gandy, that G. W. Bush should have been compelled to nominate all of the people Clinton originally nominated, but that Republicans in the Senate refused to confirm purely for political gain: "It isn't right not to hold hearings. But having had the Republicans block so many qualified nominees . . . my view would be [to hold hearings] on the Clinton people before or at the same time as the Bush people. Push them [Clinton and Bush nominees] all through. Give them all hearings" (Aron interview, 2002).

Conclusion

The third elite mobilization strategy to develop in the modern political era is obstructing the confirmation of a particular nominee through the use of a variety of tactics, including forcing roll-call votes, using delay tactics, exercising blue-slip privileges, mounting filibusters, and refusing to log-roll. Nominees are first targeted by interest groups aligned with the opposite party of the president; such objections are largely based on the activists' conclusion that the nominee will decide cases in a manner inconsistent with the activists' political agenda. Senators then "score points" with these key political elites by using whatever tactics available to obstruct the nominee's confirmation. Unlike the other elite mobilization strategies, however, this strategy is a confirmation-based strategy, not a nomination-based strategy, and is focused on defeating a nomination, rather than choosing a nominee. It is also a strategy aimed at a specific nomination, rather than one designed according to a broad normative goal applicable to all nominations.

CHAPTER 7

Lower Court Judicial Selection
as a Campaign Issue

BEFORE THE 1960S, it was not uncommon in American history for Supreme Court decisions to become fodder for a presidential election. In his book *Campaigns and the Court* (1999), Donald Grier Stephenson Jr. documents seven such instances: in 1800 (the Court's refusal to declare the Alien and Sedition Acts unconstitutional); in 1832 (the Court's finding that the federal bank was constitutional); in 1860 (the Court's finding that slavery was constitutional); and in 1896, 1912, 1924, and 1936 (the Court's power to overturn commercial statutes on Fourteenth Amendment substantive due process grounds). Other scholars often point to the 1964 election as one in which the Supreme Court played an important role. As stated in Chapter 2, in that election, Republican nominee Goldwater attacked the Warren Court's spate of "liberal" decisions on a number of salient issues, most notably the civil liberty rights of criminal defendants. In each of the elections mentioned above, the presidential challenger raises the judicial issue, and holds the incumbent president or his party responsible for objectionable Supreme Court rulings made by the incumbent's judicial appointees to the high court.

This fairly common campaign tactic did not, however, carry over to lower federal court decisions until fairly recently. Before the modern political era, there was but one occasion where a presidential challenger made lower federal court rulings a campaign issue. In the 1896 election, the Democratic Party platform called for an end to life tenure for lower court judges and for legislation curbing the power of these judges to issue injunctions in labor disputes (Hall, 1985). In short, the lower federal courts were not seen as important players in national policy-making, and so their decisions were not thought important enough to become presidential campaign issues. But beginning with Nixon's 1968 run for the presidency, the lower federal courts would become the target of campaign rhetoric in *every* presidential election. Today, they are also a fixture of key senatorial campaigns, mostly in the South. And in the November 2003 election cycle, we even saw this issue raised in a gubernatorial race for the first time.

That the lower federal courts finally emerged as a campaign issue in the 1960s is no coincidence given the historic transformation in American institutions occurring during this period. In short, with the traditional party system breaking down, with political issue activists taking over the role of party activists, and with the Supreme Court opening the floodgates for these issue activists to begin lawsuits in federal court to achieve their policy goals, presidential challengers of both parties, starting with Nixon, used the lower court selection process as a means to "signal" important activists. These challengers would promise that if elected, they would employ a "new" judicial selection strategy that would put judges on the bench who would deliver more favorable policy outcomes for the candidate's affiliated activists. Similarly, senatorial challengers of both parties, starting in the 1980s, used the lower court confirmation process to send cues to their activists that if elected, they would have voted differently than the incumbent had on a controversial nominee and, going forward, will vote for nominees who support the activists' policy goals. In this chapter, we will see how candidates for public office—both presidents and senators and now even governors—from Nixon through G. W. Bush have exploited the judicial selection issue in political campaigns against incumbents.

The Republican Party's Use of the Lower Federal Courts in Election Campaigns

REPUBLICAN PRESIDENTIAL CANDIDATES

Nixon's Presidential Campaigns

The selection of lower federal court judges was an integral part of Nixon's "southern strategy," which was designed to break the Democratic Party's century-old monopoly on conservative, white southern votes. With the old party system beginning to break down, Nixon hoped to form a new Republican coalition, and so he made America's crime "problem" one of his major campaign themes (Beckett, 1997).[1] To this end, he promised to appoint "law and order" judges to all levels of the federal bench. It was Nixon's stated intent to appoint lower court judges who would exercise the broad discretion accorded them in a series of Supreme Court cases in the 1960s in a manner that would curb civil liberties protections granted criminal defendants. These cases included *Mapp v. Ohio* (allowing the exclusion of evidence obtained in violation of a defendant's Fourth Amendment rights), *Gideon v. Wainwright* (mandating appointment of counsel to indigent defendants) and *Miranda v. Arizona* (allowing the exclusion of confessions obtained without informing suspects of their Fifth and Sixth Amendment rights, among other things, to remain silent and to have legal counsel appointed).

Although it is doubtful that the judicial selection component of Nixon's southern strategy, standing alone, would have had a direct impact in swaying southern voters, without question, Nixon's focus on combating street crime (part of which would be accomplished through careful judicial selection) was a decisive factor in contributing to Nixon's victory as it played on the country's racial tensions. Furthermore, it would begin a process—later crystallized by Reagan in the 1980 election—of attracting white southerners permanently to the Republican Party. In his 1972 reelection campaign, Nixon repeated the strategy; the Republican platform proclaimed that Nixon was winning the war on crime because of his appointment of "judges whose respect for the rights of the accused is balanced by an appreciation of the legitimate needs of law enforcement."[2]

Reagan's and G. H. W. Bush's Presidential Campaigns

In its 1980 platform, under the party leadership of candidate Reagan, the Republican Party called for "the appointment of judges *at all levels* of the judiciary who respect traditional family values and the sanctity of innocent life";[3] in other words, Reagan would use a nominee's stand on *Roe v. Wade* as a litmus test for judicial appointments. As we saw in Chapter 3, Reagan kept his campaign promise as his appointees indeed are decisively pro-life.

In 1988, under the leadership of G. H. W. Bush, the Republican Party platform promised to continue the "Reagan-Bush team['s]" record for naming judges who believe in "judicial restraint, the rights of law-abiding citizens, and traditional family values."[4] Here, candidate Bush suggests he will use three litmus tests in choosing lower federal court judges: Reagan's abortion test, Nixon's crime test, and a new Republican test—judges who ascribe to a legal philosophy of judicial "restraint." This third litmus test simply reflects the growing influence that the Federalist Society enjoyed in the inner circles of Republican power beginning with the Reagan administration (see Chapter 5). And as we saw in Chapter 3, like Reagan, Bush also kept these campaign promises; his judicial appointees are quite conservative on issues of crime, civil rights, abortion, and states' rights. Again, in the 1992 platform, Bush promised "the appointment of judges who respect traditional family values and the sanctity of innocent human life."[5]

Dole's Presidential Campaign

After losing the White House in the 1992 election, Republicans started to expand on the traditional way the party had used judicial selection in political campaigns—that is, by promising to employ ideological litmus tests in judicial selection. In 1996, Republican nominee Robert J. Dole actually made the judicial ideology of *specific* Clinton judges a focal point of his presidential campaign. We also begin to see Republicans use judicial selection as an issue in statewide Senate races; here, Republican Senate candidates would attack their opponents for voting to confirm liberal judges to the lower federal courts. In both instances—Dole in the presidential race and Republican candidates in Senate races—Republicans appear to resort to this strategy when they are unable to attack their opponents for being liberal themselves; instead, they impute liberalness to their opponents because of their support of liberal lower court judges or their opposition to conservative judges.

Like Nixon, Dole focused his presidential campaign attacks on charges that Clinton's judicial appointees were "soft" on crime. But without question, Dole took the issue much farther than even Nixon, and certainly farther than any other Republican in the modern political era. Specifically, he made the ideology of Clinton's judicial appointments a *cornerstone* of his presidential campaign, singling out specific Clinton lower court judges for attack on the campaign trail, rather than attacking the ideology of the lower federal courts as a whole.

The first hint that Dole was going to make judicial ideology a campaign theme came in his response to Clinton's 1996 State of the Union Address. Countering Clinton's achievements in lowering the crime rate and signing into law a tough crime bill, Dole told the American public that the "liberal" Clinton administration was out of touch with the values of Americans:

> [Clinton] has put liberal judges on the bench to war with our values . . . President Clinton shares a view of America held by our country's elites . . . It is as though our government, our institutions and our culture have been hijacked by liberals and are careening dangerously off course . . . Whether it's deficit spending or the welfare bureaucracy or our liberal courts or the trouble in our schools—what's wrong is that the elites in charge don't believe in what the people believe in. (Quoted in Kamen and Brown, 1996)

Except for vague promises in his stump speech during the Republican primary season—that he would appoint "tough" and "conservative" judges (Harden, 1996a)—Dole did not unveil his anti-Clinton judicial strategy until he had locked up the Republican nomination and his only opponent was Clinton himself. On April 19, 1996, in a speech to the American Society of Newspaper Editors, Dole sharply criticized Clinton for appointing "liberal" judges. He again zeroed in on these judges' criminal law rulings in an effort to undermine Clinton's crime policies.

First noting that Americans "feel increasingly at risk," Dole went on to charge, among other things, that liberal judges were the "root causes of the crime explosion" (Lewis, 1996); that Clinton's judicial appointees show an "outright hostility to law enforcement" (King, 1996); and that if Clinton were reelected, the Clinton-packed judiciary would be "an all-star team of liberal leniency" (Lewis, 1996) and "could lock in liberal judicial activism for the next generation, and the social landscape could dramatically change" (King, 1996).

Singling out specific examples of "soft on crime" and "pro-defendant" judges, Dole named his first choices for what he called his judicial "Hall of Shame" (Hall, 1996; Jackson, 1996; King, 1996). Dole's five "inductees" were Third Circuit judge Lee Sarokin, Eleventh Circuit judge Barkett, New York district court judge Harold Baer, and two Virginia district court judges, Leonie M. Brinkema of Alexandria and Raymond A. Jackson of Norfolk (Hall, 1996; King, 1996). For each of these judges, Dole recited specific criminal rulings in which the judges overturned criminal convictions on procedural grounds or gave criminals allegedly light sentences. He promised to expand his list as the campaign continued (King, 1996).[6]

Early on, the Dole campaign indicated that its candidate would continue this strategy throughout the election (Hallow, 1996). But Clinton did not want to give Dole any time for this issue to resonate with the American public, and he and his campaign strategists quickly responded with a five-pronged counterattack. First, they pointed out that Dole had voted to confirm 98 percent of Clinton's judicial appointees (*Buffalo News*, 1996). Second, they cited statistics demonstrating that crime had been dropping since Clinton took office (Harden, 1996b). Third, Clinton political advisors reminded the American public that Clinton, and not the Republicans in the Senate, was responsible for adding one hundred thousand more police officers to the streets to regulate handgun sales and to eliminate certain types of assault weapons (Chernoff, Kelly, and Kroger, 1996). Fourth, Democrats were quick to point out that the very federal programs Dole denounced on the campaign trail as "intrusive into the lives of average Americans" and indicative of more "centralized power in Washington"—for example, federally mandated set-asides of minority business, the Voting Rights Amendments of 1982, the expansion of federal criminal jurisdiction and federal civil rights protections for the disabled, women, and minorities—were federal programs Dole supported in the Senate (Rosen, 1996). And fifth, the Clinton justice department took extraordinary steps to pressure one of Dole's

"Hall of Shame" judges (Judge Baer of New York) to reverse his decision suppressing incriminating evidence of drug dealing on Fourth Amendment grounds (Greenhouse, 1996b). Clinton even went so far as to threaten to ask for the judge's resignation in the event he did not overturn his ruling (Mitchell, 1996).[7]

In response to the Clinton strategy, Senate Judiciary Committee Chairman Hatch issued an attack on Clinton's judicial appointees, claiming that the "defining" difference between Democrats and Republicans in the 1996 national election was their views on judicial philosophy:

> The philosophy that a president's judges bring to the bench should be one of the central issues for public debate; long after a president has left office, his judges will still be deciding cases. To this end, many Republicans, including me, have criticized President Clinton's selections for the federal judiciary. Mr. Clinton has appointed judges who have voted to use harmless technicalities to overturn criminal convictions and have imposed their own policy preferences on the law. By my count, about two-thirds of the Clinton appellate judges have shown their colors by writing or joining activist opinions.
>
> President Clinton's response . . . has relied on a number of misleading myths. Instead of hiding behind weak arguments and unconvincing statistics, the president should explain why he believes his choice of judicial activists is good for the nation. In this election year, judicial selection is a defining issue between Democrats and Republicans . . .
>
> Judges Sarokin, Barkett and Daughtrey are only the most egregious examples, but their performances have been matched by other judges who have carried forward the Clinton liberal activist agenda. Judges such as David Tatel and Judith Rogers of the D.C. Circuit, Guido Calabresi and Pierre Leval of the Second Circuit, Theodore McKee of the Third Circuit, Diana Motz and Blane Michael of the Fourth Circuit, Karen Nelson Moore of the Sixth Circuit, Diane Wood of the Seventh Circuit, Michael Hawkins of the Ninth Circuit, and Carlos Lucero and Robert Henry of the 10th Circuit have written or joined opinions seeking to free defendants on harmless technicalities or to stretch the law to fit their policy ends.
>
> I could go on, but there is no need. The views of such judges are part of a pattern and practice of activism that characterizes the Clinton appellate judiciary. Mr. Clinton has chosen to pursue his liberal agenda through the appellate judges, who make rulings on issues of law that will bind the other judges in that circuit . . .
>
> If anyone has been soft on crime, it is Mr. Clinton. His appointments to the federal bench have only compounded the damage already done on the crime front by his absence of leadership in the war on crime and on drugs. Come November, the voters can force a change in administration; unfortunately, Mr. Clinton's judges will be with us for life. (Hatch, 1996)

Perhaps recognizing the inherent disingenuousness of Dole's strategy to attack Clinton's federal court appointees, given his votes to confirm all of these judges, by the time of the Republican National Convention in August, many Republicans—though certainly not the party's right-wing base[8]—had been urging Dole to abandon this campaign strategy. In his acceptance speech at the convention, Dole spoke directly to these mainstream Republicans and told them that he would continue waging his battle over the federal judiciary:

> I have been asked if I have a litmus test for judges. I do. My litmus test is that they be intolerant of outrage, that their passion is not to amend but to interpret the Constitution, that they are restrained in regard to those who live within the law and strict with those who break it.
>
> And for those who say that I should not make Bill Clinton's liberal judicial appointments an issue of this campaign, I have a simple response. I have heard your argument: the motion is denied.
>
> I save my respect for the Constitution, not for those who would ignore it, violate it or replace it with conceptions of their own fancy. My administration will zealously protect civil and constitutional rights while never forgetting that our own primary duty is protecting law-abiding citizens. (Associated Press, 1996)

And as was true of every Republican platform since 1980, the platform in 1996 again called for the "appointment of judges who respect traditional family values and the sanctity of innocent human life."[9]

Despite Dole's continued cries questioning Clinton's commitment to combating crime when Clinton was also appointing "liberal" judges to the lower federal courts (see, for example, Harden, 1996b), Clinton was winning the crime battle with Dole. Just as he had successfully shed the Democratic Party's image as being "soft" on crime in the 1992 election, public opinion polls during the 1996 presidential campaign indicated that Clinton was again convincing Americans that he was a "new" Democrat (Harden, 1996b). Try as he might to repeat Nixon's successful 1968 campaign strategy, Dole never closed the gap in Clinton's lead, and Clinton was reelected in November.

2000 and 2004 Presidential Campaigns

Despite the ineffectiveness of Dole's strategy of using Clinton's lower federal court judges as a major presidential campaign theme, Judiciary Committee Chairman Hatch, too, sought to use Clinton's lower federal court judges as a presidential campaign issue when he ran for the Republican nomination in 2000. But he did so from a different angle than had Dole. Hatch believed that his experience in shepherding through Clinton judicial nominees demonstrated his ability to attain interparty consensus and thus distinguished him from an already crowded field of Republican candidates who would further polarize politics in Washington. However, the very constituency that Hatch needed to win the Republican nomination—conservative elites—felt strongly that Hatch should have been blocking, not promoting,

Clinton's judicial nominees and so were not persuaded that Hatch should be their candidate for president. An editorial in the *Wall Street Journal* characterized two different Hatches:

> It's time someone had a heart to heart political chat with Senator Orrin Hatch. Our first choice for the job is—Presidential candidate Orrin Hatch!
>
> Only weeks ago, on the campaign trail in Iowa, the Utah Republican taped a scorching half-hour TV ad expressing his outrage at the Clinton Administration's many legal and ethical evasions. But back chairing the Judiciary Committee last week, the same man forgot all that unpleasantness and whisked through two liberal judicial nominees, including one who had signed off on the wrist-slap plea bargain for [1996 Clinton campaign finance-related convict] John Huang.
>
> Will the real Orrin please stand up? . . .
>
> Once back in the Beltway something happens and the Utah flame-thrower becomes Ms. Reno's "friend." The truth-teller of the campaign trail becomes just one more Clinton enabler.
>
> This helps explain Mr. Hatch's decision to approve Judge Richard Paez to the Ninth Circuit Court of Appeals. Mr. Hatch and Pennsylvania liberal Arlen Specter were the only two Republicans to vote for him on the Judiciary Committee. Eight others voted no on grounds that he was a very model of a judicial activist, having spoken out against California Propositions 187 and 209 while a sitting judge . . .
>
> What must truly blow the other Orrin's mind, however, is that this Beltway alter ego also overlooked Judge Paez's role in the John Huang sentencing . . .
>
> Alabama Republican Jeff Sessions found this so outrageous he made a big flap about it on the Senate floor. The former prosecutor says Judge Paez violated federal sentencing guidelines in essentially giving Mr. Huang a get out of jail free card . . .
>
> Senator Hatch—not the campaign ethicist—never even mentioned the Huang matter in his own Senate statement supporting Judge Paez's nomination. Not a word. So the loyal Clinton servant won his promotion to the nation's appellate bench, 59–39.
>
> No wonder Bill Clinton and friends think they can get away with anything. Republicans keep letting them. (Editorial, *Wall Street Journal*, 2000)

Accordingly, with the conservative base of the Republican Party extremely dissatisfied with Hatch's bipartisanship as chairman of the Judiciary Committee, his presidential candidacy failed. After coming in last place in the Iowa caucuses in January 2000, Hatch was the first Republican presidential candidate to pull out of the race (Dewar, 2000).

Though G. W. Bush did not make lower court nominations a focal point in either the 2000 or 2004 general elections, the Republican platforms in both years spoke to the issue. Notably, in 2004, the party's platform had an entire section entitled "Supporting Judges Who Uphold the Law." Building on the strategy now favored by conservative elites involved in appointment politics (see Chapter 5), this section denounced the appointment of "activist" federal court judges, and cited particular rulings of sitting judges that were salient with mainstream American voters, including striking down the pledge of allegiance and upholding partial birth abortions.[10] Moreover, unlike Dole and Hatch, G. W. Bush did not focus on specific confirmation battles in his two campaigns for president. Rather, like Reagan and G. H. W. Bush, G. W. Bush simply laid out a broad normative goal to appoint "strict constructionist" judges to the federal bench (e.g., Egelko, 2004).

REPUBLICAN SENATE CAMPAIGNS

The 1994 California and Connecticut Senate Races

It is interesting that Dole was not, in fact, the first political candidate to use specific Clinton lower court appointees as a major campaign theme. As early as the 1994 midterm elections, several conservative Republican Senate challengers made an issue of their Democratic opponents' roll-call votes in favor of confirming Eleventh Circuit judge Rosemary Barkett—a Clinton appointee labeled by conservative activists as "soft on crime" because of her decisions while a Florida Supreme Court justice. Specifically, this tactic was tried by Republican candidates Michael Huffington in his race against Dianne Feinstein (D-CA) (Daly, 1994) and Gerald Labriola in his race against Joseph Lieberman (D-CN) (Lecher, 1994).

Like Clinton, however, both of these incumbent Democratic senators were not traditional liberal Democrats when it came to criminal law enforcement, but rather, were "new" Democrats. Notably, both senators were firm supporters of the death penalty. And so, just as Dole would do two years later in his campaign against Clinton, not able to attack these Democratic senators' crime positions on crime directly, these conservative Republican candidates instead tried to paint the Democratic incumbents as "soft" on crime through the back door—by pointing to their votes to confirm a "pro-criminal" judicial nominee. But like Dole in the 1996 presidential election, both Republican challengers lost their Senate races.

The 2002 Texas, Georgia, and Tennessee Senate Races

In the 2002 midterm elections, the Republican Party made a strategic decision to make judicial selection on the lower federal courts a central campaign theme in hotly contested Senate races, particularly in the South. In short, Republican strategists believed that the Democrats' refusal to confirm two conservative Bush appointees to the Fifth Circuit Court of Appeals— Pickering of Mississippi and Owen of Texas—could prove to be critical. According to Republican pollster Whit Ayres, the issue would be "potentially a very significant campaign issue, particularly in generating intensity among Republican voters" (quoted in Goldstein, 2002). Both judicial candidates had been defeated at the committee level by 10–9 votes on straight party lines. Democrats claimed that Pickering's prior decisions as a district court judge demonstrated an insensitivity to minorities; they claimed that Owen's prior decisions as a Texas Supreme Court judge demonstrated a hostility to a woman's right to choose abortion.

However, unlike previous Senate campaigns—in which incumbents were attacked for how they *actually* voted on judicial confirmations on the floor of the Senate—pursuant to this latest strategy, Republican Senate candidates in the South attacked Democratic opponents for how they *might have voted* on controversial lower court confirmations that never made it to the Senate floor for roll-call votes. Specifically, this strategy played out in three Senate races in 2002: Texas, Georgia, and Tennessee. Republicans won all three critical races, allowing the party to reclaim control of the Senate by a slim 51–49 lead.

The Texas Race The 2002 Texas Senate race, between Republican John Cornyn and Democrat Ron Kirk, was for an open seat vacated by Republican senator Gramm. Beginning early in the campaign, both candidates used the Pickering and Owen nomination fights that were brewing in the Senate to mobilize their respective party bases. And the judicial selection issue would continue to play a significant role throughout the campaign.

Pursuant to the Republican Party's global strategy, immediately after the Democrat-led Judiciary Committee defeated nominee Pickering for a seat on the Fifth Circuit, Cornyn stated: "Yesterday's unanimous Democratic committee vote rejecting Judge Charles Pickering is an outrage. By remaining silent, my potential Democratic opponents are effectively endorsing a litmus test that eliminates qualified nominees unless they are liberal activists."[11] But Kirk, then only one of two Democratic candidates vying in a primary to challenge Cornyn, did not remain silent for long. Although not directly stating how he would have voted on the Pickering nomination, Kirk did send out a fund-raising letter criticizing Republican attempts to "pack the courts with conservative jurists who oppose Democratic rights and principles, including a woman's right to choose" (Robison, 2002). This was generally assumed to be an attack on both Pickering and Owen. On March 28, 2002, at a fund-raiser for Cornyn, President G. W. Bush also made mention of the Pickering nomination, saying, "We need people like John Cornyn in the United States Senate, who will work with the White House to have a solid judiciary, to make sure that the judges do what they're supposed to do in the United States and not overstep their bounds" (Bumiller, 2002).

With the Senate Judiciary Committee still considering the Owen nomination, Cornyn spoke at a rally in her support at Southern Methodist University in Dallas on May 9, 2002:

Nothing gives me more pride . . . as a Texan, as a colleague, as one who believes in the rule of law and the role of the courts . . . than to be able to stand here to-day in support of the nomination of Priscilla Owen to the Fifth Circuit Court of Appeals . . . Simply put, Priscilla Owen is an outstanding jurist, one who knows that the role of a judge is to interpret the law, not make law. There is no good reason why, a full year after she was nominated, this eminently qualified woman should not be sitting on the federal bench . . . It is time that the politicians stop playing politics with our judicial system. Justice Owen deserves better. The American people must demand better . . . Help is on the way.[12]

With respect to the Owen nomination, Kirk was in a difficult position. To declare his support for the nominee would surely alienate Democratic activists who were then busy raising money and rallying support for Kirk around the country and in Texas, but who also vehemently opposed the Owen nomination. Indeed, in July 2002, a coalition of civil rights, women's rights, labor, reproductive rights, and consumer organizations announced a plan to actively oppose Owen's confirmation, including traveling to Washington to educate the media and the Judiciary Committee about Owen's record.[13]

On the other hand, for Kirk to declare opposition to Owen—a fellow Texan—would surely alienate swing votes in Texas. Accordingly, Kirk tried to play both sides of the fence. In June 2002, he sent a letter to Republican and Democratic leaders, asking that they "move expeditiously to provide hearings for qualified judicial nominees" (quoted in Robison, 2002). He also declared support for another G. W. Bush nominee, David Godbey, nominated by the president for a district court judgeship in Dallas. Kirk called him a "common sense jurist" who will "fairly interpret the law" (quoted in Robison, 2002). But since Kirk had previously declared his opposition to pro-life judicial candidates, the Republican leadership was not about to let him off the hook that easily. As long as Democrats on the Judiciary Committee continued to stall the Owen nomination, Republican leaders would continue to exploit Owen to Kirk's disadvantage.

On July 20, 2002, Vice President Richard B. Cheney, during a fund-raising luncheon for Cornyn, stated: "just this week, Ron Kirk said that if he were elected to the U.S. Senate, and I quote, 'There will be many times, probably more times than not, that I will be supporting the president.' Yet, the first opportunity he has to forecast how he will work with the president, he came out against the president's first rate nominee [Owen]"(quoted in Williams, 2002). By this time, Cornyn and Republicans packaged the issue as one of supporting or opposing President G. W. Bush. Republicans were so sure that this issue would play well with the conservative base of the Republican Party in Texas that they went so far as to run television advertisements during the election accusing Kirk of opposing G. W. Bush's lower court judicial nominees because he had been captured by northeastern liberals; this attack was intended to tie Kirk to Senator Hillary R. Clinton (D-NY), who had done fund-raising for the Kirk campaign.

The television advertisement was paid for by a newly formed conservative judicial umbrella group known as the Committee for Justice, headed by C. Boyden Gray, former White House counsel to G. H. W. Bush. A whistled tune in the background suggests an Old West theme and high-noon shootout. A voice says, "A new gang's riding into Texas, gunning for our judge." The ad then accuses Senate Democrats of joining with liberal special interests to block Owen's confirmation to the Fifth Circuit Court of Appeals, and the voice says: "Now they're being helped by one of Texas's own. At first, Ron Kirk said the Senate needed to confirm judicial nominees. Then he met the East Coast Liberal Gang . . . took their money, and changed his mind." The "East Coast Liberal Gang" presumably included Hillary Clinton.

On September 5, 2002, the Judiciary Committee finally voted on the Owen nomination. Like Pickering, she was defeated 10–9, with votes cast along party lines. Sensing that this vote would directly affect Kirk's chances of being elected, Judiciary Committee Chairman Leahy issued a statement declaring Owen's record as "too extreme even for the very conservative Texas Supreme Court" and noting that even Cornyn, a former Texas State Supreme Court justice, once "lectured" Owen about adhering to Texas precedents (quoted in Martin, 2002). Cornyn denounced Leahy's attempt to undermine his support of Owen as "a pathetic attempt by Senate Democrats to try to take political heat off Ron Kirk and themselves" (quoted in Martin, 2002). A White House spokesperson predicted that the Owen vote was the turning point in the Texas Senate race, saying, "Ron Kirk just lost the election" (quoted in Martin, 2002) And the chairman of the Republican Party of Texas stated, "While Texans of both parties were advocating on behalf of Justice Owen, Democratic Senate nominee Ron Kirk refused to lift a finger" (quoted in Mason, 2002). Cornyn went on to defeat Kirk by a margin of 54 percent to 46 percent. And once he took office, the Republican leadership put him on the Judiciary Committee.

The Georgia Race The Georgia Senate race in 2002 was between Republican challenger C. Saxby Chambliss and Democratic incumbent Max Cleland. Notwithstanding the fact that Cleland did not sit on the Judiciary Committee and thus never had the opportunity to vote on either the Pickering or Owen nomination (since they never got floor votes), the Republican leadership attacked him because he remained silent while fellow Democratic Georgia senator Zell Miller went on record saying that he would have voted to confirm Pickering and Owen had the Democratic leadership sent the nomination to the floor. At a fund-raiser for Chambliss's Senate bid, President G. W. Bush said, "I put up a good man from Mississippi the other day [for a seat on the Fifth Circuit], and I don't remember the senior senator from Georgia [Cleland] defending this man's honor" (quoted in Bumiller, 2002).

Conservative Georgia elites were so outraged with the state of affairs on the Judiciary Committee after the Owen defeat that some saw the Georgia election as a referendum on the work of the Judiciary Committee: "The Georgia race for the U. S. Senate, pitting U.S. Rep. Saxby Chambliss against incumbent Max Cleland, is not really about Cleland. At issue is whether the [Democratic] ideologues of the Senate Judiciary Committee will continue to rain terror on judicial nominees who fail their litmus tests" (Wooten, 2002). Liberals believed Miller's support of Pickering and Owen to be the downfall of the Cleland campaign: "So far, the chief victim of Miller's actions has been his Senate colleague, Max Cleland. Miller's right-wing [views] made Democrat Cleland appear radical in his fall campaign, even though Cleland embraced many of President Bush's initiatives and stood firmly in the center of the political landscape" (Griffis, 2002).

Chambliss went on to defeat Cleland by a margin of 53 percent to 46 percent. And like Cornyn of Texas, Chambliss was rewarded with a seat on the Judiciary Committee in the 108th Congress.

The Tennessee Race   Lamar Alexander used the Pickering nomination not against a Democratic challenger for Tennessee's open seat, but rather against a conservative Republican challenger for the party's Senate nomination. After declaring his candidacy for the Senate in March 2002, Alexander's Republican opponent, Edward G. Bryant, questioned Alexander's conservative credentials, and this theme was picked up by some conservative radio talk show hosts in Tennessee (Humphrey, 2002). According to one such host, Alexander was surrounding himself with the "income tax crowd"—that is, Tennessee Republicans who support a state income tax (Humphrey, 2002).

Alexander's response to these attacks was to air radio ads on the same conservative talk shows in which, among other things, he stated: "President Bush was right about Judge Pickering. And he's right about fixing schools, cutting taxes and creating jobs. I'm running for the Senate to support him, and to represent Tennesseans with conservative principles and an independent attitude" (quoted in Humphrey, 2002).

After winning the Republican primary, Alexander continued to make the Pickering and Owen confirmation votes by the Judiciary Committee a campaign issue against his Democratic challenger, Robert N. Clement. In a speech to district attorneys in Tennessee, Alexander proclaimed: "The liberal crowd that runs the Senate will not confirm President Bush's nomination of law-and-order judges who will enforce the law instead of making it up as they go along . . . She [Owen] was doing her job, upholding the law, and because liberals don't like that, they wanted to stop her from becoming a federal judge. That's just wrong" (quoted in Humphrey, 2002). Then at a $1,000-a-plate fund-raising event on Alexander's behalf in September 2002, President G. W. Bush—just as he had done in Texas and Georgia—urged critical Republican voters to support Alexander:

> I appreciate the fact that I'll be able to work with Lamar on making sure the good people who I nominate to our federal benches will not only get a fair hearing, but a speedy hearing, and will get approved. The country got to see what happens when the Senate gets so politicized that they won't give people a fair hearing when it comes to judicial nominees.
>
> I named a fabulous woman out of Texas, named Priscilla Owen to the 5th Court. And they distorted her record. She had the highest ranking from the ABA, and yet having listened to the rhetoric coming out of a highly politicized and polarized committee, you never would have realized how qualified she is. She was turned down for purely political purposes. For the sake of a federal judiciary that is strong and solid, we need United States senators like Lamar Alexander who will be fair and reasonable and realistic, and will not play politics with the President's judicial nominees.[14]

Faced with the same dilemma that Kirk faced in Tennessee—not wanting to criticize the committee vote for fear of alienating Democratic activists, but at the same time, not wanting to appear aligned with liberal interest groups—Clement followed the same script as Kirk. First, he pledged his support for another Bush nominee to a district court in Knoxville, Tennessee. Second, he criticized the Judiciary Committee for not filling vacant positions fast enough (Humphrey, 2002). But Clement met the same fate as Kirk; he lost to Alexander by a margin of 55 percent to 44 percent.

THE MISSISSIPPI GUBERNATORIAL CAMPAIGN

For the first time in the modern political era, a contentious Senate battle over a court of appeals nomination played a significant role in a *gubernatorial* campaign. That election pitted one of the Republican Party's favorite sons, former Republican Party chairman Haley Barbour, against incumbent Democrat Ronnie Musgrove. At the center of this election controversy was, yet again, the Pickering nomination. This time, however, the campaign rhetoric surrounded not the action of the Democrats on the Senate Judiciary Committee, but rather, all Democrats in the Senate.

Having failed to gain approval from the Judiciary Committee in the 107th Congress, the Pickering nomination died at the end of the congressional session. However, armed with a new Republican majority in the 108th Congress—a majority gained in three critical Senate campaigns in which the Pickering nomination was a topic of much political debate— President G. W. Bush renominated Pickering for the same vacant judgeship. This time around, Pickering cleared the Judiciary Committee with a 10-9 vote recommending his confirmation, with the vote going along party lines (Dewar, 2003). Accordingly, Pickering's nomination would make it to the Senate floor for the first time. But before this initial hurdle had even been cleared, Democrats vowed to block this nomination (Pettus, 2003). Lacking the necessary fifty-one votes to defeat Pickering in a roll-call vote, Democrats planned to mount a filibuster against Pickering—a tactic they had already used against three other court of appeals nominations by G. W. Bush— Estrada (D.C. Circuit), Owen (Fifth Circuit), and Pryor (Eleventh Circuit). Accordingly, just by virtue of the fact that Pickering hails from Mississippi, the Pickering nomination would become a campaign issue in the Mississippi gubernatorial race.

At a fund-raising event for Barbour on September 12, 2003, the president called on Senate Democrats to allow Pickering's nomination to proceed to a roll-call vote: "He's [Pickering's] a man who will interpret the law, not legislate from the bench. Some senators are playing politics with America's justice. They did this man and this country a disservice" (quoted in Pettus, 2003). Having witnessed the damage that this campaign issue caused three Democrats in the South running for the Senate in 2002, Musgrove tried to level the playing field by coming to Pickering's defense. In a letter sent to Senate Democratic leader Thomas Daschle on March 24, 2003, Musgrove, along with four other Democrats seeking statewide office in Mississippi, expressed their support for Pickering and dismissed charges by Senate Democrats that he was a racist: "Charles Pickering was, before rising to the federal bench, an active Republican. It is our hope that party labels can be transcended in this fight over his nomination. We should cast a blind eye to partisanship when working to build a fair and impartial judiciary." The letter further stated that "Mississippi has made tremendous progress in race relations since the 1960s and Charles Pickering has been part of that progress. We ask the United States Senate to stand up to those that malign the character of Charles Pickering, and give him an up or down vote on the Senate floor" (quoted in Pettus, 2003).

Notwithstanding the fact that the Republican majority knew it lacked the sixty votes needed to end the filibuster (Kane, 2003)—indeed, it had failed to end the filibusters against Estrada, Owen, and Pryor on numerous occasions—the Republican leadership decided to hold a floor vote on a cloture motion on the Pickering nomination on October 30, 2003, just five days before the Mississippi gubernatorial election. The timing of this vote was no accident. As former Senate Majority Leader Lott (R-MS) acknowledged, the Mississippi race was "tight" and he believed the Pickering filibuster vote "could be the difference" to put Barbour over the top (Kane, 2003). Another conservative strategist concurred with this assessment, saying that the Pickering vote "is a big deal in the Mississippi gubernatorial race" (quoted in Kane, 2003). Again wanting to neutralize the issue for Musgrove, Democrats in Mississippi took out print ads touting Musgrove's support of Pickering.

As expected, Republicans failed to muster the nine Democratic votes it needed to end the Democrats' filibuster (Holland, 2003a); only three senators from the other side of the aisle wound up voting for Pickering (Miller [D-GA], Jeffords [I-VT], and John Breaux [D-LA]). So as not to alienate southern Democrats, two Senate Democrats running for president missed the vote (Edwards [D-NC] and John Kerry [D-MA]). After the vote, the ranking Democratic member of the Judiciary Committee, Leahy (D-VT), expressed outrage that Republicans were timing this vote to aid Barbour in his gubernatorial campaign: "I would hope that we're not using the U.S. Senate to get involved in a gubernatorial election in Mississippi" (quoted in Holland, 2003b). Lott believed that the Democrats' filibuster would ultimately hurt Democrats: "I'm sure it's [the Pickering vote] going to contribute some anger toward Democrats who blocked a good and decent man" (quoted in Holland, 2003c).

The gubernatorial candidates themselves also spoke out on the vote. Barbour immediately tried to tie Musgrove to liberal Democrats who are out of touch with southern values: "liberal national Democrats have made it clear of their position that if you are pro-life, conservative, Southern and Christian, then you are not qualified or trusted to serve our country" (quoted in Harrist, 2003). Despite Musgrove's public support for Pickering, Barbour won the election.

The Democratic Party's Use of the Lower Federal Courts in Political Campaigns

PRESIDENTIAL CAMPAIGNS

As we saw in Chapter 3, Democratic presidents, unlike Republicans, have been much more reluctant about representing to the party's base that they use ideological litmus tests in making judicial selections for the lower federal courts. Instead, they tend to stress their commitment to diversify the federal bench (see Chapter 4). Nonetheless, all Democratic presidential candidates since 1980 have promised to appoint only pro-choice justices to the Supreme

Court. In fact, abortion and the Supreme Court became a hot campaign topic in the 1992 presidential race during which the Court handed down its decision in *Planned Parenthood v. Casey*, which many feminists believed to be an anti–abortion rights decision. Fearing that he would lose women's votes, G. H. W. Bush shied away from the abortion issue in that campaign, while Clinton made it a central campaign promise to appoint only Supreme Court justices who would protect a woman's right to choose abortion (Ayres, 1992). And, when Democratic presidential candidates Clinton (in 1992) and Kerry (in 2004) attempted to soften this position, they were immediately called to task by liberal activists (Egelko, 2004).

The 1986 Washington Senate Race

As discussed in Chapter 5, one of the most controversial and toughest confirmation fights of Reagan's presidency involved Seventh Circuit nominee Daniel Manion. To avoid another embarrassing defeat of one of his judicial nominees—an Alabama district court nominee, Jefferson B. Sessions, had just been defeated—Reagan was willing to engage in a log-roll that would lock up the necessary votes needed to confirm Manion. In exchange for the vote of moderate Republican Gorton of Washington—who had been opposed to Manion's confirmation before the trade—Reagan agreed to move along the nomination of a moderate lawyer Gorton had handpicked for a Washington State district court seat—a candidate previously rejected by the White House because he had once represented a man suing a conservative Republican for libel in a high-profile case in Washington State (Gailey, 1986; Turner, 1986). Accordingly, when the first of two roll-call votes on Manion was taken on June 26, 1986, Gorton cast his vote with Reagan; he did so again when the second vote was taken on July 24, 1986.[15] With Gorton's support, the second vote on Manion's nomination was 50–49, with Vice President G. H. W. Bush breaking a tie. But what Gorton probably did not anticipate was that this political horse-trade would ultimately become one of the major campaign issues of his 1986 bid for reelection to the Senate.

Immediately after the Manion vote, nearly every newspaper in the state of Washington denounced Gorton, nicknaming him "Slippery Slade" (Apple, 1986). His opponent in the Senate race, Brock Adams, now believed he had stumbled on a winning issue, and his campaign team decided to make Gorton's change of vote on Manion a major theme of the campaign. Among other things, Adams accused Gorton of "selling out on his principles" by voting for Manion (quoted in Turner, 1986). Later, he would say that "Gorton sold the nation short when he traded politics for principle and delivered

Manion to the federal bench" (quoted in Schwartz, 1988). Further compounding Gorton's campaign problems, many conservatives in Washington State suggested that they would not vote for Gorton in the November election because he was backing a liberal, William Dwyer, for the federal bench: "Dwyer is a left-wing liberal and a Democrat, and why would a Republican Senator want to nominate a man like that?" asked (Ashley Holden, director of the Washington Conservative Council, quoted in Turner, 1986).

Only one year before the Manion vote, Gorton looked unbeatable to the Democratic Party. In a poll conducted in July 1985, Adams, a former congressman and secretary of transportation during the Carter administration, trailed Gorton by 22 percentage points (King and Weaver, 1986). Nonetheless, Adams volunteered to be his party's challenger to the formidable Gorton in 1986. Not surprisingly, trailing his opponent by such a huge margin, Adams also found it difficult to raise money, while Gorton was considered a rising star of the Republican Party; Gorton thus enjoyed a sizable lead in fund-raising as well (Apple, 1986). After the Manion trade, however, everything changed. By August 1986, Gorton led Adams by only 42 percent to 38 percent, with 20 percent undecided (Apple, 1986). By October, pollsters were saying that turnout would be the key to winning the race, and since Gorton had alienated conservatives as well as liberals in Washington State with the Manion deal, high turnout for Gorton was unlikely. Adams went on to win the election 51 percent to 49 percent, which some political analysts believed to be "in considerable part" due to the Manion vote (Lewis, 1986). Ironically, Gorton would be elected to Washington's other Senate seat in 1988, and while serving in the Senate for the second time, he would engage in another high-profile log-roll with President Clinton to secure the nomination of his preferred candidate for the Ninth Court of Appeals (see Chapter 6).

The 2000 Missouri Senate Race

As discussed in Chapter 4, on October 7, 1999, the Senate rejected the nomination of Ronnie White, the first black to serve on the Missouri Supreme Court, for a judgeship on the U.S. District Court for the Eastern District of Missouri. Although days before the roll-call vote it had looked as if White would be confirmed—after being reported favorably out of the Judiciary Committee not once but twice, and receiving the backing of Republican Missouri senator Bond—several key Republican senators, including Bond and Judiciary Chairman Hatch, switched their votes at the behest of the other Republican Missouri senator, Ashcroft. Ultimately, the vote on the White nomination went along party lines, and he was defeated 54–45. Critically, Ashcroft could have killed the nomination simply by not returning his blue slip, as the home state senator for the White nomination. But instead, he chose to take the issue to the floor where his opposition to White would gain more publicity, as no judicial nomination had been defeated on the floor since the nomination of Bork to the Supreme Court in 1987.

At the time of the vote, Ashcroft no doubt believed that engaging in a high-profile floor debate against an allegedly "pro–death penalty" judicial nominee would send an important signal to conservative activists—constituents whom Ashcroft desperately needed to mobilize as he was then engaged in a hotly contested reelection race with Democratic Missouri governor Mel Carnahan (see Chapter 4). But what Ashcroft and fellow Senate Republicans did not foresee was the role their actions would ultimately play in causing Ashcroft's defeat in the 2000 senatorial election. In short, Ashcroft and his colleagues did not anticipate the impact their public actions would have in mobilizing Missouri's black activists against Ashcroft, which led to a record number of black voters turning out for Carnahan.

Governor Carnahan called Ashcroft's actions "a desperate effort to save his own political career" and "character assassination at its worst" (Shesgreen, 1999a). Senate Minority Leader Daschle (D-SD) echoed Carnahan's sentiments, calling it "a dark day" in the Senate:

> The [Ronnie White] vote tells minority judicial candidates, "do not apply" . . . I'm not calling them [the Republicans] racist, but . . . it raises some very serious questions about the perception, the attitude of some on the other side when it comes to minorities. There is very little sensitivity, whether it's Ronnie White, Judge Paez . . . Carol Moseley Braun. You can go on down the list. I think there's a pattern here, and I think we ought to be given some explanation for why this pattern has become so apparent and so dangerously ill-considered. (Quoted in Abrams, 1999)[16]

Devastated by White's defeat, and spurred on by Democratic Party leaders—who were quick to characterize the Republicans' actions as racist (see Chapter 4)—black civil rights activists immediately went into action against Ashcroft. At a news conference on October 7, 1999, James Morgan, president of the St. Louis branch of the NAACP, warned that Senator Ashcroft's actions would be redressed at the polls the following November: "It's too late to affect the nomination of Judge White, but it's not too late to affect the election of Senator Ashcroft" (quoted in Shesgreen, 1999a). Morgan also indicated that the White vote was on the agenda of the Missouri NAACP conference scheduled to take place the following weekend (Shesgreen, 1999a). And on October 9, black political and religious leaders in St. Louis gathered on the steps of the Old Courthouse to rally against the White vote (Shesgreen, 1999b).

The Black Leadership Forum, a Washington-based coalition of three dozen civil rights organizations, planned an emergency meeting for October 7—the same day as the floor vote—to discuss a strategy of response. The executive director of the forum made it clear that she considered the Republicans' actions to be racially motivated, despite protestations from some Republican senators that they did not know of Justice White's race before casting their vote: "What happened was a racist vote on a black nominee. I cannot believe the nonsense about the detractors of Justice White saying that they did not know that he was black" (Yvonne Scruggs-Leftwich, quoted in Shesgreen, 1999b).

On October 9, black religious leaders jumped into the fray.[17] At the Forty-fourth annual NAACP Fight for Freedom Fund Dinner in Ohio, the Rev. Joseph E. Lowery—who founded the Southern Christian Leadership Conference in 1957 with the Rev. Dr. Martin Luther King Jr.—characterized the treatment of Justice White as "judicial lynching" and said that White "has been made a scapegoat for Republican political chicanery" (quoted in McCain, 1999).

Black clergy in Missouri felt particularly betrayed by Senator Bond's vote. In an unusual move, some black religious leaders had pledged support for Republican candidate Bond in his successful 1998 senatorial election against Democrat Jay W. Nixon; Bond went on to garner an unusually high 33 percent of the African American vote in that election (Kraske, 1999). But such support came only after Bond met with, and promised, leading black clergy from the state that he would support the White nomination (Goldstein, 1999). After Bond switched his vote, these black religious leaders condemned Senator Bond as well as Ashcroft.

The Reverend W. Bartalette Finney Sr., a presiding elder of the African Methodist Episcopal Church in western Missouri, stated that Bond is "dead in the African American community" (quoted in Goldstein, 1999). Former Kansas City mayor Emanuel Cleaver, who then became minister of the St. James United Methodist Church in Kansas City, convened a meeting of black clergy that week to develop an "action plan" designed to redress the White episode (Goldstein, 1999). About this meeting, Rev. Finney said: "We're clergy persons. We've had prayer about this. We've turned it over to God. But we're going to be a God squad. That means anybody we can tell about this awful, terrible experience we're going to do it. Do not trust Christopher Bond on any issue" (quoted in Goldstein, 1999). Black clergy from St. Louis expressed similar sentiments. At the October 9 rally at the courthouse in St. Louis, event organizer Reverend B. T. Rice, president of the St. Louis Clergy Coalition, said, "Senator Bond's words are not his bond" (quoted in Shesgreen, 1999b). Consequently, Bond garnered only fifteen percent of the African American vote in his 2004 reelection bid (Jonsson, 2004).

Having spent the first week after White's defeat expressing their outrage at Senators Ashcroft and Bond, black leaders in Missouri then turned their attention to taking positive steps against Ashcroft in his bid for reelection. At a meeting of thirty black political and religious leaders in Kansas City on October 15, black officials promised to mount a vigorous challenge to Senator Ashcroft in the senatorial election of 2000 (Kraske, 1999). As former Kansas City mayor and now clergyman Emanuel Cleaver said: "Do not get angry. Do not get even. Get active" (quoted in Kraske, 1999). At the October 15 meeting, the African American officials decided to fax protest letters to the four Republican senators from Missouri and Kansas who opposed White. They also decided to mount voter-registration and get-out-the-vote drives against Ashcroft, the only one of these four senators up for reelection in 2000. This prompted one Washington commentator to note that "Senate Republicans may have done more for the cause of black voter registration and turnout in next year's Senate races in Missouri and other key states than anything Democrats might have done for themselves" (King, 1999). Echoing these thoughts, Kelvin Simmons, a Kansas City councilman attending the conference, said: "Thank you, Mr. Ashcroft. You just energized a sleeping giant" (quoted in Ayres, 1999).

Mobilization efforts, however, were not limited to the state of Missouri. Black lawyers and law students in Washington, D.C., also organized a protest on October 22, 1999, over the White nomination; black political elites at this event again called for African American voters in Missouri to unseat Senator Ashcroft in the 2000 election (Shesgreen, 1999c). Donald Temple, one of the rally's organizers, also stated that he and other Washington lawyers had started making fund-raising calls for a get-out-the-vote effort in Missouri against Ashcroft; to that end, the Washington lawyer group raised in just one week five thousand dollars to fund this mobilization effort and hoped to raise several hundred thousand dollars before the 2000 elections (Shesgreen, 1999c).

Now sensing that the White vote could mean important electoral gains for blacks at the polls in the 2000 election, black Democratic Party leaders stepped up their mobilization efforts by attacking Ashcroft and the Republican-led Senate as racists. At the October 22 Washington rally, the Congressional Black Caucus called for President Clinton to appoint more blacks to the federal bench, including the seat for which White had been nominated, through his power to make recess appointments (Shesgreen, 1999c).[18] Two days later, House members William Clay of St. Louis (D-MO) and

Maxine Waters (D-CA) publicly labeled Ashcroft a racist (Kraske, 1999).[19] And as Gore's presidential campaign advisors recognized that high black turnout in the 2000 election would be crucial for Gore, the vice president held a private conference call with more than one hundred prominent African Americans to voice his opposition to the Senate's actions over the White nomination, as well as the troubled nomination of former senator Carol Moseley Braun as ambassador to New Zealand (Novak, 1999).

By year's end, the Republican Party began to acknowledge that Ashcroft's and Bond's actions may have permanently damaged Republican Party efforts to court the black vote in the 2000 elections (Shesgreen, 1999d). As one anonymous Republican activist lamented: "Kit Bond made tremendous inroads in the African American community in the last election. There were a lot of [black leaders] who . . . went out on a limb for him and feel they were lied to. This was the first time they took a chance on a Republican and they got kicked in the teeth . . . [Bond] has set the Republicans back" (quoted in Shesgreen, 1999d). A prominent black Republican, James Buford, head of the Urban League, agreed: "This will have a rippling effect on all Republican candidates running in the near future. It's a major blow and it really pretty much solidifies the African American vote against Republicans" (quoted in Shesgreen, 1999d).

It would appear that Republicans, especially in Missouri, had a lot to fear, as black activists in Missouri followed through on their promises made in October 1999; by the beginning of 2000, a formidable statewide organization had been put in place to mobilize black voters against Ashcroft (Sherman, 2000). Political strategists acknowledged that a high black turnout in the Missouri election would likely spell defeat for him (Dine, Lambrecht, and Samuel, 2000). Moreover, President Clinton, enjoying unusually high approval ratings among black Americans, as high as 87 percent in some polls (Sherman, 2000), in the last year of his presidency, would not let the White issue die. At a speech made on April 30, 2000, at the NAACP Fight for Freedom Fund Dinner, Clinton again reminded African American leaders that he and the Democratic Party were actively trying to appoint and confirm minority judges, only to be stonewalled by a Republican-led Senate intent on keeping these nominees off the federal bench (U.S. Newswire, 2000). Several months later, at the annual convention of the NAACP, Clinton again reminded black political elites that Republican senators were biased against blacks and other minority judicial candidates (Houston Chronicle News Service, 2000).[20]

Black mobilization efforts against Ashcroft continued into the waning days of the 2000 election. On September 14, 2000, the president of the St. Louis chapter of the NAACP proclaimed that "we have signed up 1,000 voters since Labor Day in St. Louis alone" (Brogan, 2000). The Rev. Jesse Jackson also joined in the fight, leading a voter-registration rally in downtown St. Louis in September (Brogan, 2000). In October, opponents of Ashcroft circulated thousands of fliers accusing the senator of "racial insensitivity," as evidenced, in part, by his actions aimed at defeating the White judicial nomination (Mannies, 2000). The fliers' distributors—including the Association of Community Organizations for Reform Now, Pro-Vote, and the Coalition of Black Trade Unionists—also vowed to continue their efforts right up to Election Day.

Ultimately, black turnout was high, as anticipated, in the 2000 Missouri election, and Ashcroft was defeated, though under highly extraordinary circumstances. Only ten days before the election, Democratic challenger Carnahan was killed in a plane crash. It being too late to remove his name from the ballot, the election proceeded, with Carnahan's widow promising to assume her husband's seat should he win. Accordingly, it is difficult to assess whether black mobilization efforts prompted by the White judicial nomination ultimately caused Ashcroft's defeat, but certainly it played an important role in mobilizing black voters throughout Missouri.

Conclusion

Challengers for public office also use the lower federal court appointment process as an elite mobilization strategy. Like sitting presidents, presidential challengers take stands on broad normative nomination strategies they would use if elected; like sitting senators, senatorial challengers take public positions on controversial confirmation proceedings. Both types of stands serve as important cues to signal their party's respective activists that once in office they will ensure that the "right" kind of judges will get nominated or confirmed for the federal bench.

CHAPTER 8

The Impact of Divided Government
on the Lower Court Appointment Process

ONE OF THE HALLMARKS of modern-day party politics is the predominance of divided government—where one party controls the White House and the other the U.S. Congress—at the national level. Consider that when Nixon took office in 1969, he was the first president elected in the 20th century whose party did not also control at least one of the two houses of Congress. In contrast, between 1968 and 2004, there has been some form of divided government twenty-six of thirty-six years.[1] Except for President Carter, every president during this period has had to contend with an opposition Senate for at least part of his tenure in office.

Common sense suggests that a regime of divided government could have a potentially significant impact on the way the judicial appointment process operates, given the Senate's "advice and consent" authority over the president's judicial nominations. Indeed, many judicial scholars place the blame for the "confirmation mess" that developed in the latter part of the 20th century on the existence of divided government (Bell, 2002b; Carter, 1994; Maltese, 2003). Could divided government, then, be the root cause of increased politicization of the lower federal court appointment process in the modern political era? In order to be confident in the bedrock theory of this book—that the political stakes for federal court judgeships were raised by the emergence of issue activism among party elites coupled with the activists' beliefs that the lower federal courts engage in critical policy-making—I need to assess just how divided government affects the lower court appointment process.

In this chapter, we will look at the impact of divided government on the two key institutions involved in the judicial appointment process: the Executive Branch and the Senate. If the key actors involved in judicial appointment politics adopt elite mobilization strategies during divided government and cease using such strategies during unified government, this would lend support to the notion that the predominance of divided government in the modern political era has caused the judicial appointment process to break down. If, however, elite mobilization strategies continue in full force regardless of a shift from unified to divided government (or vice versa), then we may reject the alternative theory that divided government is at the heart of increased politicization of the lower court appointment process. As we will see below, empirical studies indicate that the presence or absence of divided government does not affect the use of elite mobilization strategies: Presidents continue to use the same controversial litmus tests to choose nominees and the likelihood that a given nominee will not be confirmed by the Senate remains unchanged. In short, elite mobilization strategies do not go away simply because we are under a regime of unified government.

Divided government does, however, affect one aspect of elite mobilization. Specifically, depending on the type of governing regime, we see senators shifting the tactics that they use to obstruct confirmation of nominees that interest groups aligned with their party have designated as objectionable. What is important to emphasize, however, is that senators continue to engage in this third type of elite mobilization strategy—confirmation obstruction—regardless of the type of ruling regime.

Prior Research on Divided Government

The first thorough examination of the impact of divided government came with David Mayhew's book *Divided We Govern* (1991), in which he challenged the conventional wisdom that divided government results in legislative gridlock. He argued that, to the contrary, during a period of divided government, congressional leaders of the opposite party of the president seize the opportunity to gain national attention—perhaps in contemplation of runs for the presidency—by leading the way to the passage of major legislation. Similarly, Fiorina (1992) found that divided government leads to heightened partisan competition, which in turn leads to greater government activism, neither party wanting to be held responsible by the electorate for failing to pass a popular legislative proposal.

Other scholars have challenged Mayhew's findings. Cameron (2000) found that presidents are more likely to veto legislation when there is a divided government, thus producing legislative impasse. Epstein and O'Halloran (1996) reported that presidents have much less success in getting their policy initiatives passed during a period of divided government. Sundquist

(1992) questioned Mayhew's conclusions because Mayhew failed to consider the delay in the passage of legislation when there is divided government; in other words, while legislation might ultimately pass, passage will take much longer under divided government than under unified government. Finally, Edwards, Barrett, and Peake (1997) found that while simple legislation may regularly pass under divided government, landmark legislation is much less likely to pass under these circumstances.

We now examine what the literature on judicial politics says about the impact of divided government on the behavior of the two key players in judicial appointment politics: the president and the Senate.

PRESIDENTIAL REACTIONS
TO SHIFTS IN RULING REGIME

In theorizing about how the president's appointment strategy might change when his party does not control the Senate, we start with the indisputable fact that a president makes hundreds of lower court appointments in the course of a single term. Accordingly, it is unrealistic to assume that the Senate majority in a divided government has the resources—that is, the time, the money, or the political capital—to successfully challenge the scores of lower court nominations made by the president, and the president is well aware of this fact (Hansen, 1991). Moreover, interest groups concede that they lack the resources to mount confirmation battles against every lower court nominee of an opposition president (see Chapter 5). Interest group leaders also understand that senators are loath to vote "no" to a president's lower court nominees too many times because they do not wish to be labeled as an obstructionist come election time (Gandy, Cavendish, Jipping interviews). Accordingly, it is fair to say that lower court nominations have a presumption favoring confirmation.

Recognizing the limitations on the Senate's willingness and available resources to fight every judicial nominee, former Senate Judiciary Committee Chairman Orrin Hatch has remarked that "there is no substitute for holding, and exercising, the power to *nominate* federal judges."[2] Thus, why should we expect the president to alter his nominating behavior simply by virtue of his party not controlling the Senate? In other words, the president is likely to employ the same ideological litmus test or affirmative action strategy he would use under unified government as he would under divided government knowing that most of his nominees will ultimately get confirmed. This is particularly true when one considers that interest groups aligned with the president will continue to pressure him to appoint lower court judges pursuant to a uniform litmus test. Thus, we should not expect to find any statistically signicant difference in the voting behavior of judges appointed by the same president under a unified government and those appointed under a divided government. And, in fact, prior research confirms just this point (Scherer, 2001).

As detailed in my 2001 article in the *Law and Society Review*, I advance the notion that when party leadership in the Senate shifts during a single presidency, we have a perfect opportunity to test whether the president alters nominating behavior to accommodate this change in legislative power. By comparing the decision-making behavior of the president's judges appointed under unified government versus those appointed under divided government, we can test whether divided government forced the president to appoint more moderate judges. Fortunately, extensive data are available in two such instances: during the Reagan and the Clinton administrations. Using substantially the same voting data on courts of appeals judges to which I have referred throughout this book (see Chapters 2, 3, and 4), I tested whether the ideology of the Republican Senate majority drove Clinton to appoint more conservative federal court judges than he appointed when he served under a unified government during the first two years of his presidency. I also tested whether the Democratic Senate majority that took power in 1987 effected a shift in nominating behavior by Reagan during the last two years of his presidency. Since the issue areas used for this analysis—once again, search and seizure cases, race discrimination cases, and states' rights cases[3]— are those for which issue cleavage between conservative and liberal positions is most pronounced, it is reasonable to conclude that if there is no difference in voting behavior between the unified-divided presidential cohorts in these three issue areas, there is not likely to be any difference in other issue areas. Using the same voting behavior models employed in Chapter 3, I added a control variable for divided government. Consistent with expectations, there was no meaningful difference in the voting behavior between the two Clinton cohorts (judges appointed under divided and unified government) in any of the three issue areas considered. Nor was the Reagan cohort under divided government significantly different from the Reagan cohort under unified government in any of the three issue areas. Thus, we can conclude that presidents use the same judicial selection criteria whether government is unified or divided.

SENATE REACTIONS TO SHIFTS IN REGIMES

Much of the research on Senate judicial confirmation behavior focuses on Supreme Court nominations. Scholars have tested a host of factors that make it more likely for a senator to vote "no" to a Supreme Court nominee. Regarding the effect of ruling on Supreme Court roll-call votes, scholars have found that divided government has a statistically significant impact on the likelihood that a senator will vote against a Supreme Court nominee (Cameron, Cover, and Segal, 1990; Ruckman, 1993). A more recent study, however, concludes that divided government has no impact on whether or not a Supreme Court nominee is ultimately confirmed (Shipan and Shannon, 2003). Another study found that divided government does not affect the level of constitutional questioning of Supreme Court nominees at confirmation hearings (Ogundele and Keith, 1999).

As stated in Chapter 5, however, a presumption of confirmation exists at the lower court level that does not necessarily exist at the Supreme Court level. This is principally a function of the sheer number of lower court nominations a president makes in a term and the resources that interests groups and senators would need to expend to challenge every lower court nomination deemed objectionable. In contrast, because Supreme Court nominations are so rare, resources can be mustered each time a Supreme Court nomination is made and interest groups believe the nominee's ideology to be hostile to their policy objectives. Consider that since *Roe v. Wade*, every Supreme Court nominee believed to oppose that decision has been challenged by pro-choice interest groups, such as Planned Parenthood and NARAL Pro-Choice America. Given the different treatment of lower court nominations versus Supreme Court nominations, it is not surprising that prior research indicates that, all things being equal, a court of appeals nominee is not less likely to be confirmed because of the existence of divided government (Krutz, Fleisher, and Bond, 1998). Similarly, with scores of high-level agency nominees to consider each presidential term, the Senate is not more likely to reject an executive agency nomination under divided government (McCarty and Razaghian, 1999). This makes even more sense when one considers that interest groups continue pressuring senators to block objectionable nominees with equal force regardless of whether government is unified or divided. Accordingly, the literature, and common sense, suggests that confirmation outcomes for lower court nominees do not vary on the basis of ruling regime.

There is, however, one area in which divided government has consistently been found to have a statistically significant impact on Senate confirmation behavior: Research has shown that the length of time to be confirmed increases during periods of divided government (e.g., Bell, 2002a; Binder and Maltzman, 2002; Shipan and Shannon, 2003). Given that divided government was previously shown to have no impact on presidential elite mobilization strategies, this evidence on confirmation delay suggests that we need to further explore the effect of divided government on Senate confirmation behavior. As discussed below, we find that senators are, in fact, forced to shift obstructionist tactics when we move from divided to unified government.

They do not, however, abandon our third elite mobilization strategy altogether. To do so, of course, would seriously jeopardize their standing with key activists needed to mobilize voters on Election Day. Consider what occurred when we moved from divided to unified government in January 2003.

Although Democratic senators had successfully forestalled hearings and roll-call votes on many of G. W. Bush's most controversial nominees under divided government in the 107th Congress (2001–2002)—consistent with the findings of prior studies on divided government and confirmation delay—Democrats lacked the power to delay hearings and votes once the Republicans took control of the Senate in the 108th Congress (2003–2004). But this simply led the Democratic minority to shift tactics, and instead, to filibuster many of the same nominees that they had been holding up in the previous congressional session. Accordingly, even under unified government, the Democrats were able to execute an elite mobilization strategy: denying confirmation to nominees that liberal interest groups had pegged as objectionable. The tactics used to accomplish this goal may have been different, but the results were the same. In fact, given that interest groups prefer votes (even cloture motion votes) over delay so that they can know specifically where each senator stands on a judicial candidate (see Chapter 5), in some sense the filibuster tactic used under unified government may well have served Democratic senators better than the delay tactics used under divided government.

BLUE-SLIP VETOES INCREASE
DURING DIVIDED GOVERNMENT

Besides confirmation delay, there is another obstructionist tactic that senators use less frequently during unified government: the blue slip. As discussed in Chapter 6, the Senate's blue-slip procedure that was first initiated in the 1950s allowed one home state senator to effectively veto a president's lower court nomination. Although this rule accorded home state senators a great power, before the modern political era, blue slips were rarely used to block a lower court nomination. The original rule was amended for the first time in 1980 by Judiciary Committee Chairman Edward Kennedy (D-MA) to facilitate President Carter's efforts to diversify the federal bench. Thus, Kennedy made it more difficult for a senator unilaterally to block a Carter nominee by refusing to kill a nomination on a single blue slip. By amending the blue-slip rule to favor the president in his own party, rather than his fellow senators, Kennedy opened a Pandora's box that future chairs of the Judiciary Committee would feel free to follow.

As shown in Table 8-1, there has been a pattern since 1980 of amending the blue-slip rule upon a change from divided to unified government or vice

TABLE 8-I
Blue-Slip Procedures in the U.S. Senate, 1968–2003

President (Party)	Judiciary Chairman (Party)	Ruling Regime	Blue-Slip Rule★
Nixon/Ford (Republican)	James Eastland (Democrat)	Divided	One negative blue slip *blocks* nomination
Carter (Democrat)	James Eastland (Democrat)	Unified	One negative blue slip *blocks* nomination
Carter (Democrat)	Edward Kennedy (Democrat)	Unified	1978–79, one negative blue slip *blocks* nomination 1979–80, one negative blue slip *does not block* nomination
Reagan (Republican)	Strom Thurmond (Republican)	Unified	One negative blue slip from *Republican* senator *blocks* nomination One negative blue slip from *Democratic* senator *does not block* nomination
Reagan/G. H. W. Bush (Republican)	Joseph Biden (Democrat)	Divided	One negative blue slip *does not block* nomination
Clinton (Democrat)	Joseph Biden (Democrat)	Unified	One negative blue slip *does not block* nomination
Clinton (Democrat)	Orrin Hatch (Republican)	Divided	One negative blue slip *blocks* nomination
G. W. Bush (Republican)	Orrin Hatch (Republican)	Unified	One negative blue slip *does not block* nomination
G. W. Bush (Republican)	Patrick Leahy (Democrat)	Divided	One negative blue slip *does not block* nomination
G. W. Bush (Republican)	Orrin Hatch (Republican)	Unified	Two negative blue slips *do not block* nomination

★Rule allowing one negative blue slip to block nomination favors home state senator; rule not allowing one negative blue slip to block nomination favors president.

versa. Under unified government, the rule tries to rein in the blue-slip practice, thereby aiding the president's nomination strategy and inhibiting the minority party's ability to block those nominations; the rule does not allow a single blue slip to kill a nomination. Under divided government, the rule fosters the blue-slip practice, thereby aiding the majority party in the Senate and inhibiting the president's ability to effect a nomination strategy; this rule accords a single blue slip veto power. The only exception to this pattern is found in the years 1987–92, when Senator Joseph Biden, a Democrat, chaired the Judiciary Committee during the Reagan and G. H. W. Bush presidencies.[4] Simply stated, after 1980, blue-slipping was a much more effective tactic for obstructing confirmation during divided government than it was during unified government because a single senator could hold up a nominee's confirmation. But even under unified government, senators in the opposite party of the president could still veto a lower court nominee provided both home state senators rejected the president's choice for a vacant judgeship.

In the current administration, for the first time, the blue slip is not even available to senators in the opposite party of the president. This is because in the 108th Congress, Chairman Hatch refused to delay hearings and roll-call votes even when both home state senators blue-slipped a lower court nomination. Such was the case in Michigan. Again, the transition to unified government in 2003 highlights that even though blue-slipping may not be an available tactic in a senator's arsenal for blocking confirmation during unified government, senators denied their blue-slip veto will simply shift gears and turn to the filibuster to block these same nominees. As detailed in Chapter 6, there has been an ongoing battle between the White House and Michigan senators over nominations to the Sixth Circuit since 1998. Because a Republican senator blue-slipped two of Clinton's Michigan nominees to the Sixth Circuit (Helene White and Kathleen McCree Lewis), the two current Democratic senators from Michigan have refused to give their consent to all four of G. W. Bush's Sixth Circuit nominees from Michigan (Henry Saad, David McKeague, Richard Griffin, and Susan Nielsen). Three of these nominees (Saad, Griffin, and McKeague) have also been opposed by leading liberal interest groups. During divided government in 2001–2002, Democratic Judiciary Chairman Leahy honored the home state senators' wishes. However, notwithstanding the fact that *both* home state senators refused to consent to these nominations, Chairman Hatch gave all four Michigan nominees hearings and, once approved by the Judiciary Committee along party lines, sent the nominations to the floor for roll-call votes. Michigan senators Stabenow and Levin joined forces with fellow Democrats and filibustered three of the four Michigan nominees (Saad, Griffin, and McKeague). Not surprisingly, these are the same three nominees opposed by liberal activists.

THE USE OF FILIBUSTERS INCREASES
DURING UNIFIED GOVERNMENT

As discussed in Chapter 6, although the filibuster has long been a tactic available to senators to stave off passage of legislation, the filibustering of judicial nominations is a phenomenon that began in the modern political era. Since the filibuster against Abe Fortas in 1968, twenty-five more judicial nominees have been filibustered.[5] Table 8-2 shows all judicial nominations that have been subjected to cloture motions, the governing regime at

TABLE 8-2

Judicial Nominations Subject to Cloture Motions, 1968–2004

Nominee (Court Nominated to)	Nominating President	Ruling Regime	Outcome of Confirmation
Abe Fortas (Supreme Court)	Johnson	Unified	Cloture motion failed; nomination withdrawn
William Rehnquist (Supreme Court, AJ)	Nixon	Divided	Confirmed
Stephen Breyer (First Circuit)	Carter	Unified	Confirmed★
William Rehnquist (Supreme Court, CJ)	Reagan	Unified	Confirmed
J. Harvie Wilkinson (Fourth Circuit)	Reagan	Unified	Confirmed
Daniel Manion (Seventh Circuit)	Reagan	Unified	Confirmed
Sidney Fitzwater (NDTX)	Reagan	Unified	Confirmed
Edward Carnes (Eleventh Circuit)	G. H. W. Bush	Divided	Confirmed
Rosemary Barkett	Clinton	Unified	Confirmed
H. Lee Sarokin	Clinton	Unified	Confirmed
Richard Paez (Ninth Circuit)	Clinton	Divided	Confirmed
Marsha Berzon (Ninth Circuit)	Clinton	Divided	Confirmed
Ted Stewart (D UT)	Clinton	Divided	Confirmed★
Lavenski Smith (Eighth Circuit)	G. W. Bush	Divided	Confirmed★
Richard Clifton (Ninth Circuit)	G. W. Bush	Divided	Confirmed★
Julia Smith Gibbons (Sixth Circuit)	G. W. Bush	Divided	Confirmed★
Miguel Estrada (D.C. Circuit)	G. W. Bush	Unified	Cloture motion failed; nomination withdrawn
Priscilla Owen (Fifth Circuit)	G. W. Bush	Unified	Cloture motion failed; renominated in 109th Congress
William Pryor (Eleventh Circuit)	G. W. Bush	Unified	Cloture motion failed; received recess appointment
Charles Pickering (Fifth Circuit)	G. W. Bush	Unified	Cloture motion failed; received recess appointment
Carolyn Kuhl (Ninth Circuit)	G. W. Bush	Unified	Cloture motion failed; not renominated in 109th Congress
Janice Rogers Brown (D.C. Circuit)	G. W. Bush	Unified	Cloture motion failed; renominated in 109th Congress
David McKeague (Sixth Circuit)	G. W. Bush	Unified	Cloture motion failed; renominated in 109th Congress
Richard Griffin (Sixth Circuit)	G. W. Bush	Unified	Cloture motion failed; renominated in 109th Congress
Henry Saad (Sixth Circuit)	G. W. Bush	Unified	Cloture motion failed; renominated in 109th Congress
William Myers (Ninth Circuit)	G. W. Bush	Unified	Cloture motion failed; renominated in 109th Congress

★Filibuster initiated by a senator in the president's party.

the time of the motion, and the ultimate outcome of the nomination. As the table reveals, of the twenty-six judicial nominations filibustered, eighteen occurred during unified government. Notably, ten of these eighteen filibusters occurred in the 108th Congress during G. W. Bush's presidency. But this is not the first time that Democrats, finding themselves the minority in the Senate, resorted to a concerted effort to use filibusters to block objectionable nominees. They followed this same strategy during the Reagan administration. During the six years of Reagan's administration when unified government prevailed (1981–86), Democrats filibustered four judicial nominations.

That the filibuster is an obstructionist tactic used predominantly during unified government should not be surprising. Consider that if the objecting senators were in the majority party in the Senate, they most likely would not need to resort to this extreme procedural maneuver to obstruct confirmation; rather, they could decline to bring the nomination up for a hearing in the committee, defeat the nomination by a majority vote in committee, decline to bring it up for a floor vote, vote it down on the floor, or have home state senators blue-slip the nominees. When the objecting senators are in the minority, however, as were the Democrats in the 108th Congress (during G. W. Bush's administration) and the 99th Congress (during Reagan's administration), they are powerless to stop the nomination from proceeding to a floor vote and will lose the floor vote on a straight up or down vote (assuming the vote goes along party lines). Filibustering, therefore, is definitely used as a tactic of last resort for the party not in power during unified government.

But why would senators ever mount a filibuster during divided government? Of the eight nominees filibustered during divided government, four (Stewart, Smith, Clifton, and Gibbons) were launched by members of the president's own party for tactical reasons not related to ideology and elite mobilization. In all four cases, members of the president's party were looking to speed up votes on other Executive Branch nominations then put on hold by another senator. Other times, filibusters are launched by members of the Senate majority party when there is a split in that caucus over the suitability of a judicial nominee. Such was the case with the remaining nominees filibustered during divided government (Rehnquist, Carnes, Paez, and Berzon). Under these circumstances, with senators in the minority party all supporting the president's nominee (since this is divided government, the Senate minority and the president share the same party) and joining together with a faction of senators in the majority party, confirmation was assured for these nominees. Those senators in the majority party who objected to the nomination were thus forced to launch filibusters as a last resort to try to stop confirmation.

At least until the 108th Congress, the filibuster was not a very effective strategy in actually keeping a nominee off the bench. Before 2003, only one nominee who was filibustered was not confirmed (Fortas). However, in the 108th Congress, the filibuster was a very effective tactic for the Democrats, denying confirmation to all ten of G. W. Bush's filibustered nominees. The president, however, has seated two of these nominees (Pryor and Pickering) on the bench through recess appointments, although they had not been confirmed for life tenure by the end of the 108th Congress. Another two of these nominees (Estrada and Kuhl) have withdrawn their names from consideration. That Democrats mounted ten filibusters simultaneously to court of appeals nominations suggests an historical change in the norms of the Senate since this once extraordinary tactic became ordinary. If Republicans have their way in the 109th Congress, Senate norms will be further eroded with eradification of the filibuster as an elite mobilization strategy, at least while unified Republican control of government remains.

Conclusion

Divided government has no statistically significant impact on most aspects of the judicial appointment process. It clearly does not undermine the theory of elite mobilization. During divided or unified government, presidents continue to select judges according to the same criteria and the Senate confirms or does not confirm nominations according to the same criteria. The only effect that divided government seems to have on the lower court appointment process is that senators may rely on certain types of obstructionist tactics during the confirmation process more or less depending on the type of ruling regime that exists. Thus, although filibusters become more prevalent during unified government, blue-slip vetoes and delay tactics are used more frequently during divided government. It is an important finding that senators in the minority party will continue to use elite mobilization tactics notwithstanding the fact that they control neither the Executive Branch nor the Senate, for this makes the nomination and confirmation phases of the appointment process equally contentious whether or not government is divided. These findings lend further support to the theory of elite mobilization.

WHY HAS THE LOWER COURT appointment process become so politicized in the modern political era? In this book, I have sought to tackle this thorny question from an entirely new perspective: that of the American party system. Because political parties have largely controlled the lower federal court appointment process at least since the Jacksonian era, I believe it is essential that we focus first and foremost on changes in the party system if we are to fully understand why the appointment process has broken down in recent years. What the research demonstrates herein is that a critical transformation in the traditional mass party system in the 1950s and 1960s is, in fact, the core explanation as to why the judicial appointment process has become so politicized.

I start from the premise that politicians have always been, and continue to be, maximizers of self-interest: They want to be reelected above all else. This means that politicians must cater to political activists who are responsible for mobilizing voters on the politicians' behalf. To ignore the activists' demands is to risk losing the next election. To this end, presidents and senators have learned to exploit lower federal court judgeships as a means of satisfying critical activists' demands for control over the selection of those positions. These fundamental premises were as true in the early 19th century as they are today in the 21st century.

When the mass party system was in place (from the Jacksonian era through the 1960s), political activists—again, those responsible for mobilizing voters on a politician's behalf—were primarily interested in acquiring material benefits in exchange for votes. They helped candidates get elected so that they could control lucrative contracts and jobs. Lower court judgeships thus were used to satisfy the patronage needs of local party and campaign elites. Political activists, working in conjunction with home state senators and the president, bestowed these jobs upon lawyers who had helped the party. Critically, with few exceptions, local political elites cared nothing about a judicial candidate's ideology or policy preferences in putting forth that candidate's name for a lower court judgeship.

With the advent of the modern party system, old-time party political elites fade from the picture. Instead, we see the advent of a new breed of political activist—that is, the issue-oriented activist (affiliated either with a specific candidate, a party, or an interest group). These individuals, in stark contrast to the old-time party elites, are solely interested in achieving policy goals through the election of their preferred candidates; they are not interested in acquiring patronage if it means compromising their policy goals. Thus, in the modern era, using lower court judgeships as patronage no longer makes sense, given that political activists are not interested in acquiring patronage.

But this does not necessarily mean that lower court judgeships would cease being exploited as a means to satisfy the demands of political activists. Indeed, because the federal courts had become much more amenable to adjudicating policy-oriented claims of underprivileged groups in society—at approximately the same time as the mass party system began breaking down—politicians saw an opportunity to continue exploiting their power over nominating and confirming judges in a variety of ways designed to satisfy the policy goals of the new breed of political activist. These various exploitation strategies I term elite mobilization strategies. One aspect of the lower court appointment process remains unchanged. These judgeships continue to have an important connection to the electoral process: They are used to mobilize elites, who then mobilize the masses.

At the beginning of the modern political era, in the 1960s and 1970s, the first two elite mobilization strategies emerge: the president's use of an ideological litmus test in the selection of lower court judges and the president's use of affirmative action in the selection of lower court judges. Although conservative activists associated with Nixon and the Republican Party wanted judges who would cut back on the broad constitutional protections accorded minorities and criminal defendants during the Warren Court era, liberal activists associated with Carter and the Democratic Party wanted progressive judges, as well as more women and minorities, on the federal bench. Both presidents were only too happy to oblige.

During Reagan's second term in office, a third elite mobilization strategy emerged as liberal activists began to press Democratic senators to use whatever procedural tactics were available to stop confirmation of Reagan's most conservative nominees. Senators quickly responded. By the end of the 1980s, not only did the lower court judicial *selection* process become infused with policy considerations, now the *confirmation* process did as well.

Finally, in the 1980s and 1990s, a fourth elite mobilization strategy comes into its own: using lower court confirmation fights on the campaign trail. Now, candidates for office can exploit lower court judgeships even before assuming any real power over the appointment process.

These political strategies have had an impact far beyond Washington, D.C. As a result of these policy-oriented selection and confirmation strategies, decision-making on the federal bench has become extremely polarized by party in the most important cases of the day. In contrast, when patronage concerns largely drove the judicial selection process (before the late 1960s), we see no statistically meaningful difference in the decision-making behavior of courts of appeals judges based on the party of the appointing president. In short, patrons did not affiliate with a party for policy purposes; with few exceptions, they were not selected by the president to sit on the bench to further a policy agenda, nor was their confirmation deemed a policy vote by the Senate. Patrons represented a wide array of regional differences that abounded in the two major parties. In short, the voting behavior of patronage appointees from the same party varies greatly, and thus, we see no statistically significant difference between the two groups.

Beginning with judges appointed by Johnson and Nixon, for the first time in history, we begin to see distinct differences in decision-making behavior of courts of appeals judges based on the party of the appointing president. In conformance with the policy demands of the new breed of political activist, Democrat-appointed judges are significantly more liberal than Republican-appointed judges in key policy areas that get litigated in the federal courts. This is not surprising, given that these judges were chosen specifically because of their support for the policy agenda of political activists affiliated with the president and his party. In short, modern-day judges deliver precisely what the activists are looking for in a judge. And because Democratic appointees will vote alike, and Republican appointees will vote alike—indeed, judicial candidates from each party were all chosen pursuant to the same litmus test—there are statistically significant differences between the two groups.

Not only do we begin to see partisan cleavages in judicial voting behavior during the Johnson/Nixon era, but those cleavages have grown deeper in the past two decades. This is not surprising, given that the policy positions of the two major parties and their activists have become increasingly polarized over time. With every change of party control in the Executive Branch since the Reagan administration, political warfare over courts of appeals judgeships has escalated as key activists become more vocal in their demands for the "right" kind of judges on the bench, and politicians' use of elite mobilization strategies become more frequent and contentious in an effort to accommodate their party's activists.

One may wonder: How do we escape this vicious cycle? Many have suggested that we need to change the institutional rules governing the confirmation process—placing the blame on the Senate. Others take presidents to task—Democrat or Republican—and challenge them to make more moderate choices for the bench in the spirit of bipartisanship. One solution so far not explored—and one that, at first glance, may seem quite radical—is to reexamine whether the lower federal courts are actually capable of effectuating social policy in our political system.

Many scholars of judicial politics question the efficacy of courts to effect social policy (see, for example, Horowitz, 1977; Rosenberg, 1991; Scheingold, 1974). These scholars argue that once activists began turning to the federal courts to achieve social policy, courts began moving away from their traditional function—adjudicating private disputes between two individuals—and taking on a broad range of cases that sought to establish new rights and obtain unconventional forms of relief. Rather than seeing this historic transformation as a positive development, these political scientists argue that the federal courts must tread carefully, as the judiciary risks institutional legitimacy by overstepping its authority (lacking the "purse and the sword"). But one political scientist goes even farther. Gerald N. Rosenberg (1991) believes that the greatest cost of this change in the American judicial system is the fact that the courts confer a "hollow hope" upon interest groups and activists—a false hope that the federal courts, rather than the other branches of government, are key to obtaining their policy goals:

> U.S. courts can *almost never* be effective producers of significant social reform. At best, they can second the social reform acts of the other branches of government. Problems that are unsolvable in the political context can rarely be solved by courts . . . Turning to courts to produce significant social reform substitutes the myth of America for its reality. It credits courts and judicial decisions with a power that they do not have. (Rosenberg, 1991, at 338; emphasis in original)

Interviews with leading activists involved in judicial appointment politics confirm that these beliefs—that the federal courts wield significant power in implementing pubic policy—remain strong today. Thus, given these beliefs, investing in the judicial appointment process makes good sense for certain interest groups. However, if Rosenberg and others who share his skepticism are correct in thinking that the federal courts cannot effect social policy, then expending precious resources on the appointment process is irrational. Were activists to share Rosenberg's way of thinking, they might be less inclined to make demands on politicians about federal court judges. It would follow, then, that absent such demands, the lower court appointment process would not be a pivotal battleground on which partisan disputes are fought. Rather, judges could be chosen on the basis of their qualifications and not their political pedigree.

Explanation and Coding of Variables:
Labor Models

Data and Methods

The units of analysis will be each judge's vote (and not the ultimate holding of the case) rendered on a three-judge or en banc panel of the U.S. Courts of Appeals. The cases included in this study are the entire universe of "nonconsensual" decisions (specifically defined below) rendered by the U.S. Courts of Appeals, including all of the eleven numbered circuits[1] and the District of Columbia Circuit. All decisions in which the plaintiff's underlying claim is one under the Fair Labor Standards Act (FLSA) are included in the analysis.

The relevant time frame is January 1, 1940, through December 31, 1947. Although the FLSA was passed in 1939, cases brought pursuant thereto did not appear with any regularity until 1940. The cases were identified through a series of comprehensive searches on the electronic database WESTLAW and include all decisions officially designated by the court for publication in the *Federal Reporter*.[2] Included in the analysis are the votes of circuit court judges in active service, circuit court judges on senior status, and U.S. District Court judges sitting by designation on the courts of appeals.

The analyses focus specifically on "nonconsensual" decisions rendered by the courts of appeals in the relevant time frame. In order to be considered a nonconsensual decision, one of two conditions must be met: (1) the appellate panel—be it a regular three-judge panel or an en banc panel—rendered a split decision (i.e., there was at least one dissenting vote against the majority ruling), or (2) the appellate panel—in all relevant cases herein, regular three-judge panels—though unanimous in its own decision, reversed or vacated the decision of the district court judge below.[3]

Explanation of Variables

DEPENDENT VARIABLE

The dependent variable is the vote of each individual judge either agreeing or disagreeing with the worker's position (or that asserted by the United States on behalf of workers) asserted on appeal where the underlying claim (though not necessarily the issue asserted on appeal) is that the defendant employer has violated the FLSA.

INDEPENDENT VARIABLES

Fact-Based Variables

The United States as Plaintiff   This variable designates whether the case was initiated by the administrator of the Wage Control Board, a presidential appointee who was permitted under the FLSA to bring cases on behalf of workers. Given that claims brought by the United States are more likely to be meritorious, judges are expected to be more supportive of workers' rights when the case is brought by the federal government.

Background-Based Variables

Appointing Presidential Party Cohort (Model 1 Only)   This group of variables designates to which political party the appointing president belonged. For each individual vote, only one of the following may be designated as the appointing presidential party: (1) Republican Party or (2) FDR–Democratic Party. Judges appointed by Republican presidents are expected to be less supportive of workers' rights than judges appointed by FDR. Table A-1 shows the total number of votes rendered by each presidential party cohort, and the number of judges in each cohort, for the labor data set.

Appointing Presidential Party Cohort (Model 2 Only)   This group of variables designates to which political party the appointing president belonged. For each individual vote, only one of the following may be designated as the appointing presidential party: (1) Republican Party, (2) FDR 1935–40–Democratic Party, or (3) FDR 1933–34, 1941–44–Democratic Party. Judges appointed by Republican presidents are expected to be less supportive of workers' rights than judges appointed by both FDR cohorts, and judges appointed by FDR in the 1935–40 period are expected to be most supportive of workers' rights. Table A-1 shows the total number of votes rendered by each presidential cohort, and the number of judges in each cohort, for this data set.

TABLE A-I
Total Votes Cast in Labor Data Set

	Percentage of Total Votes Cast	Number of Votes Cast	Number of Judges in Cohort
PRESIDENTIAL COHORTS			
Appointing Presidential Party Cohort			
FDR Appointees (Total)	63.74%	283	40
FDR 1935–40 Appointees	38.97%	173	28
FDR 1933–34, 1941–44 Appointees	24.77%	110	12
Republican Appointees	36.26%	161	27
Total	100.00%	444	67
GEOGRAPHIC COHORTS			
Southern Judge	26.1%	116	15
Non-Southern Judge	73.9%	328	52
Total	100.0%	444	67

Southern Judge This variable designates whether or not the judge rendering the decision regularly sits on the Fourth or Fifth Circuits or is a district court judge sitting by designation from a district court located in the Fourth or Fifth Circuits. Southern judges are expected to be more "conservative" than non-southern judges.

Parameter Estimates, Autocorrelation, and Heteroskedasticity Issues

Because ordinary least-squares regression is inappropriate where, as here, the dependent variable is measured dichotomously, the parameters were estimated for the independent variables by logistic regression, a maximum-likelihood estimation technique (Aldrich and Nelson, 1984). The Logit coefficients represent the estimates for the parameters of a model's independent variables in terms of the contribution each makes to the probability that the dependent variable falls into one of the designated categories (pro–criminal defendant/anti–criminal defendant). For each independent variable, a maximum-likelihood estimate (MLE) is calculated along with its standard error (SE). The MLE values divided by the SE values have a Z distribution and thus may be used for tests of significance.

Two other methodological issues are raised by virtue of the fact that each data set contains individual judges casting multiple votes. The first is heteroskedasticity. This potential problem is easily solved by using robust standard errors. Unfortunately, the second issue—autocorrelation—is not so easily solved.

Although one easy solution would be to include a dummy variable for each judge, to do so would result in the loss of a *significant* number of degrees of freedom. Without question, standard diagnostic tests for time series data are inappropriate; if anything, the potential autocorrelation problem more closely resembles spatial autocorrelation than serial autocorrelation. Nor are statistical methods designed to correct autocorrelation for panel data (such as is available on STATA) applicable because many judges in my data set render only one decision.[4] Nevertheless, there are several reasons why I believe autocorrelation does not undermine my results. In short, I must satisfy myself that I am not overestimating the impact of judges who vote multiple times versus judges who vote only one time. Accordingly, I performed several preliminary diagnostic tests to test whether there is even an indication that autocorrelation is a potential problem, and all such tests suggest it is not.

First, I introduced a dummy variable for judges who vote one time and judges who vote multiple times. This is intended to detect whether there is something unique about the voting behavior of judges who cast multiple votes versus those who cast one vote. As expected, there is nothing systematic about judges who vote multiple times compared with those who vote one time. This is not surprising, as cases are assigned to judges randomly. Second, I introduced a dummy variable for judges' first votes versus their other votes. This is intended to detect whether there is something unique about a judge's first vote versus his or her second vote, third vote, etc. Again, there is no statistical difference in a judge's voting behavior upon casting his or her first vote versus later votes. Third, I weighted each observation by the number of total votes per judge. Because this method eliminated two-thirds of my data, those presidential cohort coefficients that were previously significant were now not statistically significant. But all coefficients were qualitatively similar to those of my principal models; they had the same signs compared with my principal models and, with the exception of one coefficient in the race discrimination model, nearly the same magnitude (within the 95 percent confidence interval) as those obtained on the coefficients with no weights.[5] In sum, because none of these preliminary diagnostic tests even *hint* at an autocorrelation problem with my data, I have concluded that more complex methods to correct for spatial autocorrelation (such as constructing a matrix that treats the votes of the same judge as "neighbors," one type of fixed-effect estimator) are not warranted in this case.[6]

Coding of Variables

FACT-BASED VARIABLES

United States as Plaintiff

When the case was commenced by the administrator of the Wage Control Board, the value is 1; otherwise, the value is 0.

BACKGROUND-BASED VARIABLES

Appointing Presidential Party

For each individual vote, only one of the following appointing presidential cohorts may be coded as 1:

1. *Republican.* When an appeals court judge, or a district court judge sitting by designation, was appointed to the federal bench by Presidents Harding, Coolidge, or Hoover, the value is 1; otherwise, the value is 0.
2. *Democrat/FDR.* When an appeals court judge, or a district court judge sitting by designation, was appointed to the federal bench by President Roosevelt, the value is 1; otherwise, the value is 0.

Southern Judge

When a judge sits by permanent assignment on the Fourth or Fifth Circuits, or sits by permanent assignment on a district court in one of these two circuits, the value is 1; otherwise, the value is 0.

Explanation and Coding of Variables:
Search and Seizure Models

Data and Methods

The units of analysis will be each judge's vote (and not the ultimate holding of the case) rendered on a three-judge or en banc panel in all cases meeting certain criteria set forth below. The cases included in this study are the entire universe of "nonconsensual" decisions rendered by the U.S. Courts of Appeals, including all of the eleven numbered circuits and the District of Columbia Circuit. Nonconsensual decisions are defined in Appendix A.

The time frame for the search and seizure cases is January 1, 1994, through December 31, 2001. This time frame was chosen specifically to capture the maximum amount of votes by Clinton appointees, as well as those of the other presidents in the post-1968 period. Decisions by Clinton appointees did not begin to appear with any regularity until 1994.

Included in the analysis are the votes of circuit court judges in active service, circuit court judges on senior status, and U.S. District Court judges sitting by designation on the courts of appeals.

The legal cases from which the data were collected were identified through a series of comprehensive searches on the electronic database WESTLAW. Included in the data set were decisions officially designated by the court for publication in the *Federal Reporter*, as well as decisions not designated by the court for official publication but reprinted in full on the WESTLAW database.

Explanation of Variables

DEPENDENT VARIABLE

The dependent variable is the vote of each individual judge either agreeing or disagreeing with the criminal defendant that, by virtue of the government's violation of his or her Fourth Amendment rights, incriminating evidence of the defendant's guilt must be suppressed.

INDEPENDENT VARIABLES

Fact-Based Variables

Fact-based variables were adapted from the model developed by Segal (1983, 1986). So that the reader can understand fully why particular factual controls were chosen, I will review briefly the general legal principles governing search and seizure cases. The starting point is, of course, the text of the Fourth Amendment, which states: "The right of the people to be secure in their persons, houses, papers, and effects, against unreasonable searches and seizures, shall not be violated, and no Warrants shall issue, but upon probable cause." This "reasonableness" standard raises a presumption that, before the government can rightfully invade a person's privacy interest, a warrant, issued by an impartial magistrate on a showing of probable cause, must be obtained.[1]

The greater the privacy interest—often referred to as an "expectation of privacy"—the more strictly the government will be held to the warrant requirement.[2] The greatest expectation of privacy is in one's home—adhering to the ancient maxim that a man's home is his castle.[3]

Formal arrest of a person also presumptively requires an arrest warrant, though this type of seizure does not command the same heightened protection as when one's home is searched.[4]

Because certain situations make it impossible for the government to obtain a warrant without risking the disappearance of the person or property to be searched, the Supreme Court has carved out certain exceptions to the warrant requirement. Thus, a defendant is accorded less protection from warrantless searches of his or her person, automobile, and luggage (particularly at an airport or border crossing) because of the potential, while the government seeks its warrant, for the accused to flee the scene, for the car to be driven off, for the luggage to be secreted, and for the accused to leave the country.[5] The government is also excused from the warrant requirement when a person consents to a search.[6]

Even when an exception to the warrant requirement applies, the government must first have a sufficient quantum of evidence in its possession before it may conduct a search or seizure; that quantum depends on whether the government conducts a full-blown search or seizure (e.g., an arrest) or a limited search or seizure (e.g., a pat-down frisk). Full-blown searches require a heightened showing that a crime is being committed (probable cause) compared with limited searches (reasonable suspicion).[7]

The fact-based variables included in the search and seizure models are as follows:

Location of the Search   This group of variables designates where the search or seizure took place. For each individual vote (for or against the defendant on the search and seizure issue), only one of the following places may be designated as the place of the search: (1) home, (2) person, (3) automobile, or (4) luggage. Based on well-settled Supreme Court doctrine, defendants whose homes have been searched are expected to receive the highest amount of Fourth Amendment protection (i.e., generating the most pro-defendant voting behavior). Searches of homes will be used as the baseline against which all other places of the searches will be measured.

Presence of a Warrant   This variable designates whether the search or seizure took place after a warrant had been issued. Defendants who have been searched without a warrant are expected to receive the highest amount of Fourth Amendment protection.

Full-Blown Search Against a Defendant   This variable designates whether the search or seizure was of a limited nature or constituted a full-blown search. Defendants subjected to full-blown searches are expected to receive the highest amount of Fourth Amendment protection.

Border Search   This variable designates whether the search and seizure occurred at a point of entry into the United States. Defendants searched at the border are expected to receive the least amount of Fourth Amendment protection.

Background-Based Variables

Appointing President   This groups of variables designates which president appointed the judge rendering a given decision. For each individual vote, only one of the following may be designated as appointing president: (1) Clinton, (2) G. H. W. Bush, (3) Reagan, (4) Carter, or (5) Nixon.[8] I use the Clinton cohort as the baseline by which all other presidential cohorts are measured. Table B-1 shows the total number of votes rendered by each presidential cohort, and the number of judges in each cohort, for this data set.

TABLE B-I
Total Votes Cast in Search and Seizure Data Set

	Percentage of Total Votes Cast	Number of Votes Cast	Number of Judges in Cohort
PRESIDENTIAL COHORT			
Appointing Presidential Cohort			
Clinton	20.6%	303	69
G. H. W. Bush	16.9%	248	56
Reagan	35.5%	521	98
Carter	22.4%	329	68
Nixon	4.6%	68	24
Total	100.0%	1,469	306
RACE/GENDER COHORT			
Black Judges			
Clinton	2.7%	39	8
G. H. W. Bush	0.03%	4	2
Reagan	0.01%	2	2
Carter	3.7%	54	12
Nixon	0.0%	0	0
Total	6.4%	99	24
Female Judges			
Clinton	6.4%	93	19
G. H. W. Bush	3.3%	48	14
Reagan	2.1%	31	7
Carter	4.2%	61	14
Nixon	0.0%	0	0
Total	16.0%	233	54

Regional Background of a Judge This group of variables designates in which geographic region of the country the judge rendering a given decision regularly sits on the bench. For each individual vote, only one of the following regions may be designated as the region from which the judge hails: (1) South, (2) East, (3) Midwest, (4) Ninth Circuit, or (5) Tenth Circuit. Based on consistent findings of prior studies, southern judges are expected to render the most "conservative" voting behavior (i.e., to be the most anti-defendant in the search and seizure area). The southern region is used as the baseline against which all other geographic regions are measured.

Black Judge (Chapter 4 only) This variable designates whether the judge is African American.

Female Judge (Chapter 4 only) This variable designates whether the judge is female.

Parameter Estimates, Autocorrelation, and Heteroskedasticity Issues

As was true of the labor models explained in Appendix A, because the dependent variable is dichotomous, Logit is used to estimate the parameters. Moreover, given that again multiple votes by single judges are included in the data, there is a potential for problems with autocorrelation and heteroskedasticity. As for autocorrelation, the same diagnostic tests laid out in Appendix A were also conducted on the search and seizure data and produced no signs of autocorrelation. As for heteroskedasticity, robust standard errors are used.

Coding of Variables

DEPENDENT VARIABLE

The decision of an individual judge, and not the holding of the case, was coded 1 if the judge found against the criminal defendant and 0 if the judge found in favor of the criminal defendant. Each case normally yields three individual votes, unless the case involved an en banc court. En banc courts may range from twenty-eight votes in the Ninth Circuit to six votes in the First Circuit.

INDEPENDENT VARIABLES

Fact-Based Variables

Location of the Search   For each individual vote, only one of the following places may be designated with a value of 1:

1. *Home.* When the search or seizure took place at the defendant's home, the value is 1; otherwise, it is 0. The definition of "home" includes any type of dwelling in which the defendant was permanently or temporarily residing, including houses, apartments, trailers, motel rooms, and guest quarters. It also includes any type of building or structure that the defendant may use for commercial purposes aside from his or her dwelling place, including office buildings, individual offices, and secondary structures located on the same property as a defendant's home.
2. *Automobile.* When the search or seizure took place in the defendant's car, the value is 1; otherwise, it is 0. The definition of "car" includes any vehicle capable of transportation, including automobiles, trucks, motor homes, boats, and airplanes.
3. *Luggage.* When the search or seizure took place regarding the defendant's luggage, the value is 1; otherwise, it is 0. The definition of "luggage" includes any type of box or bag capable of concealing objects until opened,

including suitcases, briefcases, handbags, gym bags, cartons, and postal packages.
4. *Person.* When the search or seizure took place on the defendant's person in a public place, the value is 1; otherwise, it is 0. The definition of "person" includes any type of intrusion of the defendant's liberty, including arrest, detention, questioning, and frisking.

Warrant When a search or seizure took place after a warrant had been issued, the value is 1; otherwise, it is 0.

Limited Search When a limited search or seizure took place, the value is 1; otherwise, it is 0. The definition of "limited" search or seizure includes brief detention for questioning, frisking, pat-down searching, canine-sniffing, and searching solely for weapons incident to a lawful arrest.

Border Search When a search or seizure occurred at a point of entry into the United States, the value is 1; otherwise, it is 0. The definition of "border" includes any geographic border with Mexico or Canada, as well as any airport in which international travel occurs.

Background-Based Variables

Background-based variables for the search and seizure models included in Chapters 3 and 4 are coded as follows:

Appointing President For each individual vote, only one of the following appointing presidential cohorts may be coded as 1:

1. *Clinton.* When an appeals court judge, or a district court judge sitting by designation, was appointed to the federal bench by President Clinton, the value is 1; otherwise, the value is 0.
2. *G. H. W. Bush.* When an appeals court judge, or a district court judge sitting by designation, was appointed to the federal bench by President Bush, the value is 1; otherwise, the value is 0.
3. *Reagan.* When an appeals court judge, or a district court judge sitting by designation, was appointed to the federal bench by President Reagan, the value is 1; otherwise, the value is 0.
4. *Carter.* When an appeals court judge, or a district court judge sitting by designation, was appointed to the federal bench by President Carter, the value is 1; otherwise, the value is 0.
5. *Nixon.* When an appeals court judge, or a district court judge sitting by designation, was appointed to the federal bench by President Nixon, the value is 1; otherwise, the value is 0.

Region For each individual vote, only one of the following regions may be coded as 1:

1. *East.* When a judge sits by permanent assignment on the First, Second, Third, or District of Columbia Circuits, or sits by permanent assignment on a district court in one of these four circuits, the value is 1; otherwise, the value is 0.
2. *South.* When a judge sits by permanent assignment on the Fourth, Fifth, or Eleventh Circuits, or sits by permanent assignment on a district court in one of these three circuits, the value is 1; otherwise, the value is 0.
3. *Midwest.* When a judge sits by permanent assignment on the Sixth, Seventh, or Eighth Circuits, or sits by permanent assignment on a district court in one of these three circuits, the value is 1; otherwise, the value is 0.
4. *Ninth Circuit.* When a judge sits by permanent assignment on the Ninth Circuit, or sits by permanent assignment on a district court in this circuit, the value is 1; otherwise, the value is 0.
5. *Tenth Circuit.* When a judge sits by permanent assignment on the Tenth Circuit, or sits by permanent assignment on a district court in this circuit, the value is 1; otherwise, the value is 0.

Black Judge (Chapter 4 only)   When a judge is African American, the value is 1; otherwise, the value is 0.

Female Judge (Chapter 4 only)   When a judge if female, the value is 1; otherwise, the value is 0.

Explanation and Coding of Variables: Race Discrimination Models

Data and Methods

The units of analysis will be each judge's vote (and not the ultimate holding of the case) rendered on a three-judge or en banc panel in all cases meeting certain criteria set forth below. The cases included in the analyses are the entire universe of "nonconsensual" decisions rendered by the U.S. Courts of Appeals, including all of the numbered circuits, the District of Columbia Circuit, and the Federal Circuit. Nonconsensual decisions are defined in Appendix A. The time frame for the "Party in Transition" race discrimination cases is January 1, 1968, through December 31, 1974. The time frame for the "Modern Party System" race discrimination cases is January 1, 1994, through December 31, 2001. Included in all of the analyses are the votes of circuit court judges in active service, circuit court judges on senior status, and U.S. District Court judges sitting by designation on the courts of appeals.

The cases composing the data sets were identified through a series of comprehensive searches on the electronic database WESTLAW. Included in the data set were decisions officially designated by the court for publication in the *Federal Reporter*, as well as decisions not designated by the court for official publication but reprinted in full on the WESTLAW database.

Explanation of Variables

DEPENDENT VARIABLES

The dependent variable is the vote of each individual judge either agreeing or disagreeing with the minority plaintiff's position asserted on appeal in a case in which the underlying claim (though not necessarily the issue on appeal) is that the plaintiff suffered racial discrimination by virtue of the defendant's conduct in violation of the Civil Rights Act of 1964, one of the Reconstruction civil rights statutes (also known as Section 1981 or Section 1983 claims), and/or the equal protection clause of the Fourteenth Amendment. Civil rights claims asserted by prisoners and civil rights claims raised in the context of a criminal case are excluded from the analysis.

INDEPENDENT VARIABLES

So that the reader can understand why certain fact variables were chosen and coded as they were, I will briefly review the relevant law controlling race discrimination cases and civil appeals (the legal factors), and prior empirical research indicating the statistical significance of certain variables in predicting the outcome of civil appeals in general (extra-legal factors).

Legal Factors Considered for all Race Discrimination Models

Beginning with *Brown v. Board of Education* (1954), minorities were permitted to bring constitutional claims against a federal or state goverment for race discrimination based on the equal protection clause of the Fourteenth Amendment. Such claims include those for desegregation of public education and of public transportation. When, ten years after *Brown*, little progress had been made in dismantling the Jim Crow laws of the South, Congress passed several civil rights statutes designed to further ensure racial equality in the public and private sectors. First and foremost was the Civil Rights Act of 1964. This omnibus act allowed for a variety of race discrimination claims to redress, among other things, discrimination in employment practice (Title VII) and opportunities and discrimination in public accommodations (Title II). Aggrieved parties may also bring a racial discrimination suit under one or more of the federal Reconstruction civil rights statutes (42 U.S.C. Sections 1981, 1983). These claims require that the defendant be a state or local governmental entity.

Equal Protection Claim   This variable designates whether a plaintiff's principal claim is made pursuant to the equal protection clause of the Fourteenth Amendment. Since constitutional claims are generally deemed more serious than statutory claims, judges are expected to be more sympathetic to civil rights plaintiffs in constitutional cases brought under the equal protection clause.

Extra-Legal Factors Considered
for All Race Discrimination Models

Much research has been conducted in the field of judicial politics exploring whether a variety of extra-legal factors in civil cases influences a judge's vote. For instance, Perry demonstrated that judges are less likely to rule against government defendants than other types of defendants (P. Perry, 1991). Similarly, wealthier litigants have a better chance of success than poorer litigants (Lawrence, 1990). In cases involving gender discrimination, Donald Songer, Sue Davis, and Susan B. Haire found judges to be more sympathetic to female defendants than male defendants, suggesting a judicial hostility to claims of reverse discrimination (Songer, Davis, and Haire, 1994). And Lucius Barker demonstrated that interest group participation in litigation can have an important effect on the outcome (Barker, 1967).

The extra-legal variables included in the race discrimination models are as follows:

Government Defendant This variable designates whether the defendant is a government entity. Judges are expected to be less supportive of a plaintiff's position on appeal when the defendant is a government entity.

Class Action This variable designates whether the plaintiff is a class or an individual plaintiff. Judges are expected to be more supportive of a plaintiff's position on appeal when the plaintiff is not a class.

White Plaintiff (Modern Party System Only) This variable designates whether the plaintiff is white. Judges are expected to less supportive of a plaintiff's position on appeal when the plaintiff is white.

Pro Se Plaintiff (Modern Party System Only) This variable designates whether the plaintiff is represented by counsel. Judges are expected to be less supportive of a plaintiff's position on appeal when the plaintiff is represented by counsel.

Race Plus Another Discrimination Claim (Modern Party System Only) This variable designates whether the plaintiff is alleging multiple types of discrimination. Judges are expected to be less supportive of a plaintiff's position on appeal when the plaintiff alleges solely race discrimination.

Background-Based Variables

For the Party in Transition models, the background-based variables are as follows:

TABLE C-I
Total Votes Cast, Race Discrimination Data Set, Party System in Transition

	Percentage of Total Votes Cast	Number of Votes Cast	Number of Judges in Cohort
PRESIDENTIAL COHORTS			
Appointing Presidential Cohort			
Nixon	17.7%	178	42
Johnson	39.9%	403	54
Kennedy	19.5%	197	26
Eisenhower	22.9%	231	38
Total	100.0%	1,009	160
GEOGRAPHIC/PARTY COHORTS			
Southern, Republican	24.2%	244	21
Non-Southern, Republican	16.3%	165	59
Southern, Democrat	39.4%	397	28
Non-Southern Democrat	20.1%	203	52
Total	100.0%	1,009	160

Appointing Presidential Party   This group of variables designates which political party the appointing president belonged to. For each individual vote, only one of the following may be designated as the appointing presidential party: (1) Republican Party, or (2) Democratic Party. Judges appointed by Republican presidents are expected to be less supportive of the civil rights of minorities than judges appointed by Democratic presidents. Table C-1 shows the total number of votes rendered by each presidential cohort, and the number of judges in each cohort, for this data set.

Southern Judge   This variable designates whether the judge rendering the decision regularly sits on the Fourth or Fifth Circuits or is a district court judge sitting by designation from a district court located in the Fourth or Fifth Circuits. Southern judges are expected to be more "conservative" than non-southern judges.

For the Modern Party System race discrimination models, the background-based variables are the same as those used in the search and seizure models (see Appendix B). Table C-2 shows the total number of votes rendered by each presidential cohort, and the number of judges in each cohort for this data set.

TABLE C-2
Total Votes Cast, Race Discrimination Data Set, Modern Party System

	Percentage of Total Votes Cast	Number of Votes Cast	Number of Judges in Cohort
PRESIDENTIAL COHORTS			
Appointing Presidential Cohort			
Clinton	19.5%	273	72
G. H. W. Bush	19.5%	276	47
Reagan	34.5%	486	97
Carter	22.5%	317	58
Nixon	4.0%	56	20
Total	100.0%	1,408	294
GEOGRAPHIC/PARTY COHORTS[a]			
Southern, Republican	15.6%	211	37
Non-Southern Republican	40.7%	551	107
Southern Democrat	12.0%	163	39
Non-Southern Democrat	31.7%	428	91
Total	100.0%	1,353	310
RACE AND GENDER COHORTS			
Black Judges			
Clinton	3.6%	50	9
G. H. W. Bush	0.4%	5	3
Reagan	0.6%	9	2
Carter	4.9%	69	9
Nixon	0.0%	0	0
Total	8.5%	133 (out of 1,408)	23
Female Judges			
Clinton	4.7%	67	18
G. H. W. Bush	4.0%	56	14
Reagan	1.7%	24	13
Carter	4.7%	66	12
Nixon	0.0%	0	0
Total	15.1%	187 (out of 1,408)	57

[a]Excludes Nixon because party models in Chapter 2 do not include Nixon in the modern party era.

Parameter Estimates, Autocorrelation, and Heteroskedasticity Issues

Because the dependent variable is dichotomous, Logit is used to estimate the parameters. As was true with the search and seizure models (Appendix B), tests for autocorrelation were conducted and produced no signs of autocorrelation. Finally, because of potential heteroskedasticity that may arise due to the use of multiple votes by a single judge, robust standard errors are used.

Coding for Race Discrimination Models

DEPENDENT VARIABLE

The dependent variable is the vote of each individual judge either agreeing or disagreeing with the racial minority plaintiff's position advanced on appeal. When the judge disagrees with the racial minority plaintiff, the value 1; otherwise, the value is 0. In the event that the claim is one for reverse discrimination—meaning that the plaintiff is white—the dependent variable is coded 1 if the judge agrees with the white plaintiff; otherwise, the value is 0. Each case normally yields three individual votes, unless the case involved an en banc court. En banc courts may range from twenty-eight votes in the Ninth Circuit to six votes in the First Circuit.

INDEPENDENT VARIABLES

Fact-Based Variables (Legal and Extra-Legal)

Equal Protection Claim   When the principal federal claim underlying a plaintiff's lawsuit is one asserted under the equal protection clause of the Fourteenth Amendment, the value is 1; otherwise, the value is 0.

Class Action   When the underlying lawsuit is brought as a class action, the value is 1; otherwise, the value is 0.

White Plaintiff   When the plaintiff is white, the value is 1; otherwise, the value is 0.

Pro Se Plaintiff   When the plaintiff is not represented by counsel in the lawsuit, the value is 1; otherwise, the value is 0.

Race Plus Another Discrimination Claim   When the plaintiff alleges race discrimination and some other form of discrimination, the value is 1; otherwise, the value is 0. Other forms of discrimination include discrimination on the basis of sex, disability, age, and familial status.

Background-Based Variables

The background-based variables for the Modern Party System race discrimination models are coded the same as they are for the background-based variables used in the search and seizure models in Chapter 3. Coding may be found in Appendix B.

The background-based variables for the Party in Transition race discrimination models are coded as follows:

Appointing Presidential Party   For each individual vote, only one of the following appointing presidential cohorts may be coded as 1: (1) Republican—When an appeals court judge, or a district court judge sitting by designation, was appointed to the federal bench by Presidents Eisenhower or Nixon, the value is 1; otherwise, the value is 0; (2) Democrat—When an appeals court judge, or a district court judge sitting by designation, was appointed to the federal bench by Presidents Kennedy or Johnson, the value is 1; otherwise, the value is 0.

Southern Judge   When a judge sits by permanent assignment on the Fourth or Fifth Circuits, or sits by permanent assignment on a district court in one of these two circuits, the value is 1; otherwise, the value is 0.

Explanation and Coding of Variables:
States' Rights Models

Data and Methods

The units of analysis will be each judge's vote (and not the ultimate holding of the case) rendered on a three-judge or en banc panel in all cases meeting certain criteria set forth below. The cases included in this study are the entire universe of "nonconsensual" decisions rendered by the U.S. Courts of Appeals, including all of the eleven numbered circuits, the District of Columbia Circuit, and the Federal Circuit. Nonconsensual decisions are defined in Appendix B.

The time frame for the states' rights models is January 1, 1996, through December 31, 2002. The period chosen for the states' rights models reflects the fact that the Supreme Court drastically altered the balance of power between state and federal government in a series of federalism decisions. Before April 1995, the courts of appeals enjoyed little discretion under controlling law to rule in favor of the states' rights position. Thus, analysis of cases before April 1995 would provide little variation between Democrat- and Republican-appointed judges. Included in the analysis are the votes of circuit court judges in active service, circuit court judges on senior status, and U.S. District Court judges sitting by designation on the U.S. courts of appeals.

The cases composing the data sets were identified through a series of comprehensive searches on the electronic database WESTLAW. Included in the data set were decisions officially designated by the court for publication in the *Federal Reporter*, as well as decisions not designated by the court for official publication but reprinted in full on the WESTLAW database.

Explanation of Variables

DEPENDENT VARIABLES

The dependent variable is the vote of each individual judge either agreeing or disagreeing with the defendant that the state government's rights prevail over the federal government's rights. In commerce clause cases, this would mean a vote agreeing or disagreeing with the states' rights advocate that the federal government has exceeded its interstate commerce power. In Eleventh Amendment cases, this would mean a vote agreeing or disagreeing with the state defendant that the state is immune from suit and that the federal government cannot properly abrogate such sovereign immunity. Collectively, these two categories of cases are referred throughout as "states' rights" cases.

INDEPENDENT VARIABLES

So that the reader can understand why I have chosen to control for certain fact-based variables, I will briefly review the relevant law in the area of federalism.[1] Pursuant to the Eleventh Amendment of the Constitution, all states, as sovereigns separate from the federal government, are immune from suits in federal court commenced by any citizen. Thus, federal courts lack subject matter jurisdiction over such suits unless the state has waived its sovereign immunity, or alternatively, Congress has effectively abrogated the state's immunity through the enactment of a federal statute.[2] In order for Congress to abrogate legitimately the state's sovereign immunity, it must act pursuant to a valid exercise of power granted in the Constitution allowing it to alter the delicate balance between state and federal government under our system of federalism.[3] The Supreme Court has now held that the commerce clause (Article I, Section 8 of the Constitution) does not provide Congress with a valid basis to abrogate state sovereign immunity, but that Section 5 of the Fourteenth Amendment does.[4] Thus, whether a federal court will entertain a lawsuit brought against a state turns on whether the federal statute that forms the basis of the plaintiff's claim in the underlying suit constitutes a valid abrogation of the state's sovereign immunity. This issue presents the court with a clear choice between upholding the state's rights as a separate sovereign (which is the position historically advanced by the Republican Party) or the federal government's rights to protect the welfare of its citizens through national legislation (the position historically advanced by the Democratic Party).

The commerce clause also presents federal courts with thorny issues of constitutional law concerning the balance of power between state and federal government. Pursuant to the commerce clause, Congress has the power to regulate "interstate" commerce. States enjoy concurrent power to regulate commerce, provided that such regulation does not have an "extraterritorial reach"—that is, beyond the state's borders[5]—or is inconsistent with a duly passed congressional statute in the area of interstate commerce.[6] States are also forbidden from enacting commerce regulation in certain areas where the national interest in uniformity is so important as to outweigh any state interest, even where Congress has not yet acted.[7] But the federal government may also be guilty of violating the commerce clause by enacting legislation that regulates the states without any real connection to interstate commerce. When the federal government so acts, it is said to violate the Tenth Amendment, which states that "the powers not delegated to the United States by the Constitution, nor prohibited by it to the States, are reserved to the States respectively, or to the people."

Until recently, federal courts had given Congress the widest latitude under its interstate commerce power, but in the past few years, the landscape surrounding the commerce clause has significantly changed. For example, in 1995, the Supreme Court held that a federal statute (requiring gun-free school zones) was unconstitutional as going beyond Congress's interstate commerce power,[8] and in 2000, the Court struck down the Violence Against Women Act on the same ground.[9]

Fact-Based Variables

The fact-based variables included in the states' rights models for Chapter 3 are as follows:

States' Rights Issue on Appeal

This group of variables designates the legal context in which the states' rights issue is raised on appeal. For each individual vote (for or against the defendant moving to dismiss the federal claims), only one of the following may be designated as grounds for dismissal: (1) the Eleventh Amendment, or (2) the commerce clause / Tenth Amendment. Because, to date, the Supreme Court has exhibited more willingness to invalidate federal power over the states under the Eleventh Amendment, courts of appeals judges are expected to be less supportive of a defendant's claim of states' rights under the commerce clause / Tenth Amendment.

Background-Based Variables

All background-based variables used in the states' rights models are the

TABLE D-I
Total Votes Cast in States' Rights Data Set

	Percentage of Total Votes Cast	Number of Votes Cast	Number of Judges
PRESIDENTIAL COHORTS			
Appointing President Cohort			
Clinton	22.2%	75	37
G. H. W. Bush	25.6%	86	29
Reagan	32.0%	108	49
Carter	16.9%	57	26
Nixon	3.3%	11	7
Total	100.0%	337	148
RACE/GENDER COHORTS			
Black Judges			
Clinton	2.9%	10	8
G. H. W. Bush	0.0%	0	0
Reagan	0.3%	1	1
Carter	2.1%	7	4
Nixon	0.0%	0	0
Total	5.3%	18 (out of 337)	13
Female Judges			
Clinton	5.3%	18	13
G. H. W. Bush	4.4%	15	6
Reagan	1.5%	5	3
Carter	3.3%	11	8
Nixon	0.0%	0	0
Total	14.5%	49 (out of 337)	30

same as those used in the search and seizure models for Chapter 3 and are set forth in Appendix B.

Parameter Estimates, Autocorrelation, and Heteroskedasticity Issues

Because the dependent variable is dichotomous, Logit is used to estimate the parameters. As was true with the labor models (Appendix A), the search and seizure models (Appendix B), and the race discrimination models (Appendix C), tests for autocorrelation were conducted on the states' rights models and produced no signs of autocorrelation. Finally, because of potential heteroskedasticity that may arise due to the use of multiple votes by a single judge, robust standard errors are used.

Coding of Models

DEPENDENT VARIABLE

The decision of an individual judge in a states' rights case was coded 1 if the judge found in favor of the states' rights position, and 0 if the judge found in favor of the federal rights' position. Each case normally yields three individual votes, unless the case involved an en banc court. En banc panels range from twenty-eight votes in the Ninth Circuit to six votes in the First Circuit.

INDEPENDENT VARIABLES

Fact-Based Variables

The fact-based variables included in the states' rights models are coded as follows:

States' Rights Issue on Appeal   For each individual vote, only one of the following may be coded as 1: 1. *Commerce Clause.* When the defendant's motion to dismiss is based on the commerce clause, the value is 1; otherwise, the value is 0. 2. *Eleventh Amendment.* When the defendant's motion to dismiss is based on the Eleventh Amendment, the value is 1; otherwise, the value is 0.

Background-Based Variables

The background-based variables included in the states' rights models are the same as they are for the background-based variables included in the search and seizure models for Chapter 3, and are set forth in Appendix B. The number of votes per presidential cohort in the states' rights data set are shown in Table D-1.

APPENDIX E

Explanation and Coding of Variables:
Abortion Rights Data Set

Data and Methods

The units of analysis will be each judge's vote (and not the ultimate holding of the case) rendered on a three-judge or en banc panel in all cases meeting certain criteria set forth below. The cases included in this study are the entire universe of "nonconsensual" decisions rendered by the U.S. Courts of Appeals, including all of the eleven numbered circuits and the District of Columbia Circuit. Nonconsensual decisions are defined in Appendix B.

The time frame used for the abortion rights models is January 1, 1978, through December 31, 2002. The period chosen for the abortion rights models reflects the fact that the courts of appeals decide few abortion cases, and thus, in order to gather enough decisions for meaningful analysis, it was necessary to use a much broader time frame than that used for the search and seizure, race discrimination, and states' rights models. I chose 1978 as the starting point because it is the first year after the Supreme Court decided *Roe v. Wade* in which the votes of at least two of the presidential cohorts analyzed in this data set (Nixon and Carter) were regularly present.

The cases composing the data sets were identified through a series of comprehensive searches on the electronic database WESTLAW. Included in the data set were decisions officially designated by the court for publication in the *Federal Reporter*, as well as decisions not designated by the court for official publication but reprinted in full on the WESTLAW database.

Explanation of Variables

DEPENDENT VARIABLE

The dependent variable is the vote of each individual judge either agreeing or disagreeing with the plaintiff's assertion on appeal that a state or federal abortion regulation violates a woman's constitutional right to privacy under the Fourteenth or Fifth Amendments as recognized in *Roe v. Wade* and *Planned Parenthood of Southeast Pennsylvania v. Casey.*

INDEPENDENT VARIABLES

So that the reader can understand why certain fact variables were chosen and coded as they were, I will briefly review the relevant law controlling abortion cases. The Supreme Court held in *Roe v. Wade* that a woman's decision to have an abortion is a privacy right protected under the Fourteenth Amendment's due process clause. However, *Roe* cautioned that such privacy interest is not absolute; instead, the Court recognized that the state may also have an interest in protecting the health of the mother or a viable fetus (deemed to occur in the third trimester according to the *Roe* majority). Accordingly, provided the state can demonstrate that it has a compelling state interest in protecting the mother's health or a viable fetus, state regulation of abortion may be constitutional.[1] Since *Roe*, many states have enacted regulations restricting access to abortion, and it has been the duty of the federal courts to pass judgment on the constitutionality of these statutes. The Court also recognized, in *Planned Parenthood v. Danforth*, that the state enjoys greater leeway in regulating abortions for minors, given the "unique status of children under the law."[2]

Given the controlling case law, I control for the following fact-based variables in the abortion models:

Post-Casey *Period.* This variable designates whether the case was decided after the Supreme Court's decision in *Planned Parenthood v. Casey.* The expectation is that judges are more likely to uphold abortion restrictions in the post-*Casey* period.

Statute Restricting Abortions for Minors. This variable designates whether the statute under consideration by the court is one affecting only minors. The expectation is that statutes restricting abortions for minors only are more likely to be upheld by the court than one affecting adult women.

BACKGROUND-BASED VARIABLES

All background-based variables used in the abortion models are the same as those used in the search and seizure models and are set forth in Appendix B, with one exception. Regions are divided between South and non-South, and southern judges are defined as they are in Appendix B.

Parameter Estimates, Autocorrelation, and Heteroskedasticity Issues

Because the dependent variable is dichotomous, Logit is used to estimate the parameters. As was true with the labor models (Appendix A), the search and seizure models (Appendix B), the race discrimination models (Appendix C), and the states' rights models (Appendix D), tests for autocorrelation were conducted on the abortion rights models and produced no signs of auto-correlation. Finally, because of potential heteroskedasticity that may arise due to the use of multiple votes by a single judge, robust standard errors are used.

Coding for Models

DEPENDENT VARIABLE

The decision of an individual judge in an abortion case was coded 1 if the judge found that a state or federal abortion regulation was constitution, and 0 if the judge found that the regulation was unconstitutional. Each case normally yields three individual votes, unless the case involved an en banc court. En banc courts may range from twenty-eight votes in the Ninth Circuit to six votes in the First Circuit.

INDEPENDENT VARIABLES

Fact-Based Variables

The fact-based variables included in the abortion models in Chapters 3 and 4 are coded as follows:

*Post-*Casey *Period.* When a decision was rendered after the Supreme Court's decision in *Planned Parenthood v. Casey* (June 29, 1992), the decision is coded 1; otherwise, the decision is coded 0.

Statutes Restricting Abortions for Minors. When a decision passes on the constitutionality of an abortion restriction affecting only women younger than age eighteen, the decision is coded 1; otherwise, the decision is coded 0.

Background-Based Variables

The background-based variables are coded the same as they are for the background-based variables used in the search and seizure models in Ap-

TABLE E-1
Total Votes Cast in Abortion Data Set

	Percentage of Total Votes Cast	Number of Votes Cast	Number of Judges in Cohort
PRESIDENTIAL COHORTS			
Appointing Presidential Cohort			
Clinton	9.5%	17	13
G. H. W. Bush	11.2%	20	12
Reagan	36.8%	66	39
Carter	28.5%	51	28
Nixon	14.0%	25	13
Total	100.0%	179	105
GEOGRAPHIC/PARTY COHORTS			
Southern Republican	16.9%	26	18
Non-Southern Republican	39.0%	60	22
Southern Democrat	14.2%	22	14
Non-Southern Democrat	29.9%	46	27
Total	100.0%	154	92
RACE/GENDER COHORTS			
Black Judges			
Clinton	0.0%	0	0
G. H. W. Bush	0.0%	0	0
Reagan	0.0%	0	0
Carter	6.7%	12	6
Nixon	0.0%	0	0
Total	6.7%	12 (out of 179)	6
Female Judges			
Clinton	0.5%	1	1
G. H. W. Bush	1.7%	3	2
Reagan	2.2%	4	3
Carter	4.5%	8	8
Nixon	0.0%	0	0
Total	8.9%	13 (out of 179)	14

pendix B, with one exception. Regional background is divided only by southern versus non-southern judges, and southern judges are coded as set forth in Appendix B. Table E-1 shows the number of votes cast in the abortion data set.

List of Cases

Aaron v. Cooper (1958)

Adair v. United States, 208 U.S. 161 (1908)

Adkins v. Childrens Hospital, 161 U.S. 525 (1923)

Aquilar v. Texas, 378 U.S. 108 (1964)

Bakke v. Regents of the University of California, 438 U.S. 265 (1978)

Board of Education of the Township of Piscataway v. Taxman, 91 F.3d 1547 (3d Cir. 1996), cert. granted, 521 U.S. 1117 (1997)

Brown v. Board of Education (1954)

Brown v. Board of Education (Brown II) (1955)

Buckley v. Valeo, 424 U.S. 1 (1976)

Carroll v. United States, 267 U.S. 132 (1925)

Chimel v. California, 395 U.S. 752 (1969)

Cloverleaf Butter Co. v. Paterson, 315 U.S. 148 (1942)

Contractors Association of Eastern Pennsylvania v. Schultz, 442 F.2d 159 (3d Cir. 1971)

Coolidge v. New Hampshire, 403 U.S. 443 (1971)

Craig v. Boren (1976)

Davis v. Mississippi, 394 U.S. 721 (1969)

Dickerson v. United States, 530 U.S. 428 (2000)

Edelman v. Jordan, 415 U.S. 651 (1974)

Florida ex. rel. Hawkins v. Board of Control of Florida (1956)

Frontiero v. Richardson (1973)

Garner v. Louisiana (1961)

Gideon v. Wainwright (1963)

Gregg v. Georgia, 428 U.S. 153 (1976)

Griffin v. Maryland (1964)

Grove City v. Bell, 465 U.S. 555 (1984)

Healy v. Beer Institute, 491 U.S. 324 (1989)

Heart of Atlanta Motel v. United States (1964)

Notes

INTRODUCTION

1. I would characterize the figure for the Ford administration as an outlier. This is because of the unusual circumstances by which he became president (upon Nixon's resignation) and the fact that one of the two years he spent in office was a presidential election year when traditionally fewer lower court nominees are confirmed.

2. I distinguish between presidential and non-presidential election years because, traditionally, confirmations slow down during an election year, as the party not in control of the White House holds up nominations in the hopes that its preferred candidate will win the election and then fill those vacancies with judges from their own party.

3. Throughout this book, I use the term *modern political era* to mean the period 1968–2000. As explained below, I focus on this period because it is when we begin to see the use of elite mobilization strategies, and it is these strategies that have led to increased politicization of the lower court appointment process.

4. As discussed in Chapter 2, the southern strategy was Nixon's election strategy in 1968 in which he injected the race issue into the election in an attempt to woo southern Democratic voters to the Republican Party.

CHAPTER ONE

1. Some have suggested that in the modern political era, ideologically motivated local party leaders have developed quite sophisticated and professional organizations (Gibson, Frendreis, and Vertz, 1989). Thus, the terms "amateur" and "professional" are somewhat misnomers.

2. See, for example, *Brown v. Board of Education (Brown II)* (1955) (school desegregation); *Florida ex. rel. Hawkins v. Board of Control of Florida* (1956) (school desegregation); *Aaron v. Cooper* (1958) (school desegregation); *Garner v. Louisiana* (1961) (desegregation of restaurant facility); *Turner v. City of Memphis* (1962) (desegregation of restaurant facility); *Griffin v. Maryland* (1964) (desegregation of amusement park); *Heart of Atlanta Motel v. United States* (1964) (upholding constitutionality of Civil Rights Act of 1964).

3. *Mapp v. Ohio* (1961) (establishment of exclusionary rule); *Gideon v. Wainwright* (1963) (right of indigent defendants to appointed counsel); *Miranda v. Arizona*

(1966) (requirement to read defendant Fifth and Sixth Amendment rights before interrogation).

4. See, for example, *Reed v. Reed* (1971) (gender classification in statute allowing fathers, but not mothers, to serve as administrator of a child's estate held unconstitutional); *Frontiero v. Richardson* (1973) (gender classification in federal statute allowing wives of servicemen to receive benefits, but not husbands of servicewomen, held unconstitutional); *Craig v. Boren* (1976) (gender classification in state statute allowing girls between the ages of eighteen and twenty-one to drink, but not boys, held unconstitutional).

5. The two prenomination, patronage fights by liberal activists during the Clinton presidency were Gary Gaertner, chosen by House Speaker Richard Gephardt for a vacancy on the Eastern District of Missouri, and William Downes, chosen by the Democratic governor of Wyoming, Michael J. Sullivan, for a vacancy on the District of Wyoming. Clinton declined to nominate Gaertner but nominated Downes, who was subsequently confirmed by voice vote.

6. Although it is the president to whom the Constitution gives the power to appoint federal court judgeships, presidents under the old party system allowed senators in their own party to "nominate" lower court judges; in turn, a president could also count on the support of senators in his party on important legislative initiatives. In contrast, because Supreme Court positions lacked a local character, neither senators nor party activists have exercised much influence over the president's choices for the nation's highest court.

7. There is one scholar who questions the common wisdom about patronage appointments as it relates to three 20th-century administrations—that of Woodrow Wilson and the later years of the administrations of Teddy Roosevelt and FDR. Specifically, Raymond Solomon (1984) asserts that these three presidents chose courts of appeals judges predominantly on the basis of policy considerations, rather than patronage considerations. Solomon bases this conclusion on a questionable research design, however. He asserts that one can identify a patronage-driven appointment strategy by the percentage of district court judges elevated to the courts of appeals; in contrast, a policy-driven strategy can be detected by the lack of such promotions. Solomon reasons that presidents concerned with policy would not elevate district court judges previously chosen for patronage reasons to courts of appeals positions. Thus, given the low percentage of district court promotions during these three presidencies, Solomon concludes that these presidents chose courts of appeals judges primarily on the basis of policy considerations. The problem with this argument is that one could make just the opposite argument based on the same evidence: that promoting a judge from the district court to the court of appeals is a policy-driven decision. By examining the judge's prior voting record in the district court, a president could ensure that the judge, once promoted, will vote in accordance with his policy agenda. In contrast, a court of appeals nominee with no prior judicial voting record presents a much greater risk to the president. Indeed, in today's policy-driven judicial selection environment, Supreme Court justices are most often chosen from the ranks of the courts of appeals for this very reason.

8. It should be emphasized from the outset that these strategies are *not* mutually exclusive. For example, diversity appointments made by Presidents Carter and Clinton also serve the dual purpose of satisfying policy concerns of left-wing elites in the

Democratic Party. Moreover, I do not mean to suggest that patronage appointments no longer exist. To the contrary, it is well documented that more than 90 percent of judicial nominees in the modern political era belong to the same party as the president—a statistic consistent with patronage and policy strategies. Rather, I argue that, today, patronage appointees must also satisfy an ideological litmus test. For example, one of Clinton's appointees to the Ninth Circuit was William Fletcher, Clinton's former roommate at Oxford and the chairman of his California election campaign, suggesting a patronage appointment. Fletcher, however, was also a fairly liberal nominee much favored by liberal activists affiliated with the Democratic Party, suggesting an ideology appointment.

9. The other two activities members of Congress engage in are "advertising" and "credit claiming."

10. Only Edwards eventually ran for president in 2004.

CHAPTER TWO

1. See, for example, *Lochner v. New York* (1905); *Adair v. United States* (1908); *Adkins v. Childrens Hospital* (1923); and *Morehead v. New York ex. rel. Tipaldo* (1936).

2. 300 U.S. 379 (1937).

3. 29 U.S.C. sec. 201 et. seq. (2000).

4. *United States v. Darby* (1941).

5. Again, I am not suggesting that presidents before transformation of the party system in the 1960s *never* used courts of appeals appointments to further policy agendas. Rather, given the constraints of the old party system, the *majority* of lower court appointments would be made for partisan purposes.

6. Another category of decisions that would seemingly be appropriate for analysis would be search and seizure cases, given Nixon's attention to the Warren Court's criminal procedure decisions in the 1968 campaign. However, because national political debate on crime did not begin until the 1964 presidential election—after Presidents Eisenhower and Kennedy had been in office—it makes no sense to analyze whether these presidents appointed judges who would carry out a policy agenda that was not salient at the time. In contrast, the civil rights issue was a matter of concern for all four presidents under study, and thus, civil rights cases are more appropriately analyzed.

7. As explained in Chapter 5, this shift in emphasis is the result of a recognition on the part of Republican leaders that, because a majority of Americans support a woman's right to choose an abortion, it is difficult to win a confirmation battle centering around this issue.

CHAPTER THREE

1. Not wanting to appear "soft" on crime going into the 1968 election, a Democratic-controlled Congress passed this law, which characterized *Miranda* as strictly a rule of evidence, thus allowing Congress to overrule *Miranda* by statute (O'Neill, 2000).

2. *Encyclopedia of the Republican Party*, 1980 Platform (Armonk, N.Y.: Sharpe Reference), at 674. Hereafter cited as 1980 Republican platform.

3. Ibid.

4. Office of Legal Policy, U.S. Department of Justice, "Guidelines on Constitutional Litigation," February 19, 1988, at 87. Hereafter cited as Reagan Guidelines. See also, Office of Legal Policy, U.S. Department of Justice, Report to the Attorney General, "The Constitution in the Year 2000: Choices Ahead in Constitutional Interpretation," October 11, 1988, at 1–10. Hereafter cited as Report to Attorney General.

5. Ibid., at 86.

6. Ibid., at 87. In *United States v. Leon* (1984), the Court created a "good faith" exception to the warrant requirement, whereby evidence obtained pursuant to a defective warrant—but one obtained by law enforcement officers believing at the time it was a good warrant—was admissible at trial.

7. G. H. W. Bush's attack of the Massachusetts prison furlough program would take on a life of its own when Willie Horton—a convicted murderer who, when released on a weekend furlough, raped and beat a woman in Maryland—was made a centerpiece of the Bush campaign (Anderson, 1995).

8. *Encyclopedia of the Republican Party*, 1988 Platform, at 758. Hereafter cited at 1988 Republican platform.

9. In *Dickerson v. United States* (2000), the Court reaffirmed the continued validity of *Miranda*, stating that its evidentiary principles were grounded in the Fifth Amendment.

10. See *Contractors Association of Eastern Pennsylvania v. Schultz* (3d Cir. 1971).

11. Pub. L. No. 92-261, 86 Stat. 103 (1972).

12. H.R. 13916, 92d Cong. (1972); S. 3388, 92d Cong. (1972).

13. 1980 Republican platform, at 667.

14. Pub. L. No. 100-259, 102 Stat. 28 (1988).

15. *Grove City v. Bell* (1984).

16. 1988 Republican platform, at 755.

17. See *Metro Broadcasting v. FCC* (1991).

18. Pub. L. No. 102-166, 105 Stat. 1071 (1991).

19. 1980 Republican platform, at 668.

20. 3 C.F.R. 197 (1983), reprinted in 31 U.S.C. § 6506 (1994).

21. 3 C.F.R. 252 (1988), reprinted in 5 U.S.C. § 601 (1994).

22. 384 U.S. 641 (1966).

23. Reagan Guidelines, at 59–60. See also, Report to Attorney General, at 130–140.

24. 1988 Republican platform, at 757–58.

25. 1 Pub. Papers 238 (February 16, 1990).

26. 3 C.F.R. 296, 96–97 (1992).

27. Pub. L. No. 101-647, 104 Stat. 4845 (1991).

28. 514 U.S. 549 (1995).

29. 1980 Republican platform, at 689.

30. This language provoked widespread criticism, and the American Bar Association voted overwhelmingly at its annual convention to oppose judicial selection "on the basis of particular political or ideological philosophies." In addition, a group called Americans Concerned for the Judiciary placed advertisements that depicted nine justices with Reagan's face and warned that "this GOP litmus test would de-

stroy the independent federal judiciary as we know it." In response to such intense criticism of the platform's language, Reagan announced early in October, one month before the election, that he would not select judges on the basis of their opinions on any single issue (Turner, 1980). Once elected, Reagan renounced this promise.

31. Reagan Guidelines, at 82. See also, Report to Attorney General, at 11–19.

32. 1988 Republican platform, at 755.

33. In *Planned Parenthood of Southeast Pennsylvania v. Casey* (1992), the Court considered the constitutionality of a Pennsylvania statute restricting the availability of abortions, including a requirement that married women notify their husbands before having abortions. In so doing, the Court took the opportunity to revisit the decision in *Roe v. Wade*. Although reaffirming the "essential holding of *Roe*," the Court allowed state and federal legislatures more leeway in enacting statutory restrictions on abortions. The Court did, however, strike down the spousal notification provision in the Pennsylvania statute.

34. *Encyclopedia of the Democratic Party,* 1976 Platform (Armonk, N.Y.: Sharpe Reference), at 705. Hereafter cited as 1976 Democratic platform.

35. It must also be said that unlike his Democratic predecessor in the White House, Johnson, and the two subsequent Democratic presidential nominees, Walter Mondale and Michael Dukakis, Carter was, in fact, in favor of the death penalty (Charlton, 1976). Indeed, as governor of Georgia, Carter signed into law the death penalty statute that later became the test case before the Supreme Court on the constitutionality of the death penalty (*Gregg v. Georgia* [1976]).

36. 530 U.S. 428 (2000).

37. 1976 Democratic platform, at 701.

38. See Supreme Court Amicus Brief of the United States in *Board of Education of the Township of Piscataway v. Taxman* (1996). At the behest of civil rights leaders, the township settled this case before a decision was handed down in order to avoid what many legal experts expected would be another adverse affirmative action ruling by the Rehnquist Court.

39. 1976 Democratic platform, at 705 (emphasis added).

40. Ibid., at 701 (emphasis added).

41. 3 C.F.R. 146 (1998), reprinted in 5 U.S.C. § 601 (1999).

42. The Federalism Act of 1999, H.R. 2245, 106th Cong., 2d Sess. (1999); the Federalism Accountability Act of 1999, S. 1214, 106th Cong., 2d Sess. (1999); the Federalism Preservation Act of 1999, H.R. 2960, 106th Cong., 2d Sess. (1999).

43. Executive Order 13,095, 3 C.F.R. 202 (1999), reprinted in 5 U.S.C. § 601 (1999).

44. 64 Fed. Reg. 43,255 (1999), reprinted in 5 U.S.C. § 601 (1999).

45. See *United States v. Morrison* (2000); *Seminole Tribe v. Florida* (1996); and *United States v. Lopez* (1995).

46. *The Encyclopedia of the Democratic Party,* 1980 Platform, at 729.

47. Ibid., 1992 Platform, at 836.

48. Although a shift in public opinion toward a tougher stance on crime has been documented over the past three decades, the biggest movement appears to have come in the late 1960s to late 1970s, and not in the time frame between the Carter and Clinton presidencies (Page and Shapiro, 1992, at 92). The post-1980s period experiences a leveling off of public opinion on this issue.

CHAPTER FOUR

  1. In *Virginia v. Black* (2003), the Supreme Court struck down a Virginia statute criminalizing cross-burning on First Amendment grounds. Justice Thomas dissented, claiming such a statute prohibited conduct, not speech.

  2. *Weekly Compilation of Presidential Documents*, Vol. 16, No. 38, September 22, 1980.

  3. Executive Order 11,972.

  4. Beginning with the Reagan administration, senators' ability to use district court judgeships as patronage also began to erode. First, Reagan insisted that home state senators from his party submit not one name for a district court judgeship, but several names, from which the Reagan administration would choose its preferred candidate (Goldman, 1997). Thus, senators had to be mindful of the ideological litmus test Reagan used in choosing lower court judges, or else risk having the president choose none of the senators' candidates. Second, during the 1980s, interest groups began to get involved not just in judicial nomination politics, but in judicial confirmation politics as well (see Chapter 5). Thus, senators who supported ideologically objectionable judicial candidates to the district courts would be held accountable by interest groups on which senators relied for reelection. Thus, like presidents, senators were forced to be mindful of the policy objectives of sympathetic interest groups. Today, while patronage is still a consideration of home state senators in proposing multiple district court nominees to the president, senators must also make sure that their preferred candidates are in line with the ideological objectives of the appointing president and the activists engaged in judicial appointment politics (see Chapter 1).

  5. Although originally appointed to the Fifth Circuit, Judge Hatchett moved to the Eleventh Circuit when it was created in 1981. He was thus the first African American to sit on the Eleventh Circuit as well.

  6. Like Judge Hatchett, Judge Kravitch also moved to the Eleventh Circuit in 1981 and became the first woman on that circuit court.

  7. The lack of a causal relationship between socioeconomic status and political ideology among African Americans is contrary to what is observed among white voters—where increased income and education have been shown to increase conservativeness. This contrary finding among African Americans is perhaps best explained in Dawson's *Behind the Mule: Race and Class in African-American Politics* (1994). There, he demonstrates that African American political ideology is shaped by the individual's perception of "linked fate" with the black race as a whole and that blacks' feelings of "linked fate" do not significantly vary across socioeconomic classes. Thus, for example, because highly educated African Americans are about as likely as high school–educated blacks to feel a "linked fate" with the black race, both educational groups are likely to share the same political ideology. And as public opinion polls demonstrate, African Americans are overwhelmingly aligned with the liberal wing of the Democratic Party (Bolce, De Maio, and Muzzio, 1992).

  8. Gregory was a recess appointee of Clinton's. Because G. W. Bush made Gregory's appointment one for life, Gregory is included in the G. W. Bush column in Table 4-1.

9. As described in Chapter 6, this tactic—of soliciting help from blacks at the grass-roots level—is precisely the strategy that key interest groups use when mounting a fight against an objectionable nominee.

10. The praise for Clinton, however, was not unanimous among African American elites, as some black activists criticized Clinton for not appointing an African American to this civil rights position. For example, Boon-Ja-Ba, a Michigan-based group that seeks to give blacks access to the global marketplace, wrote: "the promotion of civil rights is a Black American movement created to combat racism and Jim Crow laws in the South . . . Putting a Chinese [person] in charge of our movement is tantamount to choosing us a leader . . . For President Clinton to say that Lee is the best person he could find to defend civil rights is an insult to the legacy of Martin Luther King, Medgar Evers, Emmett Till and the thousands of lynched Black martyrs of this movement" (Boon-Ja-Ba, 1998).

11. Remarks of Senator Hatch (R-UT), 142 Cong. Rec. S2790-01 (March 25, 1996).

12. Article II of the Constitution grants the president the power to "fill up all Vacancies that may happen during the Recess of the Senate, by granting Commissions which shall expire at the End of their next Session." Presidents have often used this recess appointment power to fill judicial vacancies, subject to later Senate consent. Some of the most esteemed jurists in our nation's history have initially assumed the federal bench through recess appointment, including Warren, William J. Brennan, and Marshall (when appointed to the U.S. Court of Appeals).

13. It should also be noted that although Republican senators Hatch (UT), Thurmond (SC), Grassley (IA), Specter (PA), Kyl (AZ), and Dewine (OH) voted to confirm Justice White on the Judiciary Committee, they changed their votes on the floor of the Senate at Senator Ashcroft's urging. (Remarks of Senator Leahy [D-VT], 145 Cong. Rec. S7791-01 [June 29, 1999].)

14. Carnahan, a Democrat, had pardoned a convicted murderer at the behest of the Pope (Mannies, 1999). Making much of this issue in the press, Ashcroft immediately saw his poll numbers rise (Ayres, 1999).

15. During Thomas's confirmation proceedings, the FBI uncovered a witness, Anita Hill, who would testify at the hearings that Thomas had sexually harassed her on the job while serving as her superior at the Department of Justice and the Equal Employment Opportunity Commission. Despite these allegations, the Senate voted to confirm Thomas 52–48.

16. Interviewed on *Larry King Live*, December 28, 1992 (transcript available at http://www.lexis-nexis.com).

17. Harriet Woods, president of the National Women's Political Caucus, interviewed on *Good Morning America*, January 22, 1992 (transcript available at http://www.lexis-nexis.com).

18. Interviewed on *Nightline*, February 8, 1993 (transcript available at http://www.lexis-nexis.com).

19. When it came to Supreme Court nominations, however, female activists took a different approach. When Justice Byron R. White announced his retirement only two months into Clinton's presidency, activists immediately called on the president to nominate a woman to the Supreme Court. Both Helen Neubourne, executive

director of the NOW Legal Defense and Education Fund, and Smeal stated that Clinton "*must*" appoint a woman to fill Justice White's seat (Biskupic, 1993). Clinton ultimately chose Ruth Bader Ginsburg.

20. Since the Nixon cohort includes no female judges, only the probability of a male Nixon appointee voting to regulate abortion is included in the analysis.

CHAPTER FIVE

1. In his 1995 book, *The Selling of Supreme Court Nominees*, Maltese cites just two examples of interest group involvement in the Supreme Court confirmation process before passage of the Seventeenth Amendment: Stanley Mathews, first nominated by Rutherford B. Hayes and later renominated by James A. Garfield (and opposed by the farm lobby), and Horace H. Luraton, nominated by William Howard Taft (and opposed by labor organizations).

2. The only example of concerted interest group opposition to a lower court nominee before the 1980s was in the case of Harry Wellford, nominated by Ford to the Sixth Circuit Court of Appeals in 1976. On the basis of his record as a district court judge, civil rights groups opposed the Wellford nomination on the ground that he was hostile to constitutionally protected rights for minorities (Editorial, *New York Times*, 1976).

3. See the Federalist Society website at http://www.fed-soc.org.

4. See the Alliance for Justice website at http://www.afj.org.

5. Among those 1985 conservative appointments were Frank H. Easterbrook (Seventh Circuit), John F. Noonan (Ninth Circuit), J. Daniel Mahoney (Second Circuit), Bobby Ray Baldock (Tenth Circuit), James L. Buckley (D.C. Circuit), and Laurence H. Silberman (D.C. Circuit) (Schwartz, 1988).

6. As discussed more fully in Chapter 7, Gorton went on to lose that Senate race; some cited his political horse-trading with judicial nominations to be one of the issues costing him the election.

7. See http://www.freecongress.org/centers/ld/jsmp/index.asp.

8. Other conservative groups joined JSMP in the fight against Guinier, seeing it as an opportunity to turn the tables on liberals and use the same tactics against her that liberals used to defeat the Supreme Court nomination of Bork in 1987 (Lewis, 1993a).

9. Specifically cited were the Clinton log-roll appointees Ted Stewart, a nominee for the Utah District Court supported by Hatch, and Barbara Durham, a nominee for the Ninth Circuit supported by former Republican Washington Senator Gorton.

10. In fact, Gandy stated that grass-roots members of NOW have even gone so far as to telephone in "anonymous" tips on where important information might be found to use against nominees who oppose NOW's civil rights agenda.

11. This new way of couching the judicial philosophy debate can be gleaned from the 1984 Republican platform, which called for the appointment of judges at all levels who respect both "the sanctity of innocent human life" and "share [Reagan's] commitment to *judicial restraint*" (*Encyclopedia of the Republican Party*, 1984 platform, at 728, 730; emphasis added).

12. Aron's message has been consistent throughout the years. Upon the forma-

tion of the Alliance for Justice, Aron was quoted as saying that the group will promote the selection of judges who are "independent, nonpartisan and believe in equal justice and fairness" (quoted in Clarity and Weaver, 1985).

13. Occasionally, cases concerning gun control and product-liability issues were also cited as examples of judicial activism.

14. Another issue cited with much less frequency is the environment.

CHAPTER SIX

1. Sometimes senators block a nomination from proceeding by placing a "hold" on the nomination. Traditionally, holds were used to block nominations not on the basis of ideology, but rather to give senators more time to review the qualifications of a candidate. However, in recent times, senators began using this tactic to delay confirmation (Bell, 2002a). Unlike a blue slip or a filibuster, which would permanently kill a nomination, a hold will only temporarily delay a vote. And because holds are anonymous, the tactic would not be a particularly effective elite mobilization strategy, which requires a public display of opposition to a nomination.

2. 142 Cong. Rec. S1161-04, at S1163 (Feb. 9, 1996).

3. 142 Cong. Rec. S3699-02 (April 19, 1996).

4. 143 Cong. Rec. S2536 (Jan. 20, 1997).

5. Remarks of Senators Sessions (R-AL), Kyl (R-AZ), Grassley (R-IA), and Thurmond (R-SC), 143 Cong. Rec. S2515-01, S2520–24 (March 19, 1997).

6. Remarks of Senator Leahy (D-VT), ibid., S2524–26.

7. Remarks of Senator Reid (D-NV), 147 Cong. Rec., S10832 (October 18, 2001); see also remarks of Senator Durbin (D-IL), 147 Cong. Rec., S13668 (December 19, 2001).

8. Remarks of Senator Leahy (D-VT), 148 Cong. Rec., S276, S277 (February 4, 2002).

9. Pub. L. No. 95-486, 92 Stat. 1629.

10. Statement of Senator Kennedy, "Selection and Confirmation of Federal Judges: Hearing Before the Senate Committee on the Judiciary," Part I, 96th Cong. (1979), at 4.

11. Ibid.

12. The *New York Times* reported that the Senate had filibustered the nomination of Thurgood Marshall for the Second Circuit Court of Appeals in 1962, but in actuality, this was a hold put on the Senate Judiciary Committee's consideration of the nomination and not a filibuster (see Editorial, *New York Times*, 1962).

13. McKeague, Griffin, and Saad were filibustered primarily because Democrats objected to Chairman Hatch's decision to send these nominations to the floor notwithstanding the fact that both home state senators from Michigan (Deborah Stabenow and Carl Levin) gave negative blue slips to these nominees. The reason that the Democratic senators were blocking these nominees is tied to a long-running feud between Republicans and Democrats over which party rightfully deserves to name judges for two of the Michigan seats on the Sixth Circuit. Because former Republican senator Spencer Abraham (R-MI) blue-slipped two of Clinton's nominees to the Sixth Circuit (Helene White and Kathleen McCree Lewis), these two seats

remained opened when G. W. Bush took office. Then, when G. W. Bush tried to fill these vacancies at the beginning of his presidency, the two Democratic senators from Michigan—Abraham was defeated in the 2000 election by Stabenow—refused to consent to any of the president's four court of appeals nominees for Michigan seats unless White and McCree Lewis were first given appointments (Pickler, 2001). The White House refused to cooperate. While the Senate was controlled by Democrats in the 107th Congress, G. W. Bush's Michigan nominations were not given Judiciary Committee hearings or floor votes. Once the Republicans took back the Senate in the 108th Congress, however, Judiciary Committee Chairman Hatch and Republican Majority Leader William Frist (R–TN) were determined to give these Michigan nominees roll-call votes (Durbin, 2003). Thus, in a showing of solidarity with their colleagues from Michigan, Democrats in the Senate agreed to support a filibuster of these nominees (Durbin, 2004).

CHAPTER SEVEN

1. In her book *Making Crime Pay* (1997), Katherine Beckett argues that the salience of the crime issue in the 1968 presidential campaign was due, not to rising crime rates, but rather to Nixon's campaign rhetoric playing on racial tensions.

2. *Encyclopedia of the Republican Party*, 1972 Platform, at 617.

3. Ibid., 1980 Platform, at 689 (emphasis added).

4. Ibid., 1988 Platform, at 758.

5. Ibid., 1992 Platform, at 801.

6. Later "inductees" included Sixth Circuit Judge Martha Craig Daughtrey (Loggins, 1996), District Judge Carl Muecke of Arizona (a Johnson appointee with whom the Clinton administration sided regarding a decision to give Arizona state prisoners greater access to prison law libraries and legal aid) (Kellman, 1996), and Fourth Circuit Judge Diana Gibbon Motz (Rosen, 1996).

7. Much to the consternation of many other federal court judges, including Chief Justice Rehnquist, Judge Baer eventually capitulated to Clinton's demands and reversed his original search and seizure decision (Goshko and Reckler, 1996; Greenhouse, 1996a).

8. Indeed, *Wall Street Journal* columnist Paul Gigot wrote, "Mr. Dole needs to find some way to energize his voters, and a battle to block a Clinton version of the Warren Court is a good bet" (Gigot, 1996).

9. 1996 Republican Party Platform, online at http://www.presidency.ucsb.edu/platforms.php, accessed January 26, 2005.

10. 2004 Republican Party Platform, online at http://www.gop.com/media/2004platform, accessed April 1, 2005.

11. Cornyn for Senate website, online at http://www.cornynforsenate.com, accessed September 8, 2002.

12. Ibid.

13. Texas Watch, online at http://www.texaswatch.org, accessed July 9, 2002.

14. G. W. Bush, quoted on the White House website, online at http://www.whitehouse.gov, accessed September 17, 2002.

15. Although the first vote was 48–46 in Manion's favor, this was the result of a

parliamentary move by Senator Robert Byrd (D-WV) intended to buy the Democrats more time.

16. On the same day of the Ronnie White vote, Democratic lawmakers and Latino civil rights activists also held a press conference accusing the Republican-controlled Senate of taking longer to confirm minority and female judges than white male judges (Simon, 1999).

17. Involvement of the black churches in this effort was critical. As far back as 1903, scholars have recognized the pivotal role that the black church plays in the political mobilization of African Americans (see, for example, Brown, 1996; DuBois [1903], 1965; Morris, 1984; McAdam, 1982).

18. Later, the Caucus would write President Clinton formally requesting such extraordinary action, stating that the party line vote against Justice White for a federal judgeship "left profound doubts about fair and unbiased treatment" for minority judicial candidates (Goldstein, 1999).

19. So dismayed by Ashcroft's actions, black Missouri political and religious leaders were not even swayed by the revelation that Ashcroft's opponent, Carnahan, had performed in black face in the early part of his political career (*St. Louis Post-Dispatch*, 1999; Bell and Schlinkmann, 1999; Associated Press, 1999).

20. This speech prompted a letter from Texas Republican senators Phil Gramm and Kay Bailey Hutchison to Clinton, accusing the president of "trading on judicial nominations as a device to generate money for Democratic political campaigns" (Houston Chronicle News Service, 2000).

CHAPTER EIGHT

1. For six years during the Reagan administration, only one legislative chamber, the House of Representatives, was controlled by the Democrats, while the Republicans controlled the Senate. From May 2001 through December 2002, during the G. W. Bush administration, the Democrats controlled the Senate but not the House. In all other years of divided government in the modern political era, both chambers of Congress were controlled by the party opposite to that of the president.

2. 142 Cong. Rec. S1161-04, at S1163 (Feb. 2, 1996).

3. I did not analyze the abortion cases because there was an insufficient number of votes in the Reagan and Clinton cohorts to obtain meaningful results once each cohort was separated by divided or unified government.

4. Biden also chaired the Judiciary Committee from 1993 to 1994 during the Clinton administration when Democrats controlled both the Executive and Legislative branches.

5. In his Congressional Research Service Report for Congress on cloture attempts, Richard S. Beth (2002) explains that identifying whether a filibuster is technically launched is often a difficult task because there are several different procedural tactics that may delay a roll-call vote; much easier to identify is whether a cloture motion is made to cut off debate. Accordingly, Beth's report focuses on the use of cloture motions to impose supermajority voting rules on presidential nominations, rather than the use of filibusters. Similarly, Table 8-2 reports cloture motions rather than filibusters.

APPENDIX A

1. Given that the Eleventh Circuit was not created until 1978, there are no Eleventh Circuit cases in this data set.

2. I would have also included "unpublished" decisions contained in the WEST-LAW database—those not designated for publication in the *Federal Reporter* but reprinted in full by WESTLAW, as I did with the other data sets used in this book, but I found no such FLSA cases in the designated time period.

3. Nonunanimous cases are limited to those in which a dissent is filed by a judge sitting on a court of appeals panel; in contrast, nonconsensual cases also include unanimous reversals by court of appeals panels of district court decisions. Unlike the Supreme Court, which has the discretion to hear only "close" cases it deems to be of national importance, the courts of appeals are the final arbiter of more than 99 percent of all federal court claims—as all federal court litigants have one appeal as of right (Goldman, 1973). Because the vast majority of these appeals are not "close" cases, but are taken so as to exhaust all possible legal avenues, there is generally but one clear decisional path available to the judges hearing these cases. In other words, the case may be finally adjudicated—and full agreement reached by the appellate panel and the district court judge—without underlying political ideologies playing a role in the decision-making process. In short, fully consensual decisions in the lower federal courts are generally deemed to reflect decisions based on precedent, statutes, or facts (Goldman, 1975, 1966; Songer, 1982). Thus, in order to answer the question—why do judges vote differently given the same case?—it is necessary to limit the analysis to nonunanimous or nonconsensual appeals cases. For purposes of my analysis, I have chosen to include all nonconsensual cases.

Although studies are more often limited to nonunanimous cases only, Goldman's seminal work on the U.S. Courts of Appeals also included nonconsensual cases (Goldman, 1966, at 375). Thus, just as nonunanimous cases serve as a proxy for "close" cases (since one of three judges deciding the same exact legal question reaches a different legal conclusion), so too do nonconsensual cases (in which at least one of four judges deciding the exact same legal question reaches a different legal conclusion).

4. Trying to find another type of data set with a similar problem to the one my data present led me to consider research in which congressional roll-call voting is the dependent variable. Like my judicial data, you would have multiple votes by the same member of Congress. A program available using STATA is intended to take care of this problem when panel data are being used, but it is also used by congressional scholars using roll-call votes as the dependent variable. This proved to not be a viable solution because, unlike panel data or congressional roll-call voting data—where every member of Congress has multiple votes—my data contain many judges who have only one vote. Thus, the STATA program automatically eliminates these single judge votes from the analysis, and to eliminate such votes would produce a biased sample.

5. That coefficient had the same sign and roughly the same magnitude but fell outside the 95 percent confidence interval.

6. In fact, some research suggests that a fixed-effect estimator is also *not* appro-

priate in this context because, in such panel data, the effect is not truly fixed (Beck and Katz, 2000).

APPENDIX B

1. *Coolidge v. New Hampshire* (1971); *Aquilar v. Texas* (1964).
2. *Katz v. United States* (1967).
3. *Silverman v. United States* (1961).
4. *Davis v. Mississippi* (1969).
5. *United States v. Ramsey* (1977); *Chimel v. California* (1969); *Davis v. Mississippi* (1969); *Carroll v. United States* (1925).
6. *Schneckloth v. Bustamonte* (1973).
7. *Terry v. Ohio* (1968).
8. Although the relevant cases collected for analysis may include votes of judges appointed by Presidents Eisenhower, Kennedy, Johnson, and Ford, the votes of these presidential cohorts were excluded from the data set, and all data sets used in the modern party era, because they produced too few votes to gain statistically meaningful results.

APPENDIX D

1. As was true of the search and seizure model (Appendix B), I cannot include many of the extra-legal factors controlled for in the race discrimination model because they either are constants in the states' rights model (e.g., there are no class action cases or pro se plaintiffs) or are facts not mentioned in the opinions and thus cannot be controlled for (e.g., race of the plaintiff). Accordingly, fact-based variables are limited strictly to legal facts.
2. *Edelman v. Jordan* (1974), at 662–63.
3. *Seminole Tribe v. Florida* (1996).
4. Ibid.
5. *Healy v. Beer Institute* (1989).
6. *Cloverleaf Butter Co. v. Patterson* (1942), at 155–56.
7. *Leisy v. Hardin* (1890), at 119.
8. *United States v. Lopez* (1995).
9. *United States v. Morrison* (2000).

APPENDIX E

1. The trimester framework enunciated in *Roe* was modified in *Casey v. Planned Parenthood* (1992). *Casey* held that the state has an interest in protecting the fetus from conception but may not unduly burden access to abortion of pre-viable fetuses.
2. *Danforth* (1976), at 75.

References

Abrams, Jim. 1999. "Nominee's Rejection Infuriates Clinton," *New Orleans Times-Picayune* (Oct. 11), p. A2.

Aldrich, John H. 1995. *Why Parties? The Origin and Transformation of Party Politics in America.* Chicago: University of Chicago Press.

Aldrich, John H., and Forrest D. Nelson. 1984. *Linear Probability, Logit and Probit Models.* Beverly Hills: Sage Press.

Alvarez, Lisette. 2001. "Ashcroft Meets with Black Lawmakers Who Opposed His Nomination," *New York Times* (Mar. 1), p. A17.

Amaker, Norman C. 1988. *Civil Rights and the Reagan Administration.* New York: Rowman & Littlefield.

Anderson, David C. 1995. *Crime and the Politics of Hysteria: How the Willie Horton Story Changed American Justice.* New York: Crown.

Apple, R. W., Jr. 1986. "Primary in Washington Could Decide Fall Race," *New York Times* (Sept. 12), p. A12.

Aron, Nan. 2002. Interview with the author. Tape recording, July 9. Washington, D.C.

Associated Press. 2001. "Bitter Senate Fight Threatens Bush's Choices for Judgeships," *St. Louis Post-Dispatch* (May 5), p. 19.

———. 1999. "Black Religious Leaders Support Carnahan," *St. Louis Post-Dispatch* (Nov. 2), p. B3.

———. 1996. "Complete Text of Dole Speech," *Arizona Republic* (Aug. 16), p. G3.

Ayres, B. Drummond, Jr. 1999. "Political Briefing; In Missouri, Religion and Politics," *New York Times* (Apr. 28), p. A18.

———. 1992. "The 1992 Campaign: Democrats; Buoyed Clinton Goes on the Offensive," *New York Times* (July 1), p. A15.

Babbington, Charles, and Joan Biskupic. 1999. "Senate Rejects Judicial Nominee; Clinton Decries 'Disgraceful Party Vote on Black Jurist,'" *Washington Post* (Oct. 6), p. A1.

Baker, Peter. 1997. "Clinton: GOP Stalling on Filling Judgeships," *Chicago Sun-Times* (Sept. 28), p. 27.

Barker, Lucius J. 1967. "Third Parties in Litigation: A Systematic View of the Judicial Function," *Journal of Politics* 29: 41–69.

Baum, Lawrence. 1990. *American Courts: Process and Policy.* Boston: Houghton Mifflin Co.

Beck, Nathaniel, and Jonathan N. Katz. 2000. "Throwing Out the Baby With the Bath Water: A Comment on Green, Yoon and Kim." Unpublished paper.

Beckett, Katherine. 1997. *Making Crime Pay: Law and Order in Contemporary American Politics*. New York: Oxford University Press.

Bell, Bill, Jr., and Mark Schlinkmann. 1999. "Carnahan Offers Apology for Wearing Black Face in Show," *St. Louis Post-Dispatch* (Oct. 26), p. A1.

Bell, Lauren Cohen. 2002a. "Senatorial Discourtesy: The Senate's Use of Delay to Shape the Federal Judiciary," *Political Research Quarterly* 55: 589–608.

———. 2002b. *Warring Factions: Interest Groups, Money, and the New Politics of Senate Confirmation*. Columbus: Ohio State University Press.

Belz, Herman. 1991. *Equality Transformed: A Quarter Century of Affirmative Action*. New York: W. W. Norton & Co.

Beth, Richard A. 2002. "Cloture Attempts on Nominations," Congressional Research Service Report for Congress, online at www.senate.gov/reference/resources/pdf/RS20801.pdf, accessed May 5, 2005.

Bickel, Alexander M. 1986. *The Least Dangerous Branch*. New Haven, Conn.: Yale University Press.

———. 1970. *The Supreme Court and the Idea of Progress*. New York: Harper & Row.

Binder, Sarah A., and Forrest Maltzman. 2002. "Senatorial Delay in Confirming Federal Court Judges, 1947–1998," *American Journal of Political Science* 46: 190–99.

Bolce, Louis, Gerald De Maio, and Douglas Muzzio. 1992. "Blacks and the Republican Party: The 20 Percent Solution," *Political Science Quarterly* 107: 63–79.

Boon-Ja-Ba. 1998. "Bill Lann Lee Appointment an Insult," *Michigan Chronicle* (April 1), p. 6.

Boyd, Herb. 1999. "Gore Irritated by Partisan Politics," *New York Amsterdam News* (Oct. 21), p. 3.

Brogan, Pamela. 2000. "Race Is a Factor in Missouri Senate Race," *Gannett News Service* (Sept. 14), p. 1.

———. 1999. "Civil Rights Groups Lash Out at Bond Over Judgeship Appointment," *Gannett News Service* (Oct. 7).

Brown, Allison Calhoun. 1996. "African American Churches and Political Mobilization: The Psychological Impact of Organizational Resources," *Journal of Politics* 58: 935–53.

Browning, Sandra Lee, and Linqun Cao. 1992. "The Impact of Race on Criminal Justice Ideology," *Justice Quarterly* 9: 685–99.

Brownstein, Ronald. 1997. "Clinton Continues Attack on Prop. 209 With TV Interview," *Los Angeles Times* (June 16), p. A3.

Brudney, James J., Sara Schiavoni, and Deborah Jones Merritt. 1999. "Judicial Hostility Toward Labor Unions? Applying the Social Background Model to a Celebrated Concern," *Ohio State Law Journal* 60: 1675–1771.

Brune, Tom. 2003. "Hatch Hopes to Fast Track Judge Picks," *New York Newsday* (Jan. 24), p. A6.

Buffalo News. 1996. "Dole Goes Overboard About Judges," *Buffalo News* (May 5), p. 8F.

Bumiller, Elisabeth. 2002. "Bush Vows to Seek Conservative Judges," *New York Times* (Mar. 29), p. A24.

Burdette, Franklin. 1940. *Filibustering in the Senate*. New York: Russell & Russell Publishers.

Burk, Robert Frederick. 1984. *The Eisenhower Administration and Black Civil Rights*. Knoxville: University of Tennessee Press.

Caldeira, Gregory A. 1991. "Courts and Public Opinion," in *The American Courts*, edited by John B. Gates and Charles A. Johnson. Washington, D.C.: Congressional Quarterly Press.

Caldeira, Gregory A., and John R. Wright. 1998. "Lobbying for Justice: Organized Interests, Supreme Court Nominations, and United States Senate," *American Journal of Political Science* 42: 499–523.

Cameron, Charles M. 2000. *Veto Bargaining: Presidents and the Politics of Negative Power*. New York: Cambridge University Press.

Cameron, Charles M., Albert D. Cover, and Jeffrey A. Segal. 1990. "Senate Voting on Supreme Court Nominees: A Neoinstitutional Model," *American Political Science Review* 84: 525–34.

Campbell, Angus, Philip E. Converse, Warren E. Miller, and Donald E. Stokes. 1960. *The American Voter*. New York: Wiley.

Carmines, Edward G., and James A. Stimson. 1989. *Issue Evolution: Race and the Transformation of American Politics*. Princeton, N.J.: Princeton University Press.

Carp, Robert A., and Ronald Stidham. 1998. *The Federal Courts* (3rd ed.). Washington, D.C.: Congressional Quarterly Press.

Carter, Mike. 1999. "Coalition Protests Durham for Appeals Court," *Seattle Times* (Feb. 1), p. B3.

Carter, Stephen. 1994. *The Confirmation Mess*. New York: Basic Books.

Casino, Bruce J. 1988. "Federal Grants-in-Aid: Evolution, Crisis and Future," *Urban Lawyer* (Winter): 25–71.

Cavendish, Elizabeth. 2002. Interview with the author. Tape recording, July 10. Washington, D.C.

Chambers, Marcia. 1984. "Advocates for the Right to Life," *New York Times Magazine* (Dec. 16), p. 94.

Charlton, Linda. 1976. "Mondale Reports He Is Encouraged," *New York Times* (July 30), Sec. 1, p. 6.

Chase, Harold. 1972. *Federal Judges: The Appointing Process*. Minneapolis: University of Minnesota Press.

Chernoff, Harry A., Christopher M. Kelly, and John R. Kroger. 1996. "The Politics of Crime," *Harvard Journal on Legislation* 33: 527–79.

Chiang, Harriet. 2000. "Two Confirmed to Court in San Francisco After Long Battle in Senate," *San Francisco Chronicle* (Mar. 10), p. A1.

Clarity, James F., and Warren Weaver Jr. 1985. "Here Comes the Judge," *New York Times* (Jan. 18), p. A14.

Clinton, William. 1999. "President Clinton Addresses Justice System," *Criminal Justice* 14: 36-38.

———. 1992. "Judiciary Suffers Racial, Sexual Lack of Balance," *National Law Journal* (Nov. 2), p. 15.

Cohen, Lauren M. 1998. "Missing in Action: Interest Groups and Federal Judicial Appointments," *Judicature* 82: 119–20.

Conlan, Timothy. 1988. *New Federalism: Intergovernmental Reform From Nixon to Reagan.* Washington, D.C.: Brookings Institution.

Conway, M. Margaret, and Frank B. Feigert. 1968. "Motivation and Incentive System and the Political Party Organization," *American Political Science Review* 62: 1159–73.

Costain, Anne J. N. 1980. "Changes in the Role of Ideology in American Nominating Conventions and Among Party Identifiers," *Western Political Quarterly* 33: 73–86.

Crenshaw, Kimberle Williams. 1988. "Race, Reform and Retrenchment: Transformation and Legitimation in Antidiscrimination Law," *Harvard Law Review* 101: 1331–87.

Cross, Frank B. 1988. "Executive Orders 12,291 and 12,498: A Test Case in Presidential Control of Executive Agencies," *Journal of Politics and Law* 4: 483–541.

Davies, Thomas Y. 2002. "The Fictional Character of Law-and-Order Originalism: A Case Study of the Distortions and Evasions of Framing-Era Arrest Doctrine in *Atwater v. Lago Vista,*" *Wake Forest Law Review* 37: 239–437.

Davis, Abraham L. 1989. *Blacks in the Federal Judiciary: Neutral Arbiters or Judicial Activists?* Bristol, Ind.: Wyndham Hall Press.

Days, Drew S. 1984. "Turning Back the Clock: The Reagan Administration and Civil Rights," *Harvard Civil Rights–Civil Liberties Law Review* 19: 309–47.

Denning, Brannon P. 2001. "The Judicial Appointments Process: The 'Blue Slip': Enforcing the Norms of Judicial Confirmation," *William and Mary Bill of Rights Journal* 10: 75–101.

Devins, Neal. 1991. "Affirmative Action After Reagan," *Texas Law Review* 68: 353–79.

Dewar, Helen. 2003. "Panel Backs Pickering for Appellate Bench," *Washington Post* (Oct. 3), p. A21.

———. 2000. "Hatch Ends Presidential Bid, Backs Bush," *Washington Post* (Jan. 27), p. A7.

Dine, Phillip, Bill Lambrecht, and Terrence Samuel. 2000. "D.C. Connection," *St. Louis Post-Dispatch* (Feb. 6), p. A14.

Dubois, W. E. B. [1903], 1965. *The Sound of Black Folk.* New York: Avon Books.

Dudziak, Mary. 1997. "The Little Rock Crisis and Foreign Affairs," *Southern California Law Review* 70: 1641–1716.

Durbin, Dee-Ann. 2004. "U.S. Senate Democrats Block Votes on Michigan Judges," Associated Press (July 22).

———. 2003. "Michigan Judges Held Hostage by Senate Democrats, GOP Lawmakers Say" Associated Press (July 9).

Duverger, Maurice. 1964. *Political Parties.* New York: Wiley.

Editorial, *Amsterdam News.* 1992. "Federal Judiciary Appointments: An Opportunity for Clinton, Moynihan and D'Amato," *Amsterdam News* (Nov. 21), p. 12.

Editorial, *Chicago Defender,* 2000. "All's Fair in Love, War . . . and Politics," *Chicago Defender* (Aug. 15), p. 9.

———. 1999. "Clinton Leaving a Great Judicial Legacy," *Chicago Defender* (Sept. 8), p. 11.

———. 1997. "Praise Clinton for Placing Lee in Civil Rights Post," *Chicago Defender* (Dec. 22), p. 11.

Editorial, *Michigan Chronicle*. 1993. "Clinton Finds Another Turn-His-Back Way to Thank Blacks for Their Support," *Michigan Chronicle* (June 9), p. 8-A.

Editorial, *New York Times*. 2002. "An Unworthy Judicial Nomination," *New York Times* (Feb. 24), Sec. 4, p. 12.

———. 1986. "What Kind of Like-Minded Judges?" *New York Times* (May 8), p. A26.

———. 1980. "The Senate's Message to Itself," *New York Times* (Dec. 1), p. A18.

———. 1976. "A Bad Nomination," *New York Times* (Sept. 9), p. 19.

———. 1962. "Confirmation at Last?" *New York Times* (Aug. 23), p. 28.

Editorial, *The Record*. 1992. "Quotas, Qualifications and Building a Cabinet," *The Record* (Dec. 23), p. B6.

Editorial, *Wall Street Journal*. 2000. "Hatch Versus Hatch," *Wall Street Journal* (Mar. 17), p. A34.

———. 1997. "End, Mend, Whatever," *Wall Street Journal* (Oct. 20), p. A22.

Editorial, *Washington Post*. 2001. "The First Batch," *Washington Post* (May 13), p. B6.

———. 1986. ". . . And the Screening of Judges," *Washington Post* (Nov. 11), p. A20.

Editorial, *Washington Times*. 2001. "Mr. Leahy's Fuzzy Math," *Washington Times* (Dec. 3), p. A18.

Edsall, Thomas Byrne, and Mary Edsall. 1992. *Chain Reaction: The Impact of Race, Rights and Taxes on American Politics*. New York: W. W. Norton & Co.

Edwards, George C., III, Andrew Barrett, and Jeffrey Peake. 1997. "The Legislative Impact of Divided Government," *American Journal of Political Science* 41: 545–63.

Enda, Jodi. 1992. "Women Flex Political Muscle," *The Record* (Nov. 1), p. A37.

Epp, Charles R. 1998. *The Rights Revolution*. Chicago: University of Chicago Press.

Epstein, David, and Sharyn O'Halloran. 1996. "Divided Government and the Design of Administrative Procedures: A Formal Model and Empirical Test," *Journal of Politics*. 58: 373–97.

Epstein, Lee. 1985. *Conservatives in Court*. Knoxville: University of Tennessee Press.

Evans, Evan A. 1948. "Political Influences in the Selection of Federal Judges," *Wisconsin Law Review* 1948: 330–51.

Feder, Don. 1997. "GOP Will Cave on Naming Lee," *Boston Herald* (Dec. 15), p. 23.

Finn, Chester E., Jr. 1982. "Affirmative Action Under Reagan," *Commentary* (April), pp. 17–28.

Fiorina, Morris. 1992. *Divided Government*. New York: Macmillan.

Fleming, Roy B., and B. Dan Wood. 1997. "The Public and the Supreme Court: Individual Justice Responsiveness to American Policy Moods," *American Journal of Political Science* 41: 468–98.

Franklin, Ben A. 1985. "Senate Confirms Appellate Judge," *New York Times* (Nov. 8), p. B10.

Frolick, Joe. 1992. "Feminists Says Fight Can't End With Election," *Cleveland Plain Dealer* (Nov. 17), p. 1D.

Frymer, Paul, and Albert Yoon. 2002. "Political Parties, Representation and Federal Safeguards," *Northwestern University Law Review* 96: 977–1027.

Gailey, Phil. 1986. "G.O.P. Gathering Considers Political Life After Reagan," *New York Times* (June 29), Sec. 1, p. 22.

Gandy, Kim. 2002. Interview with the author. Tape recording, July 11. Washington, D.C.

Gerhardt, Michael J. 2001. *The Federal Appointments Process: A Constitutional and Historical Analysis.* Durham, N.C.: Duke University Press.

Gibson, James L., John P. Frendreis, and Laura L. Vertz. 1989. "Party Dynamics in the 1980s: Change in County Party Organizational Strength, 1980–1984," *American Journal of Political Science* 33: 67-90.

Gigot, Paul. 1996. "Buy Bill, Get Liberal Court Free," *Wall Street Journal* (April 5), p. A8.

Goldman, Sheldon. 2003. "Unpicking Pickering in 2002: Some Thoughts on the Politics of Lower Federal Court Selection and Confirmation," *University of California Davis Law Review* 36: 695–719.

———. 1997. *Picking Federal Judges: Lower Court Selection From Roosevelt Through Reagan.* New Haven, Conn.: Yale University Press.

———. 1979. "Should There Be Affirmative Action for the Judiciary?" *Judicature* 62: 488–94.

———. 1975. "Voting Behavior on the United States Court of Appeals Revisited," *American Political Science Review* 69: 491–506.

———. 1973. "Conflict on Courts of Appeals," *Cincinnati Law Review* 42: 635–58.

———. 1967. "Judicial Appointments to the United States Courts of Appeals," *Wisconsin Law Review* 1967: 186–214.

———. 1966. "Voting Behavior on the United States Courts of Appeals, 1961–1964," *American Political Science Review* 60: 374–83.

Goldman, Sheldon, and Elliot Slotnick. 1999. "Clinton's Second Term Judiciary: Picking Judges Under Fire," *Judicature* 82: 265–68.

Goldstein, Amy. 2002. "White House Pushing Harder to Confirm Judges," *Washington Post* (Apr. 15), p. A6.

Goldstein, David. 1999. "Black Clergy Feel Betrayed by Bond's Vote on Judge," *Kansas City Star* (Oct. 13), p. A1.

———. 1995. "A Warning Sign for Left of Center Judicial Candidates," *Minneapolis Star Tribune* (Jan. 21), p. 7A.

Gordon, Greg. 1995. "Hennepin Judge Alexander Withdraws Her Candidacy for the Federal Bench," *Star Tribune* (Feb. 15), p. 1A.

Goshko, John M., and Nancy Reckler. 1996. "Controversial Drug Ruling Is Reversed," *Washington Post* (Apr. 2), p. A1.

Gottschall, Jon. 1983. "Carter's Judicial Appointments: The Influence of Affirmative Action and Merit Selection on Voting on the U.S. Courts of Appeals," *Judicature* 67: 164–75.

Green, John C., and James L. Guth. 1988. "The Christian Right in the Republican Party: The Case of Pat Robertson's Supporters," *Journal of Politics* 50: 150–65.

Greenhouse, Linda. 1996a. "Rehnquist Joins Fray on Ruling, Defending Judicial Independence," *New York Times* (April 10), Sec. A, p. 1.

———. 1996b. "Judges as Political Issues," *New York Times* (Mar. 23), p. A1.

———. 1988. "Disputed Court Nominee Promises No Surprises," *New York Times* (Feb. 26), p. B8.

———. 1984. "Panel Queries Influence in A.B.A. Judge Ratings," *New York Times* (Aug. 8), p. A12.

————. 1978. "Administration Urges Newsroom Raid Ban," *New York Times* (Dec. 14), Sec. 1, p. 1.

Griffis, Kevin. 2002. "Irreconcilable Differences?" Creative Loafing Atlanta (Dec. 11), available online at http://www.atlanta.creativeloafing.com/2002-12-11/feature.html, accessed January 26, 2005.

Hager, Philip. 1985a. "Senate Panel OKs Kozinski Appeals Court Nomination," *Los Angeles Times* (Sept. 13), Part 1, p. 3.

————. 1985b. "Democrats Grill Appeals Court Nominee," *Los Angeles Times* (Nov. 2), Part 1, p. 33.

Hall, Charles W. 1996. "Lawyers Defend Virginia Judge Mocked by Dole," *Washington Post* (Apr. 23), p. B3.

Hall, Kermit L. 1985. *The Supreme Court and Judicial Review in American History.* Washington, D.C.: American Historical Association.

Hallow, Ralph. 1996. "Dole's Flubs Worry Republican Leaders," *Washington Times* (May 2), p. A4.

Hansen, John Mark. 1991. *Gaining Access: Congress and the Farm Lobby, 1919–1981.* Chicago: University of Chicago Press.

Harden, Blaine. 1996a. "Dole Plays Dour Tune in California Swing," *Washington Post* (Mar. 24), p. A8.

————. 1996b. "Criminal Justice Failing, Dole Says Eying Clinton," *Washington Post* (May 29), p. A8.

Harris, Joseph. 1953. *The Advice and Consent of the Senate.* Berkeley: University of California Press.

Harrist, Ron. 2003. "Judge Pickering Calls Filibuster Disappointing," Associated Press State and Local Wire (Oct. 30).

Hatch, Orrin. 2002. *Square Peg: Confessions of a Citizen Senator.* New York: Basic Books.

————. 1996. "Is Clinton Tough on Crime? Look at His Judges," *Wall Street Journal* (May 1), p. A15.

Henry, Ed. 1997. "His Power Being Judged, Hatch Beats Back Leaders," *Roll Call* (May 1), p. 25.

Herbert, Bob. 2002. "A Judge's Past," *New York Times* (Feb. 7), p. A29.

Higginbotham, A. Leon. 1993. "Seeking Pluralism in Judicial Systems: The American Experience and the South African Challenge," *Duke Law Journal* 42: 1028–68.

Holland, Jesse J. 2003a. "Senate Democrats Filibuster Pickering Promotion to Federal Appeals Court," Associated Press State and Local Wire (Oct. 30).

————. 2003b. "Senate Republicans Fail to Break Long-Threatened Pickering Filibuster," Associated Press State and Local Wire (Oct. 30).

————. 2003c. "GOP to Attempt to Push Pickering Through Senate, Democrats Threaten Filibuster," Associated Press State and Local Wire (Oct. 30).

————. 2001. "Daschle, GOP Come to Terms on Nominees, Senate's New Makeup," *Arkansas Democrat-Gazette* (June 30), p. A8.

Horowitz, Donald L. 1977. *The Courts and Social Policy.* Washington, D.C.: Brookings Institution Press.

Houston Chronicle News Service. 2000. "Clinton Extols VP, Hits GOP on Judgeships," *Houston Chronicle* (July 14), p. 10.

Howard, J. Woodford. 1981. *Courts of Appeals in the Federal Judicial System: A Study of the Second, Fifth, and District of Columbia Circuits.* Princeton, N.J.: Princeton University Press.

Humphrey, Tom. 2002. "Alexander Radio Ads Tout Conservative Side," *Knoxville News-Sentinel* (Mar. 27), p. B3.

Ifill, Gwen. 1992. "Clinton Chooses Two and Deplores Idea of Cabinet Quotas," *New York Times* (Dec. 22), p. A1.

Ireland, Patricia. 2003. Interview with the author. Tape recording, April 21. Miami, Florida.

Jackson, David. 1996. "Dole Hoping Clinton Judges Emerge as Issue," *Dallas Morning News* (Apr. 30), p. 1A.

Jackson, Robert L., and Philip Hager. 1985. "Senate Narrowly Confirms Kozinski as Appeals Judge," *Los Angeles Times* (Nov. 8), Part 1, p. 3.

Jacobs, John E. 1993. "Clinton's Civil Rights Challenge," *Chicago Defender* (Aug. 12), p. 14.

Jipping, Thomas. 2002. Interview with the author. Tape recording, June 6. Washington, D.C.

Jipping, Thomas, and Marianne E. Lombardi. 1994. "The Judicial Activism of Rosemary Barkett," *Washington Times* (Mar. 17), p. A19.

Johnson, Carrie. 2000. "Clinton's Moderate Judicial Picks Place Diversity Over Ideology, Experts Say," *Fulton County Daily Report* (Mar. 24), p. 1.

Johnson, Glen. 2001. "Democrats' Walkout Signals Partisan Rupture Over Judges," *Boston Globe* (May 6), p. A6.

Kalman, Laura. 2000. "Law and Character: Does Character Affect Judicial Performance?" *Colorado Law Review* 71: 1385–1420.

Kamen, Al, and Warren Brown. 1996. "Rivals' Repeat Performance," *Washington Post* (Jan. 25), p. A23.

Kane, Paul. 2003. "Votes 'Not There' for Pickering," *Roll Call* (Oct. 22), 2003 WL 7692355.

Katz, Daniel, and Samuel J. Eldersveld. 1961. "The Impact of Local Party Activities Upon the Electorate," *Public Opinion Quarterly* 25: 1–24.

Kellman, Laurie. 1996. "Dole Launches Attack on Wide Range of Issues," *Washington Times* (Apr. 30), p. A4.

Key, V. O. 1955. "A Theory of Critical Elections," *Journal of Politics* 17: 3–18.

King, Colbert. 1999. "The Ghost of Ronnie White," *Washington Post* (Oct. 9), p. A23.

King, John. 1996. "Clinton Judicial Appointees Soft on Crime, Dole Claims," *Fort Worth Star-Telegram* (Apr. 20), p. A40.

Kirkpatrick, Jeanne. 1976. *The New Presidential Elite: Men and Women in National Politics.* New York: Russell Sage.

Klaidman, Daniel. 1993. "Liberals Hit Clinton on Judge Picks," *The Recorder* (Oct. 27), p. 1.

Kornylak, Richard. 2001. "Disclosing the Election-Related Activities of Interest Groups Through Section 527 of the Tax Code," *Cornell Law Review* 87: 230–67.

Kraske, Steve. 1999. "KC Leaders Make Ashcroft a Target," *Kansas City Star* (Oct. 15), p. A1.

Krislov, Samuel. 1974. *Representative Bureaucracy*. Englewood Cliffs, N.J.: Prentice-Hall.

Krutz, Glen S., Richard Fleisher, and Jon R. Bond. 1998. "From Abe Fortas to Zoe Baird: Explaining Why Some Nominations Fail in the Senate," *American Political Science Review* 92: 871–81.

Kurtz, Howard. 1986a. "Senate Confirms Sidney Fitzwater," *Washington Post* (Mar. 19), p. A6.

———. 1986b. "Federal Court Nominee Attacked Rights Groups," *Washington Post* (Mar. 14), p. A4.

———. 1986c. "Democrats Settle Score With Gorton on Judgeship," *Washington Post* (Oct. 11), p. A10.

———. 1985a. "Senate Committee to Reconsider Judicial Nominee," *Washington Post* (Nov. 1), p. A4.

———. 1985b. "Senator Grills Nominee," *Washington Post* (Nov. 2), p. A3.

———. 1985c. "Kozinski Judgeship Approved," *Washington Post* (Nov. 8), p. A4.

———. 1985d. "Democrats Try to Slow Confirmation of Judges," *Washington Post* (Nov. 12), p. A3.

Lauter, David. 1988. "Repeated Horton References, Prison Ad Cited," *Los Angeles Times* (Oct. 24), p. 15.

Lawrence, Susan E. 1990. *The Poor in Court: The Legal Services Program and Supreme Court Decision Making*. Princeton: Princeton University Press.

Lecher, Dave. 1994. "Huffington Attacks Rival on Judges," *Los Angeles Times* (Sept. 30), p. A3.

Leuchtenburg, William. 1995. *The Supreme Court Reborn: The Constitutional Revolution in the Age of Roosevelt*. New York: Oxford University Press.

Levin, Ann. 1987. "Libertarian Law Professor Slated for Largest Appeals Court," *Christian Science Monitor* (May 1), p. 7.

Lewis, Anthony. 1996. "Abroad at Home; The Old Dole," *New York Times* (Apr. 22), p. A13.

Lewis, Neil A. 2002. "Here Come the Judges; First the Senate, Now the Courts of Appeals," *New York Times* (Dec. 1), Sec. 4, p. 3.

———. 2000a. "Senator Vows He Will Fight Clinton's Judicial Selection," *New York Times* (Dec. 29), p. A16.

———. 2000b. "Clinton Names a Black Judge; Skirts Congress," *New York Times* (Dec. 28), p. A1.

———. 1999a. "A Nomination Is Withdrawn, and a Deal Is Threatened," *New York Times* (May 28), p. A18.

———. 1999b. "In Odd Turn, Democrats Oppose Clinton Nominee," *New York Times* (Sept. 22), p. A25.

———. 1999c. "Democrats End Threat to Block Court Nominees," *New York Times* (Oct. 2), p. A10.

———. 1997. "Move to Limit Clinton's Judicial Choices Fails," *New York Times* (April 29), Sec. D, p. 22.

————. 1995. "Partisan Gridlock Blocks Senate Confirmations of Federal Judges," *New York Times* (Nov. 30), Sec. A, p. 16.

————. 1993a. "Clinton Is Considering Judgeships for Opponents of Abortion Rights," *New York Times* (Sept. 18), p. A1.

————. 1993b. "Lani Guinier's Agenda Provokes Old Enemies," *New York Times* (May 9), Sec. 4, p. 2.

————. 1992a. "Clinton Expected to Name Woman Attorney General," *New York Times* (Dec. 9), p. A1.

————. 1992b. "Court Nominee Is Confirmed After Angry Senate Debate," *New York Times* (Sept. 10), p. A16.

Lewis, Neil A., and David Johnston. 2001. "Bush Would Sever Law Group's Role in Screening Judges," *New York Times* (Mar. 17), p. A1.

Lipshutz, Robert J., and Douglas B. Huron. 1979. "Achieving a More Representative Federal Judiciary," *Judicature* 62: 483–85.

Lithwick, Dahlia. 2002. "Personal Truths and Legal Fictions," *New York Times* (Dec. 17), p. A35.

Lott, Davis Newton. 1994. *The Presidents Speak: The Inaugural Addresses of the American Presidents From Washington to Clinton.* New York: Henry Holt Publishing.

Lunch, William M. 1987. *The Nationalization of American Politics.* Berkeley: University of California Press.

Lyons, Richard L. 1980. "On Capital Hill," *Washington Post* (Sept. 11), p. A8.

Maloney, James M. 1994. "Shooting for an Omnipotent Congress: The Constitutionality of Federal Regulations of Interstate Firearms Possession," *Fordham Law Review* 62: 1795–1834.

Maltese, John Anthony. 2003. "Confirmation Gridlock: The Federal Judicial Appointment Process Under Bill Clinton and George W. Bush," *Journal of Appellate Practice and Process* 5: 1–28.

————. 1995. *The Selling of Supreme Court Nominees.* Baltimore, Md.: Johns Hopkins University Press.

Mannies, Jo. 2000. "Political Fliers Accuse Ashcroft of 'Racial Insensitivity,'" *St. Louis Post-Dispatch* (Oct. 8), p. A7.

————. 1999. "Showing Mercy to Condemned Killer May Have Hurt Carnahan, Poll Finds," *St. Louis Post-Dispatch* (Mar. 29), p. A1.

————. 1992. "Clinton Goes on Attack Here; Bush Blasted on Thomas, Lack of Strategy on Jobs," *St. Louis Post-Dispatch* (Aug. 1), p. 1A.

Marcus, Ruth. 1992. "What Does Bush Really Believe?" *Washington Post* (Aug. 18), p. A1.

Martin, Gary. 2002. "Senate Committee Rejects Texas Judge for Court of Appeals," *San Antonio Express-News* (Sept. 6), p. 3A.

Martin, Lewis. 1993. "It's the Same Old Same Old," *Chicago Defender* (June 12), p. 20.

Mason, Julie. 2002. "Democrats Reject Owen Nomination," *Houston Chronicle* (Sept. 6), p. A1.

Masters, Brooke A. 2000. "Robb Goes to Bat for Nominee," *Washington Post* (Sept. 28), p. B1.

Matthews, Donald P. 1973. *U.S. Senators and Their World.* New York: W. W. Norton & Co.

Mayhew, David. 1991. *Divided We Govern*. New Haven, Conn.: Yale University Press.

———. 1986. *Placing Parties in American Politics*. Princeton, N.J.: Princeton University Press.

———. 1974. *Congress: The Electoral Connection*. New Haven, Conn.: Yale University Press.

McAdam, Doug. 1982. *Political Progress and Development of Black Insurgency*. Chicago: University of Chicago Press.

McAllister, Bill. 2000. "Allard Rejects Clinton Offer of Judge Swap," *Denver Post* (May 12), p. B1.

McCain, Marie. 1999. "Reverend Lowery Criticizes Senators for Blocking Nominees for Judge," *Cincinnati Enquirer* (Oct. 9), p. C6.

McCarty, Nolan, and Rose Razaghian. 1999. "Advice and Consent: Senate Responses to Executive Branch Nominations 1885–1996," *American Journal of Political Science* 43: 1122–43.

McFeatters, Ann. 2002. "Senate Panel Recommends Confirmation for Smith," *Pittsburgh Post-Gazette* (May 24), p. A1.

McFeeley, Neil D. 1987. *Appointment of Judges: The Johnson Presidency*. Austin: University of Texas Press.

Meyer, Eugene. 2002. Telephone interview with the author. Tape recording, July 30.

Mitchell, Allison. 1996. "Clinton Pressing Judge to Relent," *New York Times* (Mar. 22), p. A1.

Moore, W. John. 1993. "Judges on the Left! Hold That Line!" *The National Journal* (May 22), p. 1246.

Morris, Aldon. 1984. *The Origins of the Civil Rights Movement: Black Communities Organizing for Change*. New York: Free Press.

National Institute of Justice. 2001. *Sourcebook of Criminal Justice Statistics—2000*. Washington, D.C.: U.S. Government Printing Office.

Neas, Ralph. 2002. Interview with Amy Steigerwalt. Tape recording, August 6. Washington, D.C.

Nelson, Steve. 1983. "Judicial Skies Deserve More Than Rising Starr," *Legal Times* (July 18), p. 11.

Ness, Susan. 1978. "A Sexist Selection Process Keeps Qualified Women Off the Bench," *Washington Post* (Mar. 26), p. C8.

Neuffer, Elizabeth. 1992. "Women Press for More Nominations," *Boston Globe* (Dec. 20), p. 30.

Nix, Robert N. C. 1989. "Federalism in the Twenty-First Century: Individual Liberties in Search of a Guardian," in *Federalism: The Shifting Balance*, edited by Janice C. Griffith. Chicago: American Bar Association Publishing.

Novak, Robert. 1999. "Gore Accuses GOP of Racism," *Chicago Sun-Times* (Oct. 31), p. 31.

Ogundele, Ayo, and Linda Camp Keith. 1999. "Reexamining the Impact of the Bork Nomination to the Supreme Court," *Political Research Quarterly* 52: 403–20.

Oldfield, Duane M. 1995. "The Christian Right and the Presidential Nominating Process," in *In Pursuit of the White House: How We Choose Our Presidential Nominees*, edited by William G. Mayer. Chatham, N.J.: Chatham House Publishers, Inc.

O'Neill, Michael Edmund. 2000. "Undoing Miranda," *Brigham Young University Law Review* 2000: 185–265.

Page, Benjamin I., and Robert Y. Shapiro. 1992. *The Rational Public: Fifty Years of Trends in Americans' Policy Preferences.* Chicago: University of Chicago Press.

Parnet, Herbert S. 1990. *Richard Nixon and His America.* Boston: Little, Brown & Co.

Patterson, James T. 1967. *Congressional Conservatism and the New Deal: The Growth of the Conservative Coalition in Congress, 1933–1939.* Lexington: University of Kentucky Press.

Pear, Robert. 1996. "Governors' Plans on Welfare Attacked," *New York Times* (Feb. 14), p. A12.

Perry, Barbara A. 1991. *A Representative Supreme Court? The Impact of Race, Religion and Gender on Appointments.* New York: Greenwood.

Perry, Pamela. 1991. "Two Faces of Disparate Impact Discrimination," *Fordham Law Review* 59: 84–150.

Pettus, Emily Wagster. 2003. "Musgrove, Other Democratic Leaders Back Pickering," Associated Press State and Local Wire (Sept. 24).

Pike, David. 1983. "The Appointment Process Under Carter and Reagan," *National Law Journal* (Aug. 29), p. 26.

Pilon, Roger. 2002. Interview with the author. Tape recording, June 7. Washington, D.C.

Pinderhughes, Dianne M. 1992. "Divisions in the Civil Rights Community," *PS: Political Science & Politics* Sept.: 485–87.

Pitkin, Hanna F. 1967. *The Concept of Representation.* Berkeley: University of California Press.

Polsby, Nelson W., and Aaron Wildavsky. 1976. *Presidential Elections: Strategies of Electoral Politics.* New York: Charles Scribner's Sons.

Pritchett, C. Herman. 1948. *The Roosevelt Court: A Study in Judicial Politics and Values, 1937–1947.* New York: Macmillan.

Prysby, Charles L. 1989. "Attitudes of Southern Democratic Party Activists Toward Jesse Jackson: The Effects of the Local Context," *Journal of Politics* 51: 305–18.

Roberts, Steve. 1988. "Reagan's Social Issues: Gone But Not Forgotten," *New York Times* (Sept. 11), Sec. 4, p. 4.

Robison, Clay. 2002. "Kirk Urges Senators to Act on Bush's Court Nominees," *Houston Chronicle* (June 4), p. A17.

Romano, Michael. 2000. "Clinton Nominated Salazar Deputy to 10th Circuit Court of Appeals," *Denver Rocky Mountain News* (July 28), p. 26A.

Rosen, Jeffrey. 1996. "Dole's Judge-Bashing Doesn't Make Sense," *Dayton Daily News* (May 30), p. 11A.

Rosenberg, Gerald N. 1991. *The Hollow Hope: Can Courts Bring About Social Change?* Chicago: University of Chicago Press.

Rozell, Mark J., and Clyde Wilcox. 1999. *Interest Groups in American Campaigns.* Washington, D.C.: Congressional Quarterly Press.

———. 1996. "Second Coming: The Strategies of the New Christian Right," *Political Science Quarterly* 111: 271–94.

Ruckman, P. S., Jr. 1993. "The Supreme Court, Critical Nominations, and the Senate Confirmation Process," *Journal of Politics* 55: 793–805.

Safire, William. 2001. "Battle of the Blue Slips," *New York Times* (May 10), p. A33.

Savage, David G. 2000. "Clinton Losing Fight for Black Judge," *Los Angeles Times* (July 7), p. A1.

Scheingold, Stuart A. 1974. *The Politics of Rights: Lawyers, Public Policy and Political Change*. New Haven, Conn.: Yale University Press.

Scherer, Nancy. 2001. "Who Drives the Ideological Makeup of the Lower Federal Courts in a Divided Government," *Law & Society Review* 35: 191–218.

Schlozman, Kay Lehman, and John T. Tierney. 1986. *Organized Interests and American Democracy*. New York: Harper & Row.

Schreiber, Harry N. 1996. "Redesigning the Architecture of Federalism," *Yale Law and Policy Review* 14: 227–96.

Schulman, Bruce J. 1991. *From Cotton Belt to Sun Belt: Federal Policy, Economic Development, and the Transformation of the South, 1938–1980*. New York: Oxford University Press.

Schwartz, Herman. 1988. *Packing the Courts: The Conservative Campaign to Rewrite the Constitution*. New York: Charles Scribner's Sons.

Segal, Jeffrey A., and Harold J. Spaeth. 1993. *The Attitudinal Model*. New York: Cambridge University Press.

Senior Conservative Spokesman. 2002. Anonymous interview with Amy Steigerwalt. Tape recording, August 5. Washington, D.C.

Shenon, Philip. 1986a. "Drive on for Senate Approval of Judicial Nominee," *New York Times* (May 27), p. A16.

————. 1986b. "Reagan May Phone Senators on Court Choice," *New York Times* (June 25), p. A17.

————. 1986c. "Byrd Maneuver Stalls Approval of Judge, *New York Times* (July 2), p. A1.

————. 1986d. "Meese Denies Political Move for Judgeship," *New York Times* (July 2), p. A19.

————. 1986e. "Senate, Ending Judicial Fight, Gives Manion Approval," *New York Times* (July 24), p. A1.

Sherman, Mark. 2000. "Black Vote Is Vital for Democrats," *Atlanta Journal-Constitution* (Jan. 16), p. A1.

Shesgreen, Deirdre. 1999a. "NAACP Plans to Make White's Defeat an Issue in Ashcroft's Election," *St. Louis Post-Dispatch* (Oct. 7), p. A4.

————. 1999b. "Group Hopes to Circumvent Senate on Appointments," *St. Louis Post-Dispatch* (Oct. 22), p. A6.

————. 1999c. "GOP Fears That Blacks' Anti-Bond Sentiment Could Hurt Other Candidates," *St. Louis Post-Dispatch* (Dec. 26), p. A9.

————. 1999d. "GOP Fears That Blacks' Anti-Bond Sentiment Could Hurt Other Candidates," *St. Louis Post-Dispatch* (Dec. 26), p. A9.

Shipan, Charles R., and Megan L. Shannon. 2003. "Delaying Justice(s): A Duration Analysis of Supreme Court Confirmations," *American Journal of Political Science* 47: 654–68.

Shogren, Elizabeth. 1993. "Women Lobby Clinton on New Choice for Job," *Chicago Sun-Times* (Jan. 24), p. 6.

Silkcourts, Mark. 1991. "Why Thomas Won in the Polls and the Senate," *Atlanta Journal-Constitution* (Oct. 17), p. A17.

Silverstein, Mark. 1994. *Judicious Choices: The New Politics of Supreme Court Confirmations*. New York: W. W. Norton & Co.

Simon, Richard. 1999. "Minorities Denounce Senate Delays on Judges," *Los Angeles Times* (Oct. 6), p. 2.

Slotnick, Elliot E. 1983. "Lowering the Bench or Raising It Higher: Affirmative Action and Judicial Selection During the Carter Administration," *Yale Law and Policy Review* 1: 270–98.

———. 1980. "Reforms in Judicial Selection: Will They Affect the Senate's Role?" *Judicature* 64: 60–73.

Smith, Michael David. 1983. *Race Versus Robe: The Dilemma of Black Judges*. New York: National University Publications.

Smith, Phillip, and Al Kamen. 1985. "Silberman Backed for Appeals Court," *Washington Post* (Jan. 5), p. B1.

Solomon, Rayman L. 1984. "The Politics of Appointment and the Federal Courts' Role in Regulating America: U.S. Courts of Appeals Judgeships from T.R. to F.D.R.," *American Bar Foundation Research Journal* 1984: 285–343.

Songer, Donald. 1991. "The Circuit Courts of Appeals," in *The American Courts: A Critical Assessment*, edited by John B. Gates and Charles A. Johnson. Washington, D.C.: CQ Press.

———. 1982. "Consensual and Non-consensual Decisions of the United States Courts of Appeals," *American Journal of Political Science* 35: 225–39.

Songer, Donald, Sue Davis, and Susan Haire. 1994. "A Reappraisal of Diversification in the Federal Courts: Gender Effects in the Courts of Appeals," *Journal of Politics* 56: 425–39.

Sorauf, Frank J. 1967. "Political Parties and Political Analysis," in *The American Party System: Stages of Political Development*, edited by William N. Chambers and Walter D. Burnham. New York: Oxford University Press.

Sorauf, Frank J., and Paul Allen Beck. 1988. *Party Politics in America* (6th ed.). Boston: Scott Foresman.

Special to the *New York Times*. 1986. "The Federalist Society: Judge Scalia's Cheerleaders," *New York Times* (July 23), p. B6.

———. 1977. "Group Headed by Mrs. King Focuses on U.S. Judgeships for Blacks," *New York Times* (Sept. 4), p. 16.

St. Louis Post-Dispatch. 1999. "Reactions From St. Louis," *St. Louis Post-Dispatch* (Oct. 26), p. A6.

Staff Writer, *Washington Post*. 1985. "Disputed Judicial Nomination Sent to the Floor," *Washington Post* (Sept. 13), p. A23.

Stephenson, Donald Grier, Jr. 1999. *Campaigns and the Court*. New York: Columbia University Press.

Stone, Walter J., Ronald B. Rapoport, and Alan L. Abramowitz. 1994. "Party Polarization: The Reagan Revolution and Beyond," in *The Parties Respond: Changes in American Parties and Campaigns*, edited by L. Sandy Maisel. Boulder, Colo.: Westview.

Sundquist, James L. 1992. *Constitutional Reform and Effective Government*. Washington, D.C.: Brookings Institution Press.

Tobias, Carl. 1998. "Fostering Balance on the Federal Courts," *American University Law Review* 47: 935–61.

Tolchin, Martin. 1992. "Court Nominee Splits Advocates of Civil Rights," *New York Times* (June 11), p. A14.

Towns, Edolphys. 1993. "An Open Letter to Bill Clinton," *Michigan Chronicle* (Jan. 6), p. A7.

Turner, Wallace. 1986. "Reversal on Judicial Nominee Brings Trouble to Senator Gorton," *New York Times* (July 6), Sec. 1, p. 1.

———. 1980. "Reagan Says He Would Not Use Single Issue Test to Pick Judges," *New York Times* (Oct. 2), p. A1.

Uhlman, Thomas M. 1978. "Black Elite Decision Making: The Case of Trial Judges," *American Journal of Political Science* 22: 884–95.

United Press International. 1978. "A Black Is Confirmed as U.S. Judge in South," *New York Times* (May 18), p. B15.

U.S. Newswire. 2000. "Transcript of Clinton Remarks, April 30 at NAACP Dinner" (May 1).

Vogel, David. 1980. "The Public Interest Movement and the American Reform Tradition," *Political Science Quarterly* 95: 607–27.

Walker, David B. 1995. *The Rebirth of Federalism: Slouching Toward Washington.* New York: Chatham House Publishers.

Walker, Jack L. 1991. *Mobilizing Interest Groups in America.* Ann Arbor: University of Michigan Press.

Walker, Thomas G., and Deborah J. Barrow. 1985. "The Diversification of the Federal Bench: Policy and Process Ramification," *Journal of Politics* 47: 596–617.

Whalen, Charles, and Barbara Whalen. 1985. *The Longest Debate: A Legislative History of the 1964 Civil Rights Act.* New York: New American Library.

Wildavsky, Aaron. 1965. "The Goldwater Phenomenon: Purists, Politicians and the Two-Party System," *Review of Politics* 27: 386–413.

Williams, Lena. 1986a. "Senate Democrats Challenge Reagan Appeals Court Choice," *New York Times* (May 1), p. D27.

———. 1986b. "Key Senate Panel Balks Over Nominee to Court," *New York Times* (May 9), p. D20.

———. 1986c. "Federal Court Nominee Denies Racial Insensitivity," *New York Times* (May 7), p. A22.

Willis, Standish, Veda Britt, and Lewis Powell. 1994. "Clinton Can Make History Again," *Chicago Defender* (Jan. 3), p. 12.

Wilson, James Q. 1962. *The Amateur Democrat.* Chicago: University of Chicago Press.

Wilson, Sarah. 2003. "Appellate Judicial Appointments During the Clinton Presidency: An Inside Perspective," *Journal of Appellate Practice and Process* 5: 29–47.

Wilson, William J. 1987. *The Truly Disadvantaged: The Inner City, the Underclass, and Public Policy.* Chicago: University of Chicago Press.

Wooten, Jim. 2002. "Litmus Test Spells Doom for Nominee," *Atlanta Journal-Constitution* (Sept. 8), p. 18D.

Index

Page numbers in italics refer to tables and figures.

Southern Poverty Law Center, 149
southern strategy of Republican Party, 6, 36,
43, 50–51, 159–60, 227n4
Spaeth, Harold J., 31
Spector, 233n13
Stabenow, Deborah, 188, 235n13
Stack, Charles, *118*
Starr, Kenneth, 144
STATA, 200, 238n4
states' rights: court cases on, 239nn2–9;
and Democratic Party, 61–62, 64; expectations of judicial behavior on, 64–65;
judicial voting behavior on, 68–70, *71,
72, 219*; meaning of, for blacks, 61; and
Republican Party, 55–57, 61–62, 65; re-
search methodology on, 216–19
Steele, William, *120*
Stephenson, Donald Grier, Jr., 158
Stewart, Ted: filibuster during confirmation
process for, 149–50, *189*, 190; interest
groups' opposition to, *119*; and log-
rolling by Clinton, 63, 155, 234n9
Stimson, James A., 22
Student Transportation Moratorium Act
(1972), 53
substantive representation, 74–75, 77, 78,
84, 97–107
Sullivan, Michael J., 230n5
Sundquist, James L., 182
Sundram, Clarence, *119*
Supreme Court, U.S.: on abortion, 6,
14, 15, 19–20, 26, 29, 40, 58, 173, 221,
222, 231n33; on affirmative action, 53,
231n38; on campaign finance reform,
13; candidates for, from federal appellate
courts, 20, 230n7; on civil liberties, 14–
15; on civil rights, 54, 56; and "close"
cases, 238n3; on commerce clause, 219;
confirmation process for, 8, 234n1; on
criminal defendants' rights, 14, 51, 52–
53, 159–60, 230n9; on death penalty,
231n35; on desegregation, 14, 34; and
FDR's "court-packing" plan, 31; female
judges on, 21, 74, 230n19; on gun-free
school zones, 57, 218; impact of, on
presidential elections, 158; infrequency
of appointments to and decisions of, 1–
2, 19, 20; on interest groups, 13, 159;
interest groups/political activists and
nominations to, 3, 18, 108, 234n1; mi-

nority judges on, 74–75, 82; on New
Deal, 31; presidents' nominations to,
230n6; on property rights, 13; public
opinion poll on, 21; scholarship on,
1–2; on search and seizure, 230n6; on
women's rights, 14, 15, 218; on workers'
rights, 30, 31. *See also specific Supreme
Court justices*
Sutton, Jeffrey, *120*
Sykes, Diane, *120*
symbolic (or descriptive) representation, 74,
77–78, 83–84

Taft, William Howard, 234n1
Tatel, David, 163
Temple, Donald, 178
Tennessee election for U.S. Senate (2002),
170–71
Tenth Amendment, 50, 56, 62, 218
Tenth Circuit Court of Appeals, 81, 91, 144,
155–56
Terry v. Ohio, 239n8
Texas election for U.S. Senate (2002), 167–
69
Texas Watch, 236n12
"textualist" interpretation of Constitution,
124
Third Circuit Court of Appeals, 25, 76, 81,
86, 135
Thomas, Clarence, 75, 82, 95, 115, *118*,
233n15
Thurmond, Strom, 111, 143–44, 148, 151–
52, *187*, 233n13
Towns, Edolphys, 87–88
Treen, David, *118*
Truman, Harry S., *2*, 35, 36, 76
Turner v. City of Memphis, 227n2

United States v. Carolene Products, 15
United States v. Darby, 229n4
United States v. Leon, 230n6
United States v. Lopez, 57, 231n45, 239n8
United States v. Morrison, 231n45, 239n9
United States v. Ramsey, 239n6
Urban League, 82, 179

Violence Against Women Act, 25, 26–27,
218
Virginia v. Black, 75, 232n1
Vives, Olga, 25

The authorized representative in the EU for product safety and compliance is:
Mare Nostrum Group
B.V Doelen 72
4831 GR Breda
The Netherlands

www.ingramcontent.com/pod-product-compliance
Lightning Source LLC
Chambersburg PA
CBHW020340270326
41926CB00007B/256